Historic Preservation for Professionals

Historic
Preservation
for Professionals

Virginia O. Benson *and* Richard Klein

The Kent State University Press   Kent, Ohio

© 2008 by The Kent State University Press, Kent, Ohio 44242
ALL RIGHTS RESERVED
Library of Congress Catalog Card Number 2008014198
ISBN 978-0-87338-927-3
Manufactured in the United States of America

LIBRARY OF CONGRESS CATALOGING-IN-PUBLICATION DATA
Benson, Virginia O.
   Historic preservation for professionals / Virginia O. Benson and Richard Klein.
       p.   cm.
   Includes bibliographical references and index.
   ISBN 978-0-87338-927-3 (pbk. : alk. paper) ∞
   1. Historic preservation—United States. I. Klein, Richard, 1949– II. Title.
   E159.B42 2008
   363.6'90973—dc22   2008014198

British Library Cataloging-in-Publication data are available.

12 11 10 09 08   5 4 3 2 1

Contents

Foreword

Stanley M. Smith

During the panel discussion about revolving funds at a National Trust for Historic Preservation conference several years ago, a speaker preceding me emphasized avoiding risk. This individual outlined a plethora of procedures and controls to guarantee that preservation organizations never lose money when they lend or invest. This presentation gave me time to rethink what I would say.

When it was my turn to speak, I announced that preservation revolving funds exist to let us take risks that wise people endowed with solid business acumen would not consider reasonable or responsible investments. I was serious! The job and challenge of preservation leaders and professionals is to manage risk, not avoid it, to perpetuate the architectural heritage of diverse communities.

Preservation leaders have historically embraced visions of the future that are ahead of their time and differ substantially from accepted wisdom. Several examples:

- In the early twentieth century, some considered Victorian architecture "ugly" and worth being replaced. Today it is prized for neighborhood revitalization.
- Voltaire thought the ugly, old-fashioned gothic Notre Dame Cathedral in Paris should be demolished and replaced with a beautiful Greek-style temple of reason. Several decades later, Viollet-le-Duc implemented a preservation vision, one that makes Notre Dame rank among landmarks such as the Eiffel Tower, which define places, attract tourists, and symbolize the diverse factors that make a nation more than the sum of its people.

- The 1950s International style of architecture is out of fashion today, considered ugly by some, and sometimes endangered, unless visionary preservationists assemble strategies to assure its survival and continued use.
- An important executive from a huge foundation in a Midwest city respectfully explained to me that the upscale houses from the 1920s in a neighborhood afflicted by substantial demographic and economic changes could not be saved, "because they were constructed of wood and everyone knows that wood structures rarely last more than fifty years."

Preservation leaders have always articulated arguments and persuaded people to look differently at their surroundings, and they still need to do so.

What does it take to manage the strategic social, legal, and financial risks people must take to conserve our architectural heritages? Most preservation initiatives fall into two broad general themes:

The first is stewardship—taking good care of and protecting what we already have. The built environment continually needs cyclic new investments in care and maintenance, even though its cultural and artistic values may be generally acknowledged. The impact of deferred maintenance on old buildings is always there. The question always before us is: Can we can address deterioration of building fabrics proactively and sensitively, or do we sometimes require a crisis to get mobilized?

The second is early intervention to save often unrecognized or undervalued cultural resources. This usually entails taking major risks, striving to obtain control over buildings, changing the minds of well-placed decision makers, and/or securing funds needed to foster sustained economic feasibility.

In both cases, success in preservation requires perseverance, tenacity, mastery of the facts, and collaboration. This book is a fine starting point for people new to preservation and a valuable reference for those already deeply involved in efforts to conserve our built environment. Credible, effective organizations have leaders who do not give up easily. They seek out and test facts to guide their work and collaborate so that private, nonprofit groups complement the planning and regulatory powers of government entities. Whether by reading the entire book carefully or studying it selectively, paid professionals, members of historic commissions, and volunteers serving on nonprofit boards have the opportunity to dramatically increase their personal and collective effectiveness.

The benefits of conserving and reinvigorating living communities are not just a set of economic arguments to use with legislators or decision makers. Maintaining the identity of tangible historic places is one of the hallmarks of civilization and the antithesis of the creeping sprawl which tends to separate people and communities one from another. Understanding the content of this book is a valuable tool with which to bequeath the best of our present and past to succeeding generations.

. . .

Stanley M. Smith recently retired, after leading Historic Boston Incorporated for twenty-five years. Using a preservation revolving fund, Historic Boston has put people and resources together to preserve, usually through complex real-estate transactions, more than a dozen once-endangered historic sites. Each had a pivotal impact on its surroundings and the city in general.

In addition, after losing two battles—but in both cases winning the war—to preserve Boston's last old synagogue and a nationally significant Jesuit church, Historic Boston decided to address religious property preservation more proactively. It raised new monies for the Steeples Project, which during its first ten years awarded $1.2 million as competitive matching grants to the owners of sixty historic religious properties. These funds, accompanied by substantive technical assistance, catalyzed owners to plan and implement needed repairs for their buildings, which punctuate the skyline, define places, and house a variety of human services.

Acknowledgments

Much of the impetus for this book originated with our colleagues and students at Cleveland State University. We begin by thanking our colleague Dean Dennis Keating for his encouragement and sound counsel. We especially wish to recognize, for their patience and perseverance, our supportive spouses, Dane Benson and Jo Ann Fisher. We thank David A. Lipstreu for insightful comments related to historic land-use regulations and preservation redevelopment.

We also commend several of our students for their tremendous help. Special thanks to Heather Wallace, who did so much of the initial research. We appreciate the hard work of Jeffrey Morris and Meghan Brown, who did a superb job in research and proofreading. R. K. Bankaitis deserves special recognition for his outstanding professional photographic work and Philip Leiter for his unique photographs. We are also grateful for Morgan Harris III's excellent computer skills. Finally, we acknowledge our many preservation colleagues and friends whose encouragement was invaluable.

Chapter One

The Transforming Power
of Historic Preservation

Introduction

American cities are growing and evolving, especially at their edges. The creation of new subdivisions, shopping malls, office complexes, and highway-oriented developments appear to be endless as sprawling suburbs creep across farmlands, swallowing up small towns and countryside in an ever-expanding suburban frontier.

However, the real adventure is back in the central city, in the old ethnic neighborhoods, in the remarkable sacred landmarks, the unique school buildings, the outstanding architecture of theaters and warehouses and train stations and city parks and waterfronts. The city denizen is always uncovering some surprising aspect of art and culture, some forgotten handcrafted antique. These discoveries substantiate the story of a past that is filled with struggle, intrigue, cultural conflicts, and heroic resolutions. Transforming the centers of cities and small towns is the emerging field of historic preservation, a truly sustainable land-use ethic. Not cutting and running, the preservationists are staying for the long haul.

To prepare the enthusiast for such a noble calling, this book reveals some of the successes of recent decades and in the following chapters the methods and models that made them happen.

Storm Cunningham outlined the opportunities in the field he defined as "restorative development."[1] Although Cunningham included the restoration of natural environments, he clearly embraced the preservation of the built fabric. Opposing the dominant pioneer ethic of the United States' first centuries, Cunningham described the new development frontier, the dominant theme of the twenty-first century, as a 180-degree look behind

Restoration Development North American city. An historic building is undergoing major exterior renovation as part of overall modernization. Photo by V. Benson.

ourselves. From the westward movement of the seventeenth, eighteenth, and nineteenth centuries to the twentieth-century urban sprawl, Americans have enabled a culture of throwing away and moving on. This can no longer be sustained.

Historic preservation adds value to the existing built environment just as conservation adds it to the natural landscape. Within this new historic preservation, ethical career opportunities abound. The sustainable development of the future will require partnerships between the private, nonprofit, and public sectors. Those who prepare themselves for this creative profession will find their services in demand in business, government, and many organizations sprouting up in cities across America.

· · ·

Historic preservation is a relatively new profession. Distinct from many other fields, it has no official curriculum, certifying body, qualifying ex-

amination, or entrance fee. Although many universities offer preservation
degree programs, these vary from those connected to architecture to others with strong ties to history or archaeology to interdisciplinary degrees

Civil War Monument, Ely Square, Elyria, Ohio, c. 1888. Herman Ely donated the
site to the city in 1825. Known as Ely Square, Elyria's Parks and Recreation Department takes great pride in it. Photo by Philip Leiter.

such as urban studies. Many people have drifted into the field from aca-
deme, public administration, real-estate development, law, carpentry,
homemaking, and many other domains.

This book, unlike most that describe the preservation movement, at-
tempts to outline specific information that prepares the student for a
worthwhile career in this fascinating discipline. The term historic preservation professional (HPP), conceived by these authors to define the profession, is used here for the first time.

Opportunities in Historic Preservation

Stimulating historic preservation work is not limited to the voluntary civic
activist: well-educated and ambitious leaders in this growing enterprise can
find opportunities in all three major economic sectors: nonprofit organizations, government agencies, and private businesses.

This book emphasizes the knowledge base that the HPP needs to en-
ter this challenging career. Background information on the history of the
field; architectural concepts; legal frameworks; and a critical examination
of the HPP's work in public, private, and nonprofit employment will offer
a strong foundation to the serious student and practitioner. Each of the
chapters that follow further introduce the reader to the exciting possibilities of this career

Chapter 2 outlines the history of the preservation movement in the United
States. Why is it important to examine this process with its accomplishments
and failures? Many past trends have generated activities that still have applications today. Warnings that come from experience are also useful to prevent
repeating mistakes. This chapter reveals the changes that have transformed
historic preservation from the occasional pastime of the very wealthy to the
current economic development tool that alters downtowns and neighborhoods, creating authentic centers that attract residents and visitors alike.

Chapter 2 concentrates on the development and evolution of historic
preservation in the United States, noting that much of its success over the
past two hundred years originated with insightful leadership. These leaders
adapted their objectives to meet the nation's changing moods. They also
acknowledged the importance of effective management. From the Ladies of
Mount Vernon to the National Trust for Historic Preservation, the successful organizations focused on management efficiency and cost accounting.

The second chapter also reviews many of the legal issues HPPs are likely
to confront as they practice their profession in any of the sectors men-

tioned. The preservationists in the past have been involved in many legal battles that affect preservation practice today. An understanding of regulatory frameworks and legal constraints will aid HPPs in planning all of their preservation efforts. This chapter covers many of the important cases that affect preservation today as well as the new laws, particularly the tax incentives that stimulate current endeavors. Preservation professionals familiar with laws and public policies can very effectively accomplish their goals.

New legal procedures favoring property over preservation rights have compelled many preservationists to revamp traditional programs and strategies. This prompts diverse and highly sophisticated programming. The need for professionalizing the field has become apparent over the past quarter century, especially as it relates to planning. Establishing partnerships with allied disciplines should lower operating costs while maximizing productivity. Involved with so many aspects of development and change, the well-prepared preservationist will handle many different issues related to the United States' physical legacy.

Chapter 3 focuses on postwar U.S. development and its impact on historic preservation. Urban renewal's devastating affects on older neighborhoods receives special attention; in this instance, the bulldozing of older districts, with their significant landmarks, served as a wake-up call for preservationists. Demolition of New York City's Penn Central Station, Michael Harrington's very controversial book, the congressional junket to Europe, and the 1965 National Conference of Mayors' pointed essay all provided additional fuel for this fire. Preservationists wanted immediate action. Their demands did not go unanswered.[2] The National Preservation Act of 1966 along with a series of other related federal bills, major tax reforms, and local tax incentives—reflected this growing desire to save the United States' physical past. Once established, preservationists took the lead in preserving and maintaining this legacy.

The wide array of architectural information offered in chapter 4 will help the HPP become an intelligent consumer of design services. Architectural terminology and construction vocabulary enhance the preservationist's ability to make the case for saving old structures and sites, specifically notable buildings but also other artifacts and landscapes, including historic districts that attract considerable attention for their cultural or historical importance.

This chapter illustrates the argument that throughout the United States architectural features diverge, reflecting cultural, ethnic, and economic differences and historical events that took place in various areas. It also shows that though some preservationists come from the field of architecture, it is not necessary to have an architecture degree to find a career in this vital profession. It does discuss, too, the important role played by architectural styling in preservation. Beginning with the works of John Ruskin and Eugène Emmanuel Viollet-le-Duc and culminating with those of Robert Venturi and Denise Scott Brown, it describes the major U.S. styles and their impact on society. Styling reflects not only aesthetics and culture at critical junctures but also cost considerations, construction technology, and available building materials.

Design detailing defines the physical character of a structure. Thus, HPPs must possess much more than a cursory knowledge of design and its application to individual historic buildings. They need to be well-grounded in it—restorers and renovators demand this. Architectural integrity and style vitality are key components of preservation practice.

Chapter 5 addresses the nonprofit world and its various manifestations in the work of the HPP. Some nonprofit organizations focus specifically on preservation; many others treat preservation issues as part of their broader undertaking. Although central city organizations such as community-development corporations (CDCs) offer a wide array of services to their neighborhoods, the physical infrastructure and the important need to provide affordable housing are growing components of their development work. Revitalizing commercial areas and recycling old buildings are prominent activities in most U.S. cities. Many challenges exist within nonprofit organizations, and the well-trained HPP will find numerous career opportunities in this sector.

This chapter outlines the various levels of nonprofit organizations that employ professional preservationists. Those cases identified operate on the national, state, regional, and local levels, and the chapter recognizes numerous opportunities in such associations across the United States. It also elaborates on the organizations discussed in chapter 2 and on additional successful nonprofits.

Finally, the fifth chapter addresses the common situation of a community that needs a professional preservation organization and delineates the steps that the HPP would follow in assisting to create one and thereby creating a career for him/herself as its director. Since fundraising is a key component of success in a nonprofit, the chapter also describes the process of writing grant proposals.

Chapter 6 examines the HPP's prospects in various levels of government employment. The federal government, especially, has initiated many preservation activities, as described in chapter 2, for sentimental and patriotic reasons. Although preservation is generally a local concern, federal, state, and regional governments are becoming more aware of the economic development aspects of heritage tourism and looking for experts in this important field. Government's interest in historic preservation is reflected in the various tax-credit programs and other related incentives. The well-trained preservationist will find opportunity in many governmental bodies. Large U.S. cities are often faced with the problems of renewing old neighborhoods and providing affordable housing options for their residents. Historic districting is a growing phenomenon in many cities providing the preservation professional an opportunity in government-supported revitalization.

Chapter 6 concentrates a great deal on the local-level public sector: city, county, and township governments. Since much of the nation's sixty-year preservation movement has focused on activities at the federal and state levels through various government policies and legislation, this chapter examines the local-government methods for protecting landmarks in historic cities, towns, and rural places. With the aid of preservation leaders, cities are reclaiming areas that had been abandoned or lost to the wrecking ball. HPPs have great potential to communicate how heritage tourism, arguably a direct consequence of thoughtful preservation, affects all local government entities, whether cities, small towns or rural areas.

The main emphasis of the seventh chapter is the economic feasibility of preserving old buildings. Here, this book's focus moves to the private business approach to historic preservation, much of which falls into the category of real estate development, or some other related HPP employment. Architectural and engineering firms (A&E) employ preservationists for many tasks, especially important among them researching and writing nominations to the National Register of Historic Places.

The chapter also outlines trends in real estate development that may be expected to continue—such as urbanization, suburbanization, highway building, and contemporary housing construction. To offset some of these trends, the federal government developed the investment tax credit that can be applied to historic preservation of income-producing properties. Conservation or preservation easements are an additional economic incentive for historic projects. The economic feasibility of doing historic preservation projects is further explained in terms of market-study elements and pro forma analysis. Whether the HPP finds employment in a private-sector firm, a nonprofit organization, or a government agency, this critical information is of utmost value.

Many historic districts are the sites of private businesses that operate in interesting old buildings adapted to new uses. The preservation professional may develop expertise in assisting businesses to make these adjustments, either as a consultant or by working with the redevelopment team.

Chapter 8 prepares the HPP to practice in the United States, a large and diverse country in which the preservationist may be called upon to understand and work with many ethnic and cultural groups to maintain their individual identities. Such work may encompass many historic periods, for example: those of the original European settlements and the conflict with native populations, the Spanish settlement of Florida and California, the Civil War and the Underground Railroad, and many other specific ethnic and cultural artifacts. Here the meticulous field of anthropology and the significance of excavating evidence of previous settlements inform the knowledge base of the HPP.

Chapter 9 further describes the current career opportunities for the HPP by examining a number of contemporary trends that affect a preservationist's profession. This chapter asks some pertinent questions of HPPs as they leave their scholarly studies to become practitioners in the field. The material covered throughout the book is here applied to real-world situations fundamental to living in the United States in the twenty-first century. The HPP can make a career of improving a neighborhood, a city, or a whole region through safeguarding treasures that cannot be replicated or replaced. This final chapter predicts future preservation potential based on current trends.

HPPs no longer only dabble in cultural or historic preservation; they are serious, sophisticated planners with highly technical skills and backgrounds. They are also well versed in practical administrative procedures, whether in private, nonprofit, or public sectors. This technical expertise and administrative proficiency will increase in importance as the twenty-first century unfolds. HPPs will need to stay abreast of the latest economic, political and social changes and how these changes affect their field. This unique combination of scholarship and pragmatic approach is the premise for this book: *Historic Preservation for Professionals*.

Notes

1. Storm Cunningham, *The Restoration Economy: The Greatest New Growth Frontier* (San Francisco: Berrett-Koehler, 2002), 15.

2. Michael Harrington, *The Other America: Poverty in the United States* (New York: Macmillan, 1962).

Chapter Two

Advancing Historic Preservation in the United States

Introduction

Historic preservation in the United States is nearly as old as the nation itself. In 1643, John Winthrop, the founder of the Massachusetts Bay Colony, lamented the loss of the Castle Island fortification in Boston Harbor. He argued that the ten-year-old facility had not outlived its usefulness and that it should be refitted to protect the colonists against possible French attacks. A century later, a New York City businessman named Cadwallader Colden expressed similar sentiments when he scolded local aldermen for destroying the White Hall mansion. In the 1790s, Benjamin Latrobe, a highly respected U.S. architect, was appalled when a group of Southern gentlemen asked him to supervise the demolition of the 150-year-old Green Spring Plantation House in James City County, Virginia.[1] Built by Governor William Berkeley, Green Spring was considered a historic landmark by late eighteenth century Virginians.

Of course, these leaders were not modern-day preservationists. However, they did have a vague understanding of how the United States' architectural legacy related to the present, which led them to acknowledge these losses. Unfortunately, they did little more; it would take several national emergencies before citizens demanded action.

In 1791, the U.S. Congress, recognizing the value of preservation, allocated $300 to maintain Revolutionary War monuments, which were being vandalized. This modest allocation may have kept the spirit of the Revolutionary War alive in the young republic, but it did little to convince the general public of the importance of restoring and maintaining historic structures or sites. The economic and social advancements of the Industrial Revolution blinded most Americans to the need for preservation. Rather than devoting time to saving landmarks, they preferred to pursue the many economic and social opportunities awaiting them in the burgeoning cities and western frontiers.

Case Study: Independence Hall

It took the proposed demolition of Independence Hall in Philadelphia during the second decade of the nineteenth century before a group of enlightened citizens began to recognize the importance of preserving landmarks. Designed by Andrew Hamilton and Edmund Woolley between 1731 and 1753, Independence Hall served as the Pennsylvania State Capitol building for nearly forty-five years. Local developers first petitioned state officials to demolish the site in 1806; however, the legislature tabled all motions until 1815 when it announced plans to sell it.

National sentiment favored saving this landmark, yet nothing was done for nearly a year. Finally, a group of civic-minded Philadelphians stepped forward.[2] They argued that its importance as an election headquarters warranted saving it. State officials agreed and sold it to the City of Philadelphia for $70,000 in 1816.[3] Upon receipt, city officials rented space to Charles Willson Peale for a museum. Federal Courts also occupied the north and west rooms.

Local officials assured the public that this landmark would be restored to its original glory. However, this did not include saving its library wing: a new fireproof annex by a young Southern architect named Robert Mills soon replaced it.[4] Only with the refurbishing of its monumental bell tower and spire in 1828 did the grandeur of Independence Hall reemerge.[5] Further improvements in the 1870s and 1880s in the form of a new clock and large bell were praised by the public.

Several civic organizations sponsored major restoration efforts in the last decade of the nineteenth century. One of the most ambitious of these involved the City of Philadelphia and the National Society of the Colonial Dames of America. Beginning in 1894, they embarked on a two-year renovation of the old senate chamber, supervised by a popular local architect named George C. Mason Jr. The project's success convinced the Daughters of the American Revolution (DAR) to renovate the building's entire second floor. The DAR intended to showcase its achievement at a special

Independence Hall, Philadelphia, Pa., 1731–53. Andrew Hamilton and Edward Wooley, architects. This early rendering of Independence Hall draws attention to the original building and its two wings. Note its enormous central tower topped by an equally impressive weathervane.

July 4 celebration in 1901. A local designer, T. Mellon Rogers, received this highly prized commission.[6]

Unfortunately, the task proved overwhelming: cost overruns, bickering consultants, and incompetent local artisans led to unanticipated delays and shoddy workmanship. The DAR and city officials were not happy. In March 1898, Rogers was replaced by more experienced designers.[7] They removed all the defective moldings and wainscoting for $5,000. This additional cost brought total expenses to an unprecedented $62,000. Later renovations in the 1930s to the House of Representatives chamber were less expensive and mostly followed original design plans. This landmark remained in local hands through World War II. Independence Hall has been under the auspices of the National Park Service since 1951.

Other nineteenth-century landmarks threatened with demolition included the Old Indian House (1699) in Deerfield, Massachusetts; the Hasbrouck House (1750) in Newburgh, New York; the Hermitage (1836) in Nashville, Tennessee; Carpenter's Hall (1770) in Philadelphia, Pennsylvania; and the John Hancock House (1737) in Boston, Massachusetts. All were saved except for the John Hancock House, which was demolished in 1863: the reluctance of Boston City Council to protect this national treasure led to its demise.

The hesitation of this legislative body shocked many Bostonians. After all, less than a year earlier this same council had endorsed a motion to preserve this house as a national landmark. This proposal had called for removing it to an outlying park and refurbishing it as the "Mayor's Mansion." Unfortunately, high moving costs and mounting pressure from the local business community convinced city officials to reverse their decision. Without council support, all was lost. Local preservationists never forgot this betrayal, and the slogan "Destroyed in '63" remained a battle cry for years to come.[8]

Case Study: Mount Vernon

Another threatened landmark was Mount Vernon (1757). The rumored sale and demolition of George Washington's ancestral home first surfaced in 1846. Its owner, John Augustine Washington, a great-grandnephew of the late president, petitioned both Congress and the Virginia state legislature to purchase it for $100,000.[9] Unfortunately, neither body responded, and Washington followed by announcing plans to sell this historic plantation to developers.

In 1853, a group of wealthy women led by Ann Pamela Cunningham of South Carolina petitioned the Virginian legislature to buy the site. Unfortunately, state officials were hesitant to support them.[10] The reluctance of these legislators to approve the petition did not discourage Cunningham's group; in 1858, they approached the same body for a special charter allowing them to purchase this landmark. State officials approved this request, and they bought the site for $200,000 in 1860.

Purchasing Mount Vernon was just the beginning. They knew that their future success depended on establishing an effective organization with capable leaders at all levels.[11] Board members elected Cunningham as their official leader. They also appointed leaders for each state. Known as vice regents, these women were responsible for generating all local fund-raising activities and programming.[12] Unfortunately, ill health forced Cunningham to resign in 1874. She died a short time later; however, her untimely death did not signal the end of this new, highly energized group. In fact, the Mount Vernon Ladies' Association continues as a viable nonprofit organization to the present day. Its well-trained staff and enthusiastic volunteers are still dedicated to preserving the cultural and physical legacy of Mount Vernon as first envisioned by their founder nearly 150 years ago.[13]

Many other groups—such as the Valley Forge Association of Valley Forge, Pennsylvania, the Ladies Hermitage Association of Nashville, Tennessee, and the Site and Relic Society of Germantown, Pennsylvania—were modeled after the Ladies' Society of Mount Vernon.[14] What distinguished Mount Vernon's group from these other equally dedicated organizations was that its activities received national acclaim. Also, it enjoyed considerable political clout especially in the South.[15]

The positive publicity generated by such activity convinced others to restore landmarks throughout the United States. Some prominent national sites saved included the Lee Mansion (1802) in Arlington, Virginia; the Old Stone House (1737) in Richmond, Virginia; the Bruton Parish Church (1715) in Williamsburg, Virginia; the historic mansions of Fairmount Park (1876) in Philadelphia, Pennsylvania; General George Washington's headquarters in Morristown, New Jersey; and the Philipse Manor House (1682) in Yonkers, New York. With the exception of the Bruton Parish Church, all received some kind of public assistance.

New England Preservation

Late nineteenth- and early twentieth-century preservationists in New England followed a different course of action: they relied on their own ingenuity and private funding sources. Their independence and resourcefulness were evident as early as the 1870s, with the successful renovation of two favorite Boston landmarks, the Old South Meeting House (1876) and the Old State House (1879).[16] This cooperative spirit continued throughout New England for the rest of the nineteenth century.

The first decade of the twentieth century ushered in major administrative changes. Sophisticated new management and funding practices began to replace earlier less formal business arrangements, and these dramatic changes alarmed the old guard. Exponents of reform tried to waylay fears by saying that the new business approaches would encourage greater program opportunities while lessening daily administrative duties. There is little doubt that these efficient business practices spurred on new program initiatives. Unfortunately, they also significantly increased the daily administrative responsibilities of most preservation leaders.

However, this was not evident at the turn of the twentieth century. In fact, many aspiring preservation leaders, such as William Sumner Appleton, believed wholeheartedly in the administrative and business advantages of efficient management. They knew all too well what would happen when ineffective leadership took control. In Appleton's case, meddling by incompetent leaders had undermined his efforts to preserve the Paul Revere House in 1905. In the end, benefactors, not preservation leaders, saved the site.[17] In 1910, disgusted by outmoded business practices and less-than-enlightened leaders, Appleton founded the Society for the Preservation of New England Antiquities (SPNEA) with the support of his colleagues and friends.[18] Early critics argued that the SPNEA was power-hungry and therefore out to destroy other groups. Appleton dispelled these concerns by saying that his group wanted to help others, not hinder them. He quickly gained credibility with his peers by publishing an informative newsletter, which kept them abreast of local preservation activities and provided him with editorial space.

Supporters praised the SPNEA for identifying endangered local landmarks and initiating campaigns to save them. No other preservation group possessed such expertise. Their resourcefulness was evident as early as 1912, when members renovated an entire historic district in Concord, Massachusetts. Over the next decade, the SPNEA was to save nearly one hundred sites. One of the group's most effective strategies involved purchasing endangered structures and then mortgaging them to restorers. The revenue derived from these sales bought other historic sites. This was very similar to modern-day revolving funds, with one notable exception. Private benefactors, rather than state-regulated lending institutions, held the mortgages. Another of the SPNEA's successful approaches was to publish lists of threatened buildings and send them to potential buyers, who were encouraged to bid on them. This strategy helped to save the Boardman House (1686) in Saugus, Massachusetts; Charles Bullfinch, the First Harrison Gray Otis Townhouse (1795) in Boston, Massachusetts; and Richard Munday, the Colony House (1736) in Newport, Rhode Island.

Business and civic leaders eagerly supported the SPNEA. For example, a well-known Connecticut philanthropist, named Samuel P. Avery, established an endowment fund.[19] Others joined the board of directors, and many worked on the newsletter. In the latter case, their efforts led to an entirely new publication in 1918. This newsletter, *Old-Time New England,* featured in-depth articles and financial reports.

Major activities such as these paid off well. By the 1920s, the SPNEA was considered one of the United States' leading preservation groups. Organizations big and small asked Appleton for help. Although only a few members of his staff had any professional training in the preservation field, they still assisted other groups. Considered experts in art and fine taste, they handled a wide variety of architectural and interior-design issues and problems.

Background, education, social standing, and a sense of "good taste" prompted most of their decisions.[20] Good taste frequently resulted in beautiful structures with little historic accuracy; however, critics rarely chastised them. Expedience took precedence over other major considerations: architectural honesty, design accuracy, and structural integrity. In retrospect, it is easy to understand why this happened. Members of the SPNEA were well-intentioned elitists, and, as such, they preserved certain cherished slices of the United States' past culture and heritage while discarding others. Also, since they financed many of these projects, they believed they had the right to make all the important decisions.

Elitist leaders dominated the preservation field into the 1920s. The advent of well-paying jobs and modern, labor-saving devices gave many outsiders the finances and the time to join the cause for the first time. Special events such as the 300th anniversary of the pilgrims' landing at Plymouth, Massachusetts (1920), followed by the unveiling of McKim, Mead, and White's neoclassic portico covering Plymouth Rock in 1921 also served in this effort. In fact, membership in preservation-related organizations nearly doubled in the 1920s.

Initially, the old guard welcomed these newcomers. However, their enthusiasm soon dampened as new members began to question traditional policies. The new guard contended that traditional leaders were elitist and therefore out of step with modern thinking. The way to remedy the problem was to choose leaders based on ability and merit and not personal connections and wealth. Disagreements such as these divided groups for many years. Fortunately, these internal struggles rarely surfaced, and preservation's popularity remained unchallenged through the 1920s. The thousands of visitors to historic outdoor museums and sites such as the Wayside Inn in Sudbury, Massachusetts (1924), Colonial Williamsburg in Williamsburg, Virginia (1927), and Greenfield Village in Dearborn, Michigan (1929) reflected the public's growing interest in the nation's cultural heritage.

Case Study: Monticello

Although Sudbury, Williamsburg, and Greenfield Village received much acclaim in the 1920s there was another drama of equal importance unfolding. In 1923, a private nonprofit organization called the Thomas Jefferson Memorial Foundation purchased Monticello for just under $500,000. This represented a major victory for preservation.

First refurbished in the 1830s by Captain Uriah Levy, Jefferson's legendary home was well maintained until his death.[21] Levy stipulated in his will that federal officials renovate the mansion as an agricultural school for orphaned children. Unfortunately, Congress never acted on his bequest. In 1863, the Confederate States of America declared the site "an alien enemy," which led to extensive vandalism. Then, in 1864, Benjamin F. Ficklin, a nationally recognized business leader, bought the site for $80,500. However, less than a year later Union forces confiscated it and returned it to the Levy family.

Meanwhile, the national landmark continued to deteriorate. Further litigation in the 1870s only worsened the situation. Finally, Jefferson Monroe Levy, a nephew of the captain, purchased Monticello for $10,500 in 1879.[22] His early renovation efforts were attacked by critics, who claimed that the workmanship was shoddy and that he had no right to collect a twenty-five-cent admission charge. Levy responded that his renovations were more than sufficient and that the admission cost covered expenses.

In 1897, leading southern Democrat and former presidential candidate William Jennings Bryan tried unsuccessfully to get him to sell. Bryan's setback did not silence critics. For example, Amos J. Cummings criticized Levy for charging visitors to tour the site. However, he concluded that it did not matter since none of the furnishings in the house were original.[23] Dorothy Dix also admonished Levy for not maintaining this national treasure properly.[24]

He responded by publishing two letters he had received from a famous English visitor George Alfred Townsend. Townsend claimed that Levy was a very gracious host and that the site was well maintained. In retrospect, much of the criticism seems unwarranted. Perhaps the resurgence of anti-Semitism in the 1880s explains some of it; personal gain also may have prompted it. Whatever the motivations behind their actions, critics relentlessly pursued him to sell.

One of Levy's worst detractors was Maud Littleton. Wife of a respected New York congressman, she wrote a fifty-two-page pamphlet entitled *One*

Wish in 1911. It called for grassroots support to save both the mansion and site.[25] Its impact was small. A year later, she introduced a resolution in Congress calling for Levy to sell; it never got beyond the House Rules Committee. She then initiated a national letter writing campaign. Congressional leaders were not impressed with that, either, and the entire matter was dropped at the outbreak of World War I.[26] In the final analysis, Littleton lacked the organizational skills, political know-how, and financial resources necessary to win congressional support. A more professional approach was needed.

In April 1923 a group of influential New York attorneys, headed by Theodore Fred Kuper, met to resolve this highly controversial issue. They decided to buy the 640-acre estate and to establish a new, nonprofit organization dedicated to promoting the life and times of Thomas Jefferson. This group, named the Thomas Jefferson Foundation, purchased Monticello for $500,000. It still operates the mansion and gardens and affords a wide variety of educational, enrichment, and research programs.[27]

Preservationists in the 1920s also met increased resistance from municipal planners. An outgrowth of the City Beautiful movement, they represented a whole new breed of empiricists dedicated to efficient new business practices.[28] Obsessed with power, they allied themselves with equally ambitious business and civic leaders. These new alliances enabled them to promote new, large-scale development with minimum opposition.

City Beautiful planners claimed their actions made good business sense, but in reality, many of their decisions challenged traditional notions of progress. In most people's minds, progress meant unbridled economic, demographic, and physical expansion based on accepted laissez-faire doctrines. Efficient productivity, cheap energy and labor costs, and unlimited market potential following the Civil War prompted such thinking.

Urban planners in the 1920s rarely attacked laissez-faire doctrines directly; doing so would have labeled them radicals. They were not radicals or anticapitalists. However, they recognized that present-day capitalism could not survive without some reform. They also understood that these reforms must come from traditional leaders. With this in mind, they attacked what they believed to be the worse environmental and societal abuses in our cities, claiming that chaos was everywhere and order must be reestablished quickly. They thought reform initiated through wide-scale planning was the answer. If properly managed, it would instill in their communities new civic pride and long-term prosperity.

Many business and civic leaders concurred. They saw new development as a viable alternative to chaos. Through municipal regulatory agencies, planners introduced a multitude of new programs. These initiatives generally fit three goals. They were, first, to improve the physical quality of the environment in a direct orderly fashion, second, encourage new business development, and last, inspire civic pride. Boards of trade and chambers of commerce throughout the United States supported such actions. In fact, promotional literature of the time proclaimed that large-scale development would ensure stability and guarantee future growth and prosperity for all.

The Cleveland Municipal Stadium, promoted as the crown jewel of the 1903 Cleveland Group Plan, represented an outgrowth of such thinking. Local civic and business leaders pushed for a new municipally run stadium after World War I, and the city council responded by establishing the Cleveland Stadium Committee (CSC) in 1926. CSC recommended constructing a new $2.5 million sports facility on Lake Erie. The city council agreed and placed a stadium petition on the November 1928 ballot.

To ensure victory, CSC members launched an extensive promotional campaign. They argued that the city needs this stadium as a symbol of civic progress and pride. They also publicized the many events planned for it. Although some Clevelanders complained about its high cost, in the end the public overwhelmingly supported it. Voters in Boston, Detroit, Philadelphia, St. Louis, and San Francisco approved similar projects in the late 1920s.[29]

Undoubtedly, planners saw large-scale development as a way of guaranteeing long-term growth and prosperity. However, it meant more than that to them: they believed that, if done correctly, such planning would elevate the general public to a new moral level. Performance and permanence were viewed as stabilizing forces in an uncertain urban environment.

Because development and progress were considered interchangeable, urban planners had little toleration for skeptics, who they labeled as either fanatics or Bolsheviks. Similarly, they had little interest in saving historic buildings. In their minds, these structures only impeded progress. The public generally supported their efforts, also equating growth with prosperity.[30] Preservationists were equally cognizant of the need for new development but at what cost? They argued that saving historic structures helped preserve the United States' physical legacy and promoted patriotism by educating the public about the nation's past. They believed that with a little ingenuity many historic buildings and sites could be saved and reutilized.

Although both sides presented plausible arguments, planners ultimately won. The fact that most were college-educated men was important. The loyal opposition, made up mostly of well-meaning women, posed no direct threat. This lopsided advantage did not stop preservationists from opposing wide-scale development. Using proven business strategies, they tried to convince business and civic leaders of the value of including historic sites in new development.

Their arguments fell on deaf ears. Hindered by financial and organizational issues and blatant gender discrimination, preservationists found themselves stymied at virtually every juncture. The media also exacerbated the situation: a vital arm of the business community, it praised planners while attacking preservationists. This alliance between planners and the media continued well into the 1960s.

In spite of these problems, preservationists remained optimistic. And why not? After all, they had introduced preservation to thousands. They also played a pivotal role in educating the public about the importance of U.S. history. Unfortunately, their optimism quickly turned to pessimism after the stock market crash of 1929. Triggered by a worldwide recession, overproduction, high inventories, and stock manipulations, the Great Depression all but wiped out all the significant economic gains of the 1920s.

The 1930s proved to be a period of untold misery and suffering for millions of Americans. President Herbert Hoover attempted to lessen its impact through the Reconstruction Finance Corporation and several other stopgap measures. A conservative Republican, he hesitated to use federal tax dollars to stimulate the economy; he believed that prosperity was just around the corner and that any tampering with the economy would only delay it.

Unfortunately, the economy did not rebound, and Hoover lost his bid for reelection in 1932.[31] His successor, New York governor Franklin Delano Roosevelt, took a different approach. A liberal Democrat and disciple of the famed British economist John Maynard Keynes, Roosevelt believed that the federal government should infuse tax dollars into the economy. This resulted in the New Deal, which provided temporary work for thousands of unemployed Americans.

Preservation was not immune to the Great Depression. Few supporters remained untouched by it, yet the movement managed to survive and grow. Two important developments guaranteed its continued existence. The first occurred in 1931, when Charleston, South Carolina established one of the United States' first historic districts. Referred to as Charleston's Old and Historic District, this 138-acre neighborhood was enlarged twice, first in 1966 and then again in 1975. The original city ordinance called for the

Historic House, Charleston, S.C. This house epitomized the new Classic residences constructed in 18th century downtown Charleston. Its highly impressive open two-story side porch provided its owner, family, and guests with cooling summer breezes.

creation of a strong local architectural review board whose purpose was to oversee all building changes and new construction in this area. However, the board was unable to stop demolitions until 1966. In spite of its initial limitations, this ordinance protected many of Charleston's finest landmarks.[32] It also encouraged other communities such as New Orleans and San Antonio to expand their own preservation programs later in the same decade.

The establishment of the Historic American Buildings Survey (HABS) in 1933 was the second of these major developments.[33] HABS provided work for unemployed architects, draftsmen, and photographers. Specifically, it recorded prominent historic structures and sites for the Library of Congress archives. Originally placed under the auspices of the Civil Works Administration (CWA), it was soon turned over to the National Park Service, American Institute of Architects, and the Library of Congress. HABS funding sources included the U.S. Congress, public agencies, private foundations, advocacy groups, historical societies, and individual benefactors. Its success led to the development of a second program in 1969 called the Historic American Engineering Record (HAER). HAER deals with engineering issues and the evolution of infrastructure technology. Both programs continue to the present day.

The United States' entry into World War II in December 1941 marked the end of the Great Depression. The intensity and devastation of the war left an indelible mark on both the nation and the preservation movement. The postwar years afforded many formidable challenges. Federal officials knew that the United States' built environment, which had remained unchanged from 1930 to 1945, needed to be modernized quickly. They also recognized that returning servicemen wanted good jobs and decent housing. Congress responded to these concerns by offering affordable housing to qualified veterans through the Federal Housing Administration (FHA) and the Veterans Administration (VA). This action signaled the development of modern suburbs.[34]

Preservationists remained acquiescent during this first wave of postwar building. Occurring mostly in outlying, often rural areas, it posed no immediate threat to traditional urban settings. Congressional support in 1949 for a nationally based preservation organization also pleased supporters.[35] An outgrowth of the earlier Council for Historic Sites and Buildings, the National Trust for Historic Preservation provided leadership, education, advocacy, and assistance to preservation groups everywhere. Unfortunately, this climate of optimism soon turned to one of pessimism, when federal officials unveiled plans to demolish slum districts through urban renewal.

Title I of the National Housing Act of 1949, Urban Renewal, offered communities extensive eminent domain powers and special funding packages designed to eliminate unwanted blighted areas.[36] Preservation leaders expressed concern that eager planners might condemn all structures in targeted areas, including historic landmarks. They also questioned the courts' rights to dictate public policy; in their minds, the power of the courts must be limited to adjudication.

Preservationists suggested that municipalities should take the lead to protect their citizenry against overzealous planners by establishing their own civic watchdog organizations. Unfortunately, few followed this advice. Failure to monitor urban renewal would have dire economic and social consequences for many communities in the 1960s and 1970s. Yet, only a handful of business and civic leaders acknowledged their mistake. Preservationists were astonished that the voting public rarely chastised its leaders for such irresponsible actions. They were equally amazed that community activists did not readily challenge the legality of urban renewal in the courts. It would take the passage of the National Historic Preservation Act in 1966 and then mounting public pressure in the 1970s before the U.S. Supreme Court addressed this issue. The final, watershed case was *Penn Central Transportation Co. v. City of New York* (1978).[37]

Case Study: Penn Central

This case began in 1974, when the Penn Central Railroad launched a "takings" claim against the City of New York. The New York City Landmarks Preservation Commission had repeatedly turned down Penn Central's requests to build a new fifty-five-story office tower above historic Grand Central Station. In this case, first presented in front of the New York State Supreme Court Appellate Division, this national rail carrier argued that the city's negative response was both arbitrary and a violation of its legal right for just compensation under the Fifth and Fourteenth Amendments of the U.S. Constitution. It further stated that the city's ordinance had deprived it of any gainful use of air rights above the terminal. This kind of restriction did not apply to other non-designated sites.

Penn Central claimed that the new skyscraper would generate $3 million annually. It further argued that its contemporary design complemented the historic terminal below. It concluded that if the public wished to save landmarks such as Grand Central, then it should buy them and maintain them. The City of New York defended its action by saying that preserving historic landmarks like Grand Central was crucial to the well-being of all its citizenry and that, moreover, its actions fostered civic pride and made good business sense. In response to Penn Central's impending financial loss, New York officials claimed that its decision was not prompted by malice aforethought; they had taken every precaution possible not to penalize this property owner.

In January 1975, the New York Supreme Court ruled in favor of Penn Central. The presiding justice, Irving H. Saypol, invalidated the city's landmark ordinance. However, he did not award damages. Municipal officials had the option of appealing the decision; however, other more pressing economic and political concerns led the city not to exercise its right immediately. This delay prompted a well-known civic organization, the Municipal Art Society, to create its own special task force, the Committee to Save Grand Central. This group's membership was composed of many prominent New Yorkers, including Brendan Gill, Philip Johnson, Ed Koch, Bess Myerson, Helen Hayes, and Gloria Steinem. This task force sponsored a major media campaign that culminated in a Save Grand Central Station rally held on April 15, 1975. With this groundswell of new support, city officials decided to appeal the decision. Upon appeal, the earlier decision was overturned. This led Penn Central to take its case to the U.S. Supreme Court.

The U.S. Supreme Court, by a 6–3 decision, found in favor of the City of New York. The majority opinion, rendered by Justice William Brennan, stated that New York's Preservation Commission was within its legal rights to preserve the character and aesthetic quality of its community. In addition, he said that Penn Central was not entitled to just compensation. In fact, the current revenue generated from operating the Grand Central terminal would more than reimburse the rail carrier for any losses. However, the court failed to determine a formula for just compensation for similar cases in the future. Instead, Brennan said that the economic impact and the character of government action must be considered on an individual case basis.

Opponents claimed that the Penn Central opinion only reaffirmed the *Village of Euclid v. Ambler Realty Co.* (1926) decision. However, unlike the original case, in which Euclid was allowed to limit nuisances by protecting existing property rights through municipal zoning, this opinion was determined solely on aesthetics—no nuisances evident here. The U.S. Supreme Court quieted critics by saying that current restrictions may not apply to future construction above this or any other historic sites.

Preservationists viewed the Penn Central decision as a major victory. However, property-rights advocates were angered. They hoped that in the future the court would not so readily support the rights of preservationists over those of property owners. A more conservative Supreme Court in the 1980s and 1990s, which would uphold the legal sanctity of property rights, lessened their anxiety.

This pro-property stance alarms many preservationists, who contend that the impact of these decisions extends beyond controlling preservation. In particular, proven land-use and environmental regulations have been virtually eliminated by these recent rulings. Yet, the Supreme Court is still hesitant to overturn the fundamental basis of the Fifth Amendment jurisprudence as cited in the Penn Central case. Some recent cases upholding property rights include *First English Evangelical Lutheran Church v. County of Los Angeles*, 482 U.S. 304 (1987); *Nollan v. California Coastal Commission*, 482 U.S. 825 (1987); *Lucas v. South Carolina Coastal Council*, 501 U.S. 1003 (1992); *Dolan v. City of Tigard*, 512 U.S. 687 (1994); *Suitum v. Tahoe Regional Planning Agency*, 520 U.S. 725 (1997); *City of Monterey v. Del Monte Dunes, Ltd.*, No. 97–1235, 1998 WL 308006 (U.S. 1999), 7; and *Palazzolo v. Rhode Island*, 121 S. Ct. 2448, 2457 (2001).

Case Study: Eminent Domain, New London, Connecticut

Legal struggles continue to the present day. In the U.S. Supreme Court case *Kelo et al v. City of New London, Connecticut* (2005), the Court by a 5–4 majority ruled that "local governments may seize people's homes and businesses against their will for private development in a decision anxiously awaited in communities where economic growth often is at odds with individual property rights."[38]

Writing for the majority, Justice John Paul Stevens said, "local officials, not federal judges, know best in deciding whether a development project will benefit the community. Furthermore, states are within their rights to pass additional laws restricting condemnations if residents are over burdened. . . . It is not for the courts to oversee the choice of the boundary line nor to sit in review on the size of a particular project area."

He further stated that "promoting economic development is a traditional and long accepted function of government" and judges should give city councils and state legislatures "broad latitude in determining what public needs justify the use of taking powers." Dissenters argued that the court failed to uphold ownership rights as stated in the U.S. Constitution. Justice Clarence Thomas said minority groups and the elderly would suffer the most from these efforts.

Once a viable regional manufacturing center, New London suffered a series of economic setbacks beginning in the 1960s. Hoping to reverse these losses, city officials signed an agreement with Pfizer Pharmaceutical to redevelop part of the historic Fort Trumbull neighborhood in 1998. This successful effort led to a second proposal less than two years later. This latest package included mixed housing, a new major hotel, and additional prime office space. The for-profit New London Development Corporation handled all negotiations. Realizing that this initiative would require the demolition of historic houses and commercial blocks, local officials invoked eminent domain.

The Fifth Amendment of the U.S. Constitution sanctions eminent domain by saying, private property shall not be taken for public use without just compensation. Rarely used before World War II, urban renewal planners relied on it to acquire vast amounts of privately held property in targeted areas for public redevelopment. Over the past twenty years, municipal leaders have broadened the scope of eminent domain to include buying private parcels at cost and then turning these sites over to private investors for new development, no questions asked. Opponents claim such action is illegal and that the U.S. Constitution specifies that eminent domain should only be used by government officials to secure private property at a fair price for the public good. Critics, whose concerns are well founded, questioned whether the public good is really being served in this instance.

Over the last decade, many communities have invoked eminent domain to lure potentially profitable new development into economically distressed areas, with mixed results. In some cases, targeted neighborhoods are legally recognized historic districts. Political maneuvering such as this infuriates many preservationists; they contend that the purpose behind historic districts is to protect the rights of property owners, raise land values, increase property taxes, and stimulate new development congruent with the existing neighborhood. To not uphold the legal sanctity of these districts is to violate the law.

Pro-development advocates argue that any new investment within a distressed area is positive. Inevitably, it will stimulate the job market and expand the local tax base. Using the broad-based powers of eminent domain is essential in such development. They conclude that no matter how initially painful this process may be for some, ultimately everyone benefits. New London officials used these very arguments to justify the taking of the ninety-acre, two-block area in Fort Trumbull.

Susette Kelo and five other homeowners refused to leave the neighborhood. They claimed that city officials had no legal right to invoke eminent domain, since they could only expropriate privately held land for public-related projects. Outside preservation and lobbying groups rallied behind their cause. Their actions have paid off, at least for the foreseeable future. Fearing reprisals, the City of New London and the State of Connecticut did not proceed with evictions. Recent labor disputes and a volatile local economy may have led some to question the value of such development. Also, the U.S. House of Representatives' condemnation of the Supreme Court decision and support of a bill denying funds to municipalities that improperly use eminent domain may have prompted this moratorium.

At the same time, there are some business and civic leaders who want the preapproved plans to proceed on schedule. They contended that failure to follow through with these plans will send out a negative signal to developers everywhere: don't invest your hard earned capital here. They argue that the partisan interests of a few are delaying the city's economic rebound. Others felt that the State of Connecticut had invested $73 million in a major environmental cleanup campaign, and failure to complete this project in a timely fashion would be viewed as a terrible waste of the taxpayer's dollars. Recent discussions between the New London Development Corporation and private developers have addressed these concerns.

Nearly every state is dealing with eminent domain issues. For example, a recent ruling by the Ohio Supreme Court supports the legal sanctity of historic districts. In a unanimous decision, it reversed a series of lower court decisions favoring the use of eminent domain to stimulate private development in "blighted" areas. Justice Maureen O'Connor said that local governments do not have the legal right to invoke eminent domain solely on economic grounds. This decision is the exact opposite of the New London case.[39]

Preservation is as old as the nation itself. Its success is not based on happenstance: early on, leaders recognized that the movement's growth rested on adopting flexible goals and objectives. Drawing on traditional cultural values such as art, aesthetics, history, and patriotism, preservation leaders developed their own unique program initiatives. Creativity, timing, and patience were essential to their success.

Late nineteenth- and early twentieth-century preservation groups recognized the importance of effective leadership and organizational skills. Mastering these skills allowed groups such as the Mount Vernon Ladies' Association and SPNEA to grow and prosper. They also became recognized models of organizational efficiency for others to emulate.

A renewed public interest in American history following World War I provided further opportunities for innovative preservation leaders. It afforded them the chance to publicize recent achievements while promoting new ideas and encouraging program latitude. Opposition from prominent business groups and planners did not stop this effort. Advocates wholeheartedly supported a wide variety of cultural and educational activities, including the development of special outdoor museums. Membership in preservation organizations nearly doubled in the 1920s.

Preservationists took a different approach during the Great Depression of the 1930s. In particular, supporters worked with local business and civic leaders to enact preservation legislation in Charleston, New Orleans, and San Antonio. Also, they convinced federal officials to become involved through HABS and the National Register of Historic Places.

The establishment of the National Trust for Historic Preservation in 1949 and the widespread failure of urban renewal programs in the 1950s and 1960s led to a renewed interest in preservation throughout the United States. U.S. congressional support first through the National Historic Preservation Act of 1966 followed by other related bills and major tax reforms illustrated a new federal commitment to the movement. Preservation leaders responded by developing their own new multicultural programs.

Economic setbacks in the mid-1970s encouraged activists to partner with conservationists, environmentalists, and planners for the first time. These new efforts introduced preservation to an entirely new audience. The preservation field also became more professionalized in the 1980s; the number of schools offering advanced degrees in preservation-related fields nearly tripled.

Since the early 1980s, preservationists have been confronted with many new legal precedents. Recent U.S. Supreme Court decisions demonstrate the growing complexity of the modern American constitutional process. Preservation leaders are responding to these challenges by initiating a wide variety of new insightful programs. Advocates also serve as effective facilitators. In this capacity, they mediate difficult economic, legal, and social problems. Contemporary problems run the gamut from appropriate use of eminent domain to containment of urban sprawl and from effective management of urban development to conservation of rural areas. Controversial concerns such as these will continue to prompt discussions between pro- and anti-preservation groups for years to come. Preservation leaders must continue to present thoughtful arguments based on the intrinsic cultural, economic, and social value of preservation. Whatever the approach used, they must lead the vanguard of reform in this area. This is imperative, if historic preservation intends to remain at the forefront of U.S. cultural and historic conservancy through the twenty-first century.

Notes

1. Thomas T. Waterman and John A. Barrows, *Domestic Colonial Architecture of Tidewater Virginia* (New York: Scribner's, 1932), 13.

2. National Park Service, Independence National Historic Park, Select Committee Minutes, City of Philadelphia, Mar. 11, 1813.

3. National Park Service, *Historic Structures Report, Part II on Independence Hall,* Apr. 1962, 81–84. Courtesy of the National Park Service.

4. Ibid., 83.

5. National Park Service, "Preservation of a Shrine, Independence Hall, Philadelphia, PA," www.nps.gov/inde/preservation.html.

6. Bruce Laverty and Robert J. Hotes, "AIA Philadelphia Historic Preservation Committee," *AIA, Preservation Architect: The Newsletter of the Historic Resources Committee* (July 25, 2007): 1, www.aia.org/nwsltr-hrc.cfm?

7. National Park Service, Independence National Historic Park, Museum Collection, T. Mellon Rogers, Mar. 9, 1898, "Diary 1898."

8. Charles B. Hosmer Jr., *Presence of the Past: A History of the Preservation Movement in the United States before Williamsburg* (New York: G. P. Putnam's Sons, 1962), 39.

9. Ibid., 41.

10. Robert Poch, "The Plight of Mount Vernon," *American History Magazine* (Feb. 2004) www.historynet.com/ah/blmtvernonplight.

11. Ann Pamela Cunningham, "To the Ladies of the South," *Charleston Mercury*, Dec. 2, 1853, sec. ER I, p. 1.

12. Champion Tree Project International Official Website, "Mount Vernon Ladies Association," www.championtreeproject.org/Ford%20House/Mt%20Vernon%20Ladies.htm.

13. Ann Pamela Cunningham, "Farewell Address to the Board of Regents at Mount Vernon," in *Minutes of the Council of the Mount Vernon Ladies' Association, June 2, 1874, Reports of the Mount Vernon Ladies' Association 1853–1874* (1874): 6–7.

14. Hosmer, *Presence of the Past*, 58.

15. Mrs. Roger A. Pryor, "The Mount Vernon Association," *American Historical Register* 1 (1895): 407–20.

16. Boston City Council, *Rededication of the Old State House, Boston, July 11, 1882* (Boston: Boston City Council, 1882), 111–12.

17. "William Sumner Appleton, 1874–1947," *Old-Time New England: The Bulletin of The Society for the Preservation of New England Antiquities* 37 no. 4 (1948): 71–72.

18. William Sumner Appleton, "A Brief Account of the Society for the Preservation of New England Antiquities," typewritten manuscript for Charles Messer Stowe, ca. 1930. Courtesy of Historic New England, Boston, Mass.

19. Hosmer, *Presence of the Past*, 245.

20. Ibid., 286–87.

21. Abram Kanof, "Uriah Phillips Levy: The Story of a Pugnacious Commodore," *Publication of the American Jewish Historical Society* 39 (Sept-June 1949–50): 1–66.

22. Thomas Jefferson Foundation, "The Levys at Monticello," www.monticello.org/about/levy.html.

23. Amos J. Cummings, "A National Humiliation: A Story of Monticello," *New York Sun*, Aug. 24, 1902, 1.

24. Dorothy Dix, "Monticello: Shrine or Bachelor's Hall?" *Good Housekeeping* (Apr. 1914): 538–41.

25. Maud Littleton, *One Wish*, pamphlet Aug. 30, 1911, reprinted from *Congressional Record* (Washington, DC: GPO, 1912), 1–16.

26. U.S. Congress. *Monticello*. Debate on HR 740, 62nd Cong., 2nd sess., *Congressional Record* 49, no. 1 (Dec. 9, 1912): 347.

27. Thomas Jefferson Foundation, About Us, www.monticello.org/about/index.html.

28. William H. Wilson, "Moles and Skylarks," in *Introduction to Planning History in the United States*, ed. Donald A. Kruckenberg (New Brunswick, N.J.: Rutgers Center for Urban Policy Research, 1987), 88–89.

29. Henry S. Churchill, *The City Is the People* (New York: Norton, 1962), 84–85.

30. Richard N. Current, T. Harry Williams, and Frank Freidel, *American History: A Survey* (New York: Knopf, 1979), 639–46, 649–54.

31. Samuel G. Stoney, *This Is Charleston: A Survey of the Architectural Heritage of a Unique American City* (Charleston, S.C.: Carolina Art Association, 1960), 134–36.

32. National Park Service, Park Net, HABS, History, www.nps.gov/hpd/habs/index.htm.

33. J. John Palen, *The Urban World* (New York: McGraw-Hill, 1987), 184–87.

34. National Trust for Historic Preservation Act of 1949, Pub. Law 408, 81st Cong., 1st sess. (Oct. 26, 1949).

35. National Housing Act of 1949. Pub. Law 171, 81st Cong., 1st sess. (July 15, 1949).

36. Richard F. Babcock and Charles L. Siemon, *The Zoning Game: Municipal Practices and Policies Revisited* (Boston: Oelgeschlageer, Gunn and Hain, 1985), 58–75.

37. *Penn Central Transportation Co. v. City of New York*, 438 U.S. 104, 98 S.C. 2646 (1978).

38. *Kelo et al. v. City of New London, Connecticut*, No. 04–108 (S.Ct. June 23, 2005), www.supremecourts.gov/opinions/04pdf/04–108.pdf.

39. David Owsiany, "Ohio Court Restores Balance to Eminent Domain, Norwood Went Too Far and State Court Reels City In," *Akron Beacon Journal*, Aug. 1, 2006, 1, www.reason.org/commentaries/owsiary-20060801.shtml.

Chapter Three

Historic Preservation

Its Legislative Framework

Introduction

The twenty-five years following World War II represented a period of unprecedented economic and physical growth in the United States. Finally, the Depression and World War II were over. The nation's economy was rebounding, and the country was considered the undisputed leader of the free world. The public responded by demanding a modern society, a "brave new world" in which comfort and security would replace want and uncertainty. To them, the future provided unlimited economic and social opportunities if citizens only had the courage to pursue their dreams.

Noted architects and planners—such as Le Corbusier, Benton McKay, Lewis Mumford, and Frank Lloyd Wright—first popularized the idea of a brave new world in the late 1930s. At first glance, their description of a new world, one safe from annihilation, disillusionment, and despair may have appeared contradictory to what the British author Aldous Huxley depicted in his highly popular novel.

However, closer examination suggests just the opposite. First, all these thinkers recognized that ultimately science must become subservient to mankind, not the other way around. Second, they agreed on the necessity of educating the public to this reality as soon as possible. The New York World's Fair 1939–40 reflected this thinking. In fact, the General Motors Futurama exhibition featuring Norman Bel Geddes's larger than life three-dimensional working model of an automated future American city was the hit of the show.[1] The message conveyed to visitors at the World's Fair was direct: modern productivity was efficient, manageable, and measurable; and with proper enlightened leadership everyone would benefit. The

United States' victory in World War II, based in large measure on the ability of the nation to manufacture and distribute vital war materials on demand, added further credence to this argument.

Even though the threat of nuclear war was imminent, many postwar Americans wholeheartedly supported demilitarization. They believed that it represented the first step toward establishing a lasting peacetime economy. The question posed to the United States' postwar leadership was how best to maintain high productivity and build consumer confidence while making this transition from a wartime to a peacetime economy.

The lack of affordable good housing and well-paying jobs for returning servicemen and their families were two immediate problems. Congressional leaders enacted several major bills, beginning with the Servicemen's Readjustment Act of 1944 and the Reorganization Plans of 1947.[2] Intended to facilitate an orderly transition from wartime to peacetime, these acts set the precedent for further legislative reforms favoring new development.

The logic behind them was threefold. First, federal officials recognized that there had been no significant new construction in the United States for almost twenty years—the nation was ripe for new development. Second, they understood that the construction and building trades industry employed tens of thousands of workers and that they relied on countless outside goods and services daily. Conventional wisdom said that if Congressional leaders supported the construction and building trades industry, national prosperity would follow. Last, promoting home ownership would reinforce cultural and social values by fostering a stable family environment.

The U.S. Congress sanctioned widespread suburban development through Federal Housing Administration– and Veterans Administration–sponsored home-loan and mortgage-insurance programs.[3] Legislators also introduced special tax incentives and funding packages for growing southern and western cities. This postwar legislation culminated with President Dwight D. Eisenhower signing the Federal Highway Act on January 26, 1956.[4]

Postwar congressional leaders also approved urban renewal legislation. Under Title I of the National Housing Act of 1949, urban renewal was in direct response to public officials, planners, and developers who wanted new federal redevelopment incentives. In particular, it called for the wholesale destruction of traditional downtowns and adjacent neighborhoods for new development; proponents argued that it was a very effective way to eliminate unwanted slums in lieu of new growth.[5] This bill also called for new residential development on at least 50 percent of the cleared land.

However, few communities complied with this requirement. A 1959 study, for example, indicated that only 20 percent of all the cleared land had been set aside for new residential development and that most of it was used for public housing.[6]

Urban renewal was further strengthened in the mid-1950s when federal officials announced that the government would absorb two-thirds of all demolition costs and that the cleared inner-city land could be either leased or sold to developers. Intended to encourage new long-term investment in blighted areas, this amendment was praised by municipal officials everywhere.[7]

Business leaders also liked its informality. Non-binding contracts, or gentlemen's agreements, allowed investors and public officials to develop sites with little public interference. Once a plan received community backing then it was submitted to federal administrators for review. Rarely did federal officials reject a plan or prosecute municipal leaders for failing to complete a project. The downside was that local officials were unable to seek just compensation in the courts when an investor reneged on a plan.

However, few politicians and planners focused on the negative aspects of urban renewal. Instead, they wholeheartedly embraced it. To them, the recent proliferation of unsightly inner-city slums had led developers to invest in outlying areas. Federal programs such as these would inevitably reverse this trend. Federal officials said that funding was readily available for communities that wanted it. This idea caught on very quickly. By the mid-1950s, hundreds of communities throughout the United States had received some form of urban renewal funding.

Unfortunately, the market demand for inner-city land never reached anticipated levels. In fact, most developers shied away from these projects, preferring suburban ventures instead. The vast majority claimed that outlying development afforded them very high investment returns with limited government interference. In contrast, inner-city redevelopment was far less profitable and involved miles of bureaucratic red tape. Thus, urban renewal did not retard suburban development; it hastened it.[8] The negative impact of urban renewal first seen in the late 1950s intensified through the 1960s. This was especially true in older, less prosperous manufacturing centers.

As more historic landmarks and districts succumbed to the bulldozer, it became apparent that the nation was losing its historic physical legacy at an alarming rate. Critics argued that preservationists must act immediately or all would be lost. Preservation leaders responded by developing a new, two-pronged strategy. First, they initiated stopgap measures designed to halt further demolitions. Second, they lobbied the U.S. Congress for new comprehensive legislation.

Arbitrary actions by seemingly less-than-enlightened municipal leaders warranted such drastic action. New York City officials, for example, unveiled plans to demolish the historic Pennsylvania Railroad Station. This was January 3, 1963. Located at the corner of West 34th Street and 7th Avenue, in the heart of Midtown Manhattan, Penn Station was to be razed for a new terminal complex and a new Madison Square Garden. The public was outraged that this beautiful fifty-three-year-old Beaux-Arts station was about to be sacrificed in the name of progress. Unfortunately, this outpouring of public sympathy did little to sway public officials. Its October 28, 1963, demolition sent shockwaves throughout the preservation community nationwide. No landmark was safe from the wrecking ball.

At the same time, the early 1960s was a time of great advances within the field. For example, New York City adopted its own Landmarks Preservation Law in 1965. This impressive new ordinance set the stage for similar legislation in other cities. As was shown in chapter 2, it played a crucial role in saving Grand Central Station in 1978.[9]

New York City was not alone in saving and restoring historic sites. Similar efforts occurred in Boston's Back Bay neighborhood, Chicago's Lincoln Park district, and Philadelphia's Fairmount Park. These initiatives reflected a new spirit of cooperation between the public and private sectors. The National Trust for Historic Preservation used the destruction of historic Penn Station and these revitalization efforts to launch its own extensive lobbying efforts before Congress. Trust officials wanted the 89th Congress to pass meaningful preservation legislation before the decade's end.

Michael Harrington's *The Other America: Poverty in the United States* also helped the cause. This highly controversial book debunked myths concerning the plight of the American poor. In particular, Harrington attacked the notion that through hard work the poor could eventually overcome poverty. He said that the poor lacked the means necessary to change their economic and social condition and that poverty was a permanent part of American society.[10]

Some preservationists used Harrington's arguments to demand radical reforms; they proposed revitalizing these slums and making them profitable residential districts populated by the poor. Proponents gave three reasons for such action: it would provide the poor with a much better lifestyle, venture profits would exceed overhead costs, and the new tax revenues generated by this action would lead to expanded and improved municipal services at reasonable cost. Critics contended that current real estate market conditions did not warrant such redevelopment. However, all agreed that inner-city deterioration could no longer be tolerated and that federal intervention was necessary now.

Preservation received another major boost in 1965, when a congressional group led by Albert M. Rains, chair of the Housing Subcommittee, visited several European cities. This trip occurred in the wake of the establishment of the International Council on Monuments and Sites (ICOMOS) a year earlier.[11] ICOMOS, a nonprofit organization dedicated to the conservation of historic monuments and sites worldwide, advises the United Nations Educational, Scientific, and Cultural Organization (UNESCO). In this capacity, it selects monuments and sites for the World Heritage List. It also maintains standards for the management, preservation, and restoration of the cultural environment throughout the world.[12]

This trip to Europe proved to be a wake-up call. Congressional leaders were highly impressed with how European planners had effectively integrated historic buildings into their modern built environment. They concluded that a similar program would be very successful in the United States, so they set aside federal funds for public agencies engaged in preservation. They also expanded current home-loan programs to include property owners who were rehabilitating historic structures.

The National Trust for Historic Preservation also furthered the cause when it published *With Heritage So Rich* (1965). Sponsored by the U.S. Conference of Mayors Special Committee on Historic Preservation, this study, edited by Albert Rains and Laurence G. Henderson, called for more federal involvement in this field. It suggested three ways to do this.[13] First, it sanctioned the establishment of a permanent national register of historically significant artifacts, buildings, and districts. Second, it called for the creation of a new partnership among federal, state, and municipal government leaders. Last, it proposed significant new tax credits.

President Lyndon B. Johnson also helped preservation. In 1964, he established the President's Task Force on the Preservation of Natural Beauty, which was chaired by noted Harvard University law professor Charles M. Haar. It concluded that the federal government should become directly involved in preservation activities at all levels. Congress responded by authorizing new funding packages for communities involved in restoration projects.

The U.S. Department of Housing and Urban Development furthered this effort by mandating that all valued historic buildings in targeted urban renewal areas must be moved to safe sites, where they would be renovated and maintained by reputable preservation-related organizations. HUD's mandate, President Johnson's task force, the trust's report, the congressional junket, Harrington's book, and major urban renewal failures led the 89th U.S. Congress to approve in October 1966 the most sweeping single piece of preservation legislation to date. Known as the National Historic Preservation Act (NHPA) of 1966 (Public Law 89–665), this bill guaranteed federal support for years to come.

The National Historic Preservation Act of 1966

The NHPA set the stage for modern-day preservation in several key ways.[14] First, it ensured long-term federal, state, and municipal governmental support by rewarding preservation leaders who demonstrated outstanding management ability and budgetary responsibility.

Second, it required participation by all fifty states, the District of Columbia, the Commonwealth of Puerto Rico, the Virgin Islands, Guam, and American Samoa. Under this provision, all states and dependencies were required to appoint and support their own state historic preservation officer (SHPO). These SHPOs were responsible for coordinating all preservation activities within their jurisdiction. Their responsibilities included processing all National Register of Historic Places nominations, promoting public participation in programs, and securing matching funds for all federal grants received. SHPOs also were to maintain statewide inventories of historic buildings and sites.

Third, the act encouraged municipalities with existing preservation programs to apply for new federal assistance. A later amendment aided this process directly by establishing the Certified Local Government Program (CLG). Placed under the auspices of the National Park Service, CLG communities are entitled to special federal grants and limited technical assistance. To date, over 1,200 municipalities have received more than $40 million in federal grants.[15] This bill also afforded special U.S. Internal Revenue Service (IRS) tax credits. These programs were to be administered by the National Trust.

Last, the 1966 act did not challenge existing state and municipal land-use regulations and zoning laws. This was a prudent move; to do otherwise might have been construed as a violation of municipal legal rights. Instead, the NHPA provided generous financial and technical assistance to those communities willing to comply with these new federal guidelines. It also offered participants more input into future rehabilitation projects within targeted areas.

Traditionally, federal officials had not maintained a comprehensive record of significant historic buildings, districts, objects, sites, and structures. It took urban renewal failures in the 1950s and 1960s before government leaders acknowledged the importance of compiling such a list. The NHPA addressed this concern directly by establishing the National Register of Historic Places. Supporters believed it was imperative to save all kinds of historic buildings, landmarks, and cultural resources from the wrecking ball. A quantitative list compiled on an individual statewide basis represented a major breakthrough: placed under the auspices of the National Park Service, the National Register is the only official record of archaeological, cultural, and historic resources in the United States. Presently, there are more than 750,000 properties listed on it.

Section 108 of the NHPA detailed federal funding for the National Register and other statewide initiatives, including its grant-in-aid program. Under this provision, federal leaders were encouraged to work with state officials to formulate new programs. It also assisted National Trust leaders in achieving their program goals. Section 108 further stipulated that all grant-in-aid was not to exceed 50 percent of total program costs. The NHPA then authorized a four-year budget totaling $32 million. This initial investment grew to $100 million by 1980 and to more than $200 million by 1995.[16]

Historic districting resulted from the National Register. Prior to the passage of the NHPA, all landmarks were designated individually. However, with the adoption of the National Register the number of recorded historic buildings and sites increased significantly, calling for sweeping reforms, including district-wide designations.

The original act also insisted that aesthetics be incorporated into designation. Preservationists responded by developing their own new recording method, qualitative evaluation. Under this new process, recorders analyzed the different physical components comprising a neighborhood and how they interacted to create a distinct historic district.[17] This new approach enabled preservationists to document buildings and sites accurately and quickly. Unfortunately, it often included non-historic buildings and sites. Purists contended that the inclusion of these buildings and sites in recognized districts was inappropriate, but supporters countered by saying that many of these structures and sites were recognized local landmarks even if they were not historic.

Another major achievement of the 1966 act involved the creation of the cabinet-level Advisory Council on Historic Preservation.[18] Public demand for input into federal policy decisions prompted this action. The NHPA called for a presidential appointee to chair this seventeen-member board. Its membership was to include the secretary of the interior, the secretary of housing and urban development, the secretary of commerce, the secretary of the treasury, the U.S. attorney general, the board chairperson of the National Trust for Historic Preservation, the chief administrator of the General Services Administration, and ten other presidential appointees.[19]

Over the last forty years the size and composition of this board has changed considerably. Current members include the secretary of the interior, the secretary of agriculture, the secretary of housing and urban development, the secretary of transportation, the U.S. Capitol architect; an appointed governor and city mayor; the president of the National Conference of State Historic Preservation Officers; the board chairperson of the National Trust; various preservation experts; several at-large members; and one representative from either a Native American tribe or Native Hawaiian organization.[20]

The Advisory Council on Historic Preservation serves several important functions. First, it disseminates preservation information and materials for both the president and Congress. Second, it assists the National Trust and other preservation-related organizations in implementing new community-based projects. Last, it recommends new educational programming for preservation groups throughout the United States. These programs run the gamut from evaluating the impact of administrative statutes, laws, and regulations in the field to measuring the value of tax policies in promoting preservation.[21]

The power of the Advisory Council on Historic Preservation has been greatly expanded over the past forty years. For example, revisions to Section 106 of the review process have empowered the board to determine the potential environmental impact a new federal project might have on surrounding historic properties and sites. This additional power allows the council to safeguard endangered landmarks from destruction and obliteration. It also provides a neutral setting where opposing sides may debate the pros and cons of certain federal preservation programs in targeted areas.[22]

Section 106 also details the three-step process the advisory board must follow when reviewing a proposal. First, the lead agency must submit a formal statement to the council before initiating any new project. It describes the expected impact this new project will have on surrounding historic properties and sites. Second, the board reviews and ranks the proposal on a scale from least to most dangerous. Last, it renders a decision based on the adverse effects this project is expected to have on nearby landmarks and sites.

If the advisory council determines that a specific project will negatively affect surrounding historic sites, then the lead agency must furnish additional documentation in the form of a memorandum of agreement (MOA).[23] The MOA describes how the agency in question intends to avoid, reduce, or mitigate the potential threat. Those agencies unable to reach a satisfactory agreement with the board will be forced to comply with special guidelines imposed by this council. The enactment of Executive Order 11593 in 1971 and subsequent amendments to the original act further tightened these requirements. Specifically, these mandates spelled out the procedures all agencies must follow when revitalizing historic buildings. They also prescribed effective ways to evaluate the potential impact the new projects might have on adjacent sites.

The NHPA represented the first in a series of legislative acts and mandates intended to assist preservation. Shortly after its enactment, Congress passed a second major piece of legislation called the Department of Transportation Act of 1966 (Public Law 89–670). This bill not only established a new high-ranking cabinet position, it also addressed preservation concerns.

For example, Section 4(f) of the Transportation Act of 1966 specified that all U.S. Department of Transportation (USDOT) agencies must make every effort to preserve public historic sites. This meant that if a project would in any way harm a historic resource that is either on the National Register of Historic Places or eligible for designation then it is the responsibility of the lead agency to seek alternatives. All alternatives must be scrutinized for their potential impact on the historic resource. Those not damaging the historic resource should be adopted by the agency, and if no alternative exists, the agency in question must take every precaution to minimize the project's effect on that site. The law clearly stated that all future federal highway projects must make every "special effort to preserve the natural beauty of the countryside, public parks, recreational lands, wildlife and waterfowl refuges, and historic sites."[24]

Section 303 of the revised Transportation Act of 1966 act authorized the secretary of transportation to partner with the secretaries of the interior, housing and urban development, agriculture, and representatives of the individual states. This partnership was designed to establish measures to maintain or enhance the beauty of lands crossed by transportation activities or facilities. Ultimately, the secretary of the interior is responsible for approving or rejecting a project.

Presidential Executive Orders

Presidential executive orders further demonstrated the growing commitment of the federal government to preservation. President Richard M. Nixon signed the first one in 1971: Executive Order 11593 specified that all federal agencies maintain, preserve, and restore all historic properties within their jurisdiction. In this case, lead agencies were to work closely with the U.S. secretary of the interior and SHPOs to guarantee that all qualified sites were placed on the National Register no later than July 1, 1973.[25]

This executive order also required full documentation of all historic sites prior to alteration or demolition. The Historic American Buildings Survey (HABS) and the Historic American Engineering Record (HAER) were to retain all materials pertaining to these historic sites. The order also mandated that all federal agencies relinquish their abandoned historic properties or sites to responsible local leaders who agreed to preserve them.[26]

President James Earl Carter followed Nixon's lead and in August 1978 signed Executive Order 12072, which called for the utilization of historically, architecturally, or culturally significant buildings based on the National Register guidelines. In May 1996, President William Jefferson Clinton approved Executive Order 13006. It encouraged federal agencies to relocate to historic buildings in central cities whenever possible, and it sanctioned interior alterations in these buildings that would better serve the needs of the public. However, all alterations must follow the proscribed guidelines of the Advisory Council on Historic Preservation.

President Clinton offered additional federal support by signing Executive Order 11652 in 1998. This led to the creation of the Save America's Treasures program. Originally part of the White House National Millennium Celebration, this partnership includes representatives from the White House, the National Park Service, and the National Trust for Historic Preservation. Its goals are to foster new pride in the United States' heritage, educate the public on current preservation problems, and stimulate long-term interest in preserving our national treasures. Several major education programs and promotional campaigns have resulted from this effort.[27]

In March 2003, President George W. Bush signed Executive Order 13287. Called "Preserve America," this directive includes a variety of state, tribal, and business leaders. Its purpose is threefold. First, it sanctions local economic development through the appropriate use of historic properties. In this instance, it requires federal agencies to better manage their historic buildings and sites. Second, it officially recognizes the important role of local organizations, businesses, governments, and individuals in preserving and sustaining the United States' cultural or natural heritage. Nearly 300 communities have received this national recognition over the last three years. Third, it acknowledges outstanding achievements made by U.S. history teachers. Working in conjunction with the History Channel, it has developed its own teacher's manual, featuring lesson plans and hands-on student activities.[28]

Tax Reforms (1970s–Present)

As important as these executive orders have been in promoting and sustaining preservation, they still represented only one aspect of federal involvement. Much of the movement's initial support came from the U.S. Congress. Early on preservation leaders recognized the importance of gaining congressional support. After much debate, they decided to push for major tax overhaul. Led by The National Trust for Historic Preservation, these activists lobbied both Congress and the IRS for major tax-reform legislation beginning in the early 1970s.

They equated tax reform with large-scale rehabilitation and restoration. One could not happen without the other. Unfortunately, no such tax-relief program existed. Preservationists further contended that major federal tax reforms would help bolster the United States' slumping economy. They were not alone in this thinking. Many other influential business and government leaders advocated a restructuring of the nation's tax system. Those favoring reform saw a major tax overhaul as a positive way to fuel the economy in the wake of escalating energy costs, double-digit inflation, and increased foreign competition.

Preservationists remained vigilant in their pursuit of these reforms. Their tenacity paid off when the U.S. Congress approved the Tax Reform Act of 1976 (Public Law 94–455). This bill introduced a number of major tax revisions designed to assist owners of historic property. Investment tax credits (ITCs) for the rehabilitation and continued use of historic structures was one very popular measure; it also revised current depreciation schedules and allowances. These adjustments permitted investors to take full advantage of rapid amortization and accelerated depreciation.

Rapid amortization allowed qualified property owners to write off virtually all rehabilitation expenses incurred on certified income-producing historic buildings during the first five years of their mortgage rather than spreading them out over the lifetime of the loan.[29] Buildings and sites listed on the National Register, located in a National Register Historic District, or certified by the U.S. secretary of the interior as historically significant qualified as certified income-producing properties.

Accelerated depreciation afforded property owners a viable alternative to standard depreciation allowances. Traditionally, estimated use, wear, and obsolescence of a structure over a twenty-five- to thirty-year life span determined its allowances. As property and tax values declined the property owner was permitted additional deductions.[30] These deductions were intended to offset mounting maintenance and improvement costs. In other words, the longer one owned a historic building, the greater the potential deductions.

Given the uncertainties of the economy in the 1970s, many investors demanded faster building depreciation allowances during the first years of a structure's life cycle, not at its end. Accelerated depreciation provided a viable alternative: under this arrangement, qualified property owners received the bulk of their depreciation and rehabilitation allowances up front, with diminishing deductions over the next nineteen years of the building's life. Supporters argued that the increased capital generated by accelerated depreciation would encourage widespread rehabilitation.

Accelerated depreciation and rapid amortization appealed to many builders and developers especially as construction and labor costs soared. This bill also furthered preservation by all but eliminating tax incentives favoring the demolition of historic buildings. The only exception was when the secretary of the interior certified in writing prior to demolition that a historic structure was not significant to its surrounding neighborhood.

The volatile nature of the economy in the mid-1970s made rehabilitation very appealing to a great many new investors. The Revenue Act of 1978 (Public Law 95–600) further strengthened preservation in several crucial ways.[31] First, it placed all restoration and rehabilitation tax incentives under the U.S. federal tax code. Second, it afforded a permanent 10 percent rehabilitation tax credit for certified historic commercial and industrial buildings. Third, it allowed qualified property owners to use accelerated depreciation for demolition purposes, provided that the secretary of the interior certified that the historic structure was not important to its district. Finally, it mandated that all state and local historic districts subscribe to National Register guidelines in order to qualify for both the 1976 and 1978 tax credits.[32] An income tax incentive for investing in improvements of property is the acceleration of the depreciation expense tax deduction of the improvement cost from gross taxable income in arriving at taxable income. Also, an even more stimulating incentive is provided by the investment tax credit for historic property improvements, which differs from the tax deduction in that the credit reduces the tax liability instead of the taxable income.

The Reagan administration tried to bolster the country's economy in the 1980s by introducing several major budget cuts and tax reforms. The Economic Recovery Tax Act of 1981 (ERTA-81; Public Law 97–34) represented the first of three significant revisions. Specifically, this bill modified earlier credits by establishing one new ITC system for historic buildings determined by age. Under this new arrangement, thirty-year-old nonresidential income-producing buildings received a 15 percent credit while forty-year-old nonresidential buildings obtained a 20 percent credit. Structures and sites certified "historic" by the secretary of the interior received a 25 percent credit. Property owners claiming these credits had to use the new straight-line approach rather than the traditional accelerated method in determining building depreciation.[33]

The Tax Equity and Fiscal Responsibility Act (TEFRA) of 1982 (Public Law 97–248) further modified existing credits and depreciation allowances. Under this bill, certified property owners could only apply a 12.5 percent deduction toward rehabilitation expenditures. TEFRA also reduced the basis of depreciable assets for rehabilitation costs to a flat 50 percent.[34]

The third and most significant revision was the Tax Reform Act of 1986 (Public Law 99–514). Totally revamping the federal tax code of 1954, this bill affected the real estate industry and preservation market for years to come. It was unique in that it called for a $120 billion business tax increase, while decreasing individual taxes for the following five years. It also broadened individual and corporate tax bases while eliminating many other traditional tax shelters and incentives.[35]

It achieved its objectives in the following ways. First, it replaced the earlier confusing 15 percent tax brackets with a new two-tier system: 28 percent rate for high-income taxpayers and 15 percent for low- to moderate-income groups. This rate for the wealthiest Americans was a 22 percentage-point reduction from the 1984 level—50 percent. Second, this act reduced the maximum corporate rate from 46 percent to 34 percent. Third, it modified existing marginal tax rates, the percentage of taxes owed on earned income above the allowed deduction baseline. The new rates were 15 percent for the first $42,350, 20 percent for the next $60,000, and 31 percent to 39.6 percent for higher income. Last, the act increased the capital gains tax rate from 20 percent to 28 percent.[36]

This tax-reform package adversely impacted preservation; for the first time since the passage of the NHPA rehabilitation tax credits decreased.[37]

In reality, lower marginal rates made traditional tax incentives less imperative. It also abolished rapid amortization and accelerated depreciation. In its place, a new, standard, straight-line depreciation method determined the depreciable life of historic properties placed in service after January 1, 1987. Life spans of 27.5 years for residential properties and 31.5 years for nonresidential properties served to determine actual depreciation costs.[38]

The 1986 bill also established new criteria for passive activity loss (PAL) for historic and non-historic rental real estate. Taxpayers who actively participated in real estate ventures, as defined by the IRS, now may qualify to offset some active income by claiming annual losses up to $25,000.[39] Deductions would be attributed to real estate activities. The amount of the deduction would depend on the participant's income bracket, or at-risk factor, which would be determined by the personal liability incurred by a taxpayer, based on the sum of cash or property contributed by that individual to the project or the amount of borrowed funds applied to that project.

However, PAL rules no longer permitted property owners to offset additional liabilities from other active taxable income sources, such as direct wages. The act further stipulated that individual taxpayers—not corporations, limited partnerships, or realtors—were eligible for this deduction. Under PAL, those persons filing singly with taxable incomes of less than $50,000 and those filing jointly with taxable incomes of less than $100,000 might qualify to claim up to $25,000 in annual losses from rental property.

Historic-property owners with taxable incomes not exceeding $250,000 also may be eligible for up to $25,000 in losses from certified rehabilitation or low income housing projects. Taxpayers with annual incomes below $100,000 may qualify to utilize new passive credit exemptions up to $25,000 to offset active income taxes. However, property owners earning $100,000 to $150,000 annually or those with taxable incomes above $150,000 annually would have their exemptions reduced. ITC changes and new, stricter passive-loss rules all but eliminated traditional tax shelters.[40]

Those property owners seeking the 10 percent rehabilitation credit for noncertified historic buildings would have to comply with new federal guidelines pertaining to the allowed percentage of renovated wall surfaces on restored structures. Under this new ruling, 50 percent or more of original external walls had to remain intact. Also, 75 percent or more of the existing walls needed to be maintained as internal or external walls. Finally, 75 percent or more of the existing internal structural framework, including load-bearing internal walls, columns, girders, beams, trusses, spandrels, and other members essential to the stability of the building also were to be preserved. An earlier exemption allowing investors to retain 75 percent of the existing walls as external walls was eliminated.[41]

Another new exemption affected the acquisition, construction, and renovation of existing low-income historic housing: low-income investors with no federal assistance were entitled to receive a 9 percent annual tax credit for up to ten years, while those with existing subsidies were eligible for a 4 percent annual credit also up to ten years.[42] To qualify, an investor must show that the average cost incurred in the construction or rehabilitation of a historic multifamily structure exceeded $2,000 per unit. Deductions varied greatly, based on the unit involved. Also, investors were required to follow these rules up to fifteen years. Failure to do so might lead to recapture of some or all of the issued tax credit. Taxpayers receiving the 20 percent rehabilitation credit also were eligible.

The Revenue Reconciliation Act of 1993 (Public Law 103–66) revised some of the 1986 provisions. Specifically, it lowered individual tax-rate brackets from 28 percent to 20 percent and from 15 percent to 10 percent.[43] It also broadened PAL to allow exempted realtors to deduct historic rental properties as passive losses. Realtors who demonstrated that more than 50 percent of their work time was devoted to rehabilitation qualified for PALs.[44] This bill also increased the depreciable life span for nonresidential buildings from 31.5 years to 39 years. Additional modifications and tax revisions occurred in 1997 and 2001.[45] As of 2003, the maximum tax rate for the wealthiest citizens remained at 39.6 percent while the top corporate tax rate stood at 35 percent.

In 2000, Congress passed the New Markets Tax Credit (NMTC) Program. A part of the Community Renewal Tax Relief Act of 2000 (Public Law 106–554), it represented the first significant tax reform in nearly fifteen years. The NMTC Program provides over $15 billion in credits annually for developers wishing to invest in low-income districts.[46] Low-income districts were defined as either inner-city areas where more than 20 percent of the total population lived at or below the poverty line or neighborhoods where the median income fell 80 percent below the metropolitan average. It afforded a seven-year 39 percent tax credit for large-scale new commercial investments. Under this arrangement, locally based for-profit enterprises furnished loans to eligible businesses. Recipients, in turn, claimed a 5 percent yearly tax credit for the first three years, followed by a 6 percent annual credit for the remaining four.

To be eligible as a lender, a local enterprise must be certified as a community development entity (CDE). The U.S. Treasury Department, Community Development Financial Institute (CDFI) Fund awards these certifications. CDEs are primarily private community development corporations, financial institutions, venture capital organizations, and small businesses. They offer investment capital for major commercial development in these distressed neighborhoods. Long-term commitment in a targeted area frequently determines certification. Nominees often demonstrate their commitment by including prominent local business and civic leaders on their governing boards.[47]

Markets for NMTCs remain highly competitive. Determining factors include such things as management professionalism and proven track records of assisting disadvantaged businesses and neighborhoods. NMTCs are beneficial in two important ways: they free up capital for CDEs, which enables local developers to invest more per project, and they lessen the financial risks for those investors wishing to establish new local enterprises.

The National Trust for Historic Preservation recognized the significance of NMTCs from the beginning.[48] For example, in 2001 it received a CDFI grant totaling $127 million. Beneficiaries included the Inner City New Markets Fund, Historic Tax Credit Fund, Historic New Markets Conduit Fund, Main Street Conduit Lending Fund, and Main Street CDE Conduit Lending Fund.

In the case of the Inner City New Markets Fund, the National Trust relies on its highly successful past lending practices to leverage additional credits. It employs a similar strategy with its lucrative Historic Tax Credit Fund program. In the latter case, the National Trust encourages well-established investors to refinance their Bank of America Historic Tax Credit Funds through their organization directly, enabling these investors to receive both standard rehabilitation credits and NMTCs.

The Historic New Markets Conduit Fund is another way for lenders to receive NMTCs. Under this arrangement, lenders access NMTCs to quickly expand their current business and real estate borrowing practices. Similarly, participants in the Main Street CDE Conduit Lending Fund accelerate their own lending capabilities by drawing directly on NMTCs. Such actions benefit qualified investors.

In the final analysis, federal officials still rely on traditional ITCs to stimulate rehabilitation.[49] In fact, these credits have made possible more than 146,000 renovation projects since the mid-1980s. Taken from another perspective, nearly 60 percent of all recent construction in Baltimore, Cleveland, Detroit, Philadelphia, San Francisco, and Washington, D.C., were generated from ITCs. Innovative ITCs, expanded National Trust offerings, growing state and municipal programs, and multiple locally based organizational services have helped to offset dwindling federal tax incentives.

State preservation offices and municipal agencies play crucial roles in modern-day preservation. Much of the cooperation evident among these groups today resulted from federal action taken in the 1960s. Preservationists knew that their future success depended on teamwork at all levels. With that in mind, the NHPA empowered all government branches with broad-based authority and lucrative financial incentives. Although some of these incentives have been revised or eliminated many continue.

As stated earlier, NHPA proponents acknowledged the importance of creating a viable statewide administrative component. This led to the creation of SHPO positions. Three considerations prompted this action. First, preservationists understood that all government branches must work together. Strong SHPOs would be vital in promoting this kind of sustained partnership. Second, they understood the importance of establishing liaisons between federal and local leaders. Again, SHPOs would be very helpful in monitoring new initiatives on all levels. Third, supporters realized that all states, territories, and dependencies must become stakeholders. SHPOs would aid in this effort by guaranteeing program sustainability while minimizing outside opposition. The NHPA carefully spelled out the duties and responsibilities of SHPOs. As stated earlier, SHPOs operate viable statewide programs based on current federal legislation and guidelines, with the assistance of state-appointed historic advisory boards.

These advisory boards—made up of archaeologists, architects, civic leaders, geographers, government leaders, historians, politicians, and preservationists—serve several distinct functions. They process all National Register nominations and recommend the best for inclusion on that list. They also assist federal and state officials in investigating all alleged improprieties. Third, they act as the final board of appeal for property owners seeking redress. And, finally, they review all CLG applications and make recommendations for federal funding.

In cooperation with federal, state, and municipal agencies, preservation organizations, and interested individuals, SHPOs conduct statewide surveys of historic properties and maintain permanent property inventories.[50] They also nominate sites for the National Register and implement other statewide initiatives. SHPOs aid other government agencies, as well: working in conjunction with the secretary of the interior, the Advisory Council on Historic Preservation, individual municipalities, and other agencies,

SHPOs guarantee that eligible structures receive federal assistance. Last, they review all tax-credit applications.

Preservation officers rely on qualified academics and nonprofit leaders for assistance. These professionals often help SHPOs secure needed grants and aid in identifying historic buildings and sites. In addition, they lend their expertise in determining site eligibility, processing National Register forms, and coordinating archeological and historical programs.

SHPOs also act as liaisons between federal and municipal leaders. In this capacity, they decide important issues, including which communities qualify as CLGs.[51] Most CLGs subscribe to the following guidelines: they have effective preservation ordinances, which assist them in the designation and protection of historic landmarks and sites in their jurisdiction; they have established either a preservation agency or commission that surveys and records all landmarks and sites; and, they have encouraged public participation in every phase of their effort, which helps coordinate community efforts efficiently.

Most CLGs also have their own review boards to monitor local preservation laws and ordinances. These boards also evaluate National Register nominations, issue building and demolition permits within historic districts, and establish local rehabilitation design guidelines. CLG communities may qualify for special federal grants awarded by the secretary of the interior or for special discretionary funding from their own states.[52] Traditionally, large urban areas received the bulk of this funding. However, recent protests by small communities and rural areas have prompted many SHPOs to distribute state monies more equitably. As can be readily seen, these officials serve a multitude of functions. With their professional staffs and highly competent advisory boards, SHPOs provide a full range of programs and services.

The ever-increasing support for preservation reflects the United States' changing mood over the past four decades. In particular, high energy, labor, and construction costs encouraged many historic property owners to take full advantage of ITCs. The media also assisted by showcasing various restoration efforts to diverse audiences. The positive publicity generated by this media coverage has led to additional investment.

The National Alliance of Preservation Commissions (NAPC) also assists preservation.[53] Established in 1983 at the University of Georgia, the NAPC is the advocacy group for design review commissions throughout the United States. Its many workshops, meetings, and newsletters deal with preservation-related issues. In cooperation with the National Trust, the NAPC currently offers its membership unique educational preservation opportunities.[54]

Modern preservation leaders depend on numerous federal, state, and municipal laws to protect historic buildings and sites. What many modern-day supporters may not realize is that effective local legislation is recent. Before the passage of the NHPA, local business and civic leaders determined community-based preservation policies. Some understood the value of preservation and pushed for meaningful legislation, while many others did not. This lackadaisical approach changed dramatically in the 1960s, when the loss of numerous historic structures and sites in the wake of urban renewal made the public painfully aware of the importance of saving its physical legacy. Capitalizing on these public concerns and fears, preservation leaders lobbied Congress to pass meaningful legislation that would prevent similar cultural and historical losses in the futures.

The passage of the NHPA represented a major watershed for this movement. For the first time, congressional leaders called for protecting endangered historic landmarks and sites. From this modest beginning came other equally significant legal precedents. Preservationists used these precedents to leverage major tax reforms beginning in the mid-1970s. Its momentum continued through the 1980s and 1990s, and into the new millennium. Now considered a viable component of government at all levels, modern-day preservation with its multitude of cultural, economic, and social programs affects all Americans.

Notes

1. Raymond A. Mohl, "The Interstates and the Cities: Highways, Housing, and the Freeway Revolt," Research Report, Poverty and Race Research Action Council, 2002, www.prrac.org/pdf/mohl.pdf.

2. The Servicemen's Readjustment Act of 1944, Pub. Law 346, 78th Cong., 2nd sess. (June 22, 1944). Reorganization Plan No.3, 12 FR 4981, 61 Stat. 954 (1947).

3. Ibid.

4. Federal Highway Act of 1956, Pub. Law 627, 84th Cong., 1st sess. (June 29, 1956).

5. National Housing Act of 1949, Pub. Law 171, 81st Cong., 1st sess. (July 15, 1949).

6. National Housing Act of 1954, Pub. Law 560, 83rd Cong., 2nd sess. (Aug. 2, 1954).

7. G. William Domhoff, *Who Rules America Now? New Haven and Community Power Reexamined* (Englewood Cliffs, N.J.: Prentice Hall, 1983), 173–84.

8. Martin Anderson, *The Federal Bulldozer: A Critical Analysis of Urban Renewal, 1949–1962* (Cambridge: MIT Press, 1964), x; Jane Jacobs, *The Death and Life of Great American Cities* (New York: Random House, 1961), 4.

9. *Penn Central Transportation Co. v. City of New York*, 438 U.S. 104, 98 S.C. 2646 (1978).

10. Michael Harrington, *The Other America: Poverty in the United States* (New York: Macmillan, 1962).

11. International Council on Monuments and Sites, "ICOMOS' Mission," www.international.icomos.org/mission-eng.htm.

12. Ibid.

13. National Historic Preservation Act of 1966, Pub. Law 665, 89th Cong., 2nd sess. (Oct. 15, 1966).

14. Ibid.

15. National Park Service, Certified Local Government Program, "Program in Brief," www.cr.nps.gov/hps/clg/clg_p.htm.

16. National Historic Preservation Act of 1966.

17. Ibid.

18. Ibid.

19. Ibid.

20. United States Advisory Council on Historic Preservation, "ACHP Membership," www.achp.gov/members.html.

21. Ibid.

22. Ibid.

23. United States Advisory Council on Historic Preservation, "The Contribution of Historic Preservation to Urban Revitalization." "Section 106 Regulations Summary," www.achp.gov.html.

24. The Department of Transportation Act of 1966, Pub. Law 89–670, 80 Stat. 931, section 4(f) Policy Paper, revised June 7, 1989.

25. Executive Order 11593. 36 FR 8921, 3 CFR, 1971–1975 Comp.

26. Ibid.

27. National Park Service and the National Trust for Historic Preservation, "About Us," *Save America's Treasures*, www.saveAmericastreasures.org/about.htm.

28. "Executive Order Report to President," *Preserve America: Explore and Enjoy Our Heritage, Executive Order Report to President.*" www.preserveamerica.gov/EO.html.

29. The Tax Reform Act of 1976, Pub. Law 445, 94th Cong., 2nd sess. (Sept. 16, 1976).

30. U.S. Department of the Treasury, Internal Revenue Service, Keynote Search, Accelerated Depreciation, www.irs.ustreas.gov/business/page/o.id=134133,oo.html. Department of the U.S. Treasury, *Fact Sheet on the History of the U.S. Tax System*, www.treas.gov/education/fact-sheets/taxes/ustax.shtml

31. The Revenue Act of 1978, Pub. Law 600, 95th Cong., 2nd sess. (Nov. 6, 1978).

32. The Economic Recovery Tax Act of 1981, Pub. Law 34, 97th Cong., 1st sess. (Aug. 4, 1981).

33. Ibid.

34. Tax Equity and Fiscal Responsibility Act of 1982, Pub. Law 248, 97th Cong., 2nd sess. (Sept. 3, 1982).

35. The Tax Reform Act of 1986, Pub. Law 514, 99th Cong., 2nd sess. (Oct. 22, 1986).

36. Ibid.

37. Ibid.

38. Ibid.

39. National Park Service, Technical Preservation Society, "Historic Preservation Tax Incentives, What are Passive Activity Restrictions?" www.nps.gov/history/hps/tps/tax/IRSLIHTC.htm.

40. Ibid.

41. Ibid.

42. Ibid.

43. The Revenue Reconciliation Act of 1993, Pub. Law 66, 103rd Cong., 1st sess. (Aug. 10, 1993).

44. Ibid.

45. The Tax Reform Act of 1997, Pub. Law 34, 105th Cong., 1st sess. (Aug. 5, 1997); The Economic Growth and Tax Relief Reconciliation Act of 2001, Pub. Law 16, 107th Cong., 1st sess. (June 7, 2001).

46. National Housing and Rehabilitation Association, "New Markets,", Tax Credits, www.housingonline.com/TaxCredits/NewMarkets/tabid/40/Default.aspx.

47. U.S. Department of the Treasury, *Community Development Financial Institutions Fund*, "What We Do, New Markets Tax Credit, NMTC," www.cdfifund.gov/what_we_doprograms_id.asp?programID=5.

48. National Trust for Historic Preservation, "National Trust Community Investment Corporation," www.ntcicfunds.com.

49. Barbara Listokin and David Listokin, "Historic Preservation and Affordable Housing: Leveraging Old Resources for New Opportunities," in *Historic Facts and Findings*, ed. James Carr (Washington, D.C.: Fannie Mae Foundation, 2005).

50. National Park Service, Certified Local Government Program, www.cr.nps.gov/hps,clg/clg/quest.htm.

51. Ibid.

52. National Park Service, Certified Local Government Program, "Frequently Asked Questions," www.cr.nps.gov/hps/clg/clgquest.htm.

53. National Alliance of Preservation Commissioners, "Center for Community Design and Preservation," www.uga.edu/sed/pso/programs/napc/napc.htm.

54. Ibid.

Chapter Four

U.S. Architectural Styles

A Critical Analysis

Introduction

Over the centuries, political, military, and religious leaders have argued about which historic structures and sites should be preserved and how to do it effectively. Entire communities have been built, demolished, and rebuilt on the ashes of previous civilizations. Modern demolitions may occur in less hostile environments but the results are often the same. The question posed to preservationists, today, is how best to preserve the valuable while not obscuring progress.

Before addressing this salient point, it is important to examine some past justifications for preservation. Part of this review includes defining what constitutes modern architectural style and how it has evolved over the past several centuries. Reasons for saving and preserving historic buildings and sites came from a variety of quarters, beginning in the Middle Ages.

Medieval Popes—including John XXII, Eugene IV, and Nicholas V—supported the conservation of ancient Roman ruins, especially those related to church history. During the Age of the Enlightenment, a young Swedish monarch named Charles XI ordered all monuments in his country protected. In October 1830, the newly appointed French minister of public instruction, Francois Guizot, established the Commission des Monuments Historique to preserve the best in French architecture.[1]

Support for restoration in Europe went far beyond official laws and mandates. Two very influential nineteenth-century intellectual groups—one led by John Ruskin and the other by Eugène Emmanuel Viollet-le-Duc—enthusiastically promoted preservation but in vastly different ways. Ruskin believed that historic buildings should not be restored to their original grandeur. Rather, they should reflect the "golden stain of time" based on events occurring in them.[2]

Many of Ruskin's ideas originated from the writings of Augustus W. N. Pugin. A well-respected and highly critical English architect, Pugin designed the British House of Parliament buildings in 1834. He also was a medieval scholar and fervent advocate of Gothic styling.[3] In *The True Principles of Christian Architecture* (1841), Pugin proudly proclaimed that Gothic traditions represented the only true form of Christian architecture. This connection between the beauty of Gothic styling and "pure" Christianity did not elude Ruskin.

Idealizing morality and virtue through Gothic architecture soon became a major part of his philosophical thinking. In *The Seven Lamps of Architecture* (1849), Ruskin argued that architecture is universal and, as such, a testimony to both personal and national morality. Therefore, precise building restoration, although aesthetically pleasing, is basically dishonest. It fails to portray real-life experiences. His criticism became even sharper in *The Stones of Venice* (1851). In this writing, Ruskin argues that Venetian Gothic architecture mirrored domestic goodness and virtue, while Venetian Renaissance style reflected depravity and decadence. Disillusioned by what he perceived to be the crass materialism of his own age, Ruskin sought solace through the beauty and purity of medieval architecture.

Eugène Emmanuel Viollet-le-Duc, a highly popular French architect and author, also romanticized the past, though differently from Ruskin. He especially admired writers who captured the beauty and grace of French culture in their works. Victor Hugo was that kind of author. In *The Hunchback of Notre Dame* (1831), Hugo glorified the famous Notre Dame cathedral.[4] Unfortunately, this once-proud landmark was in a state of ruin. Outraged by its condition, the French citizenry demanded government officials restore it to its former glory. This outpouring of public sympathy so impressed Viollet-le-Duc that he devoted the remainder of his career to restoring historic structures.

From the 1830s to the 1870s, he renovated numerous buildings and sites throughout France. His achievements included Saint-Chapelle (1845) and Notre Dame Cathedral (1850), both in Paris. Viollet-le-Duc also refurbished the cathedrals at Amiens, Chartres, and Reims during the 1860s. Later renovations included the chateau at Pierrefond and the Carcassone fortifications.

Unlike Ruskin, Viollet-le-Duc believed that every detail on a historic structure must be restored to its original glory. He argued that authenticity took precedent over all other considerations.[5] Called "ensemble," this process led to meticulous restorations. It also enabled him to concentrate on the aesthetics of architecture; this ability to appreciate beautiful design for its own sake eluded Ruskin.

As influential as these two movements were in European preservation, their impact remained negligible in the United States. Rarely did nineteenth-century U.S. citizens concern themselves with the economic, political, or social impact preservation might have on their built environment. Perhaps they believed that there were few structures worth saving; more than likely their hectic lifestyles prevented them from examining the merits of this movement. Whatever the reasons, one thing was abundantly clear. Only an emergency would generate sufficient community support to save a structure on site.

The United States' indifference toward preservation afforded nineteenth-century leaders great leeway when it came to restoring landmarks. Pragmatism ruled the day. This less-than-insightful approach allowed them to downplay architectural accuracy and structural integrity. After all, saving the structure was all that mattered. This restoration philosophy often resulted in awkward restorations. Not until the 1960s did the public begin to demand accuracy in restored landmarks.

Now, however, many preservationists are keenly aware of the importance of architectural accuracy and structural integrity. The multitude of quality restorations found throughout the United States today supports this contention. Yet, there are still property owners who fail to restore structures accurately.

Adaptive reuse is a renovation process by which a historic structure is modernized internally while retaining much of its original architectural grandeur and integrity externally. Restoration, on the other hand, brings both the interior and exterior of a historic structure back to its original condition.[6] Whatever the desired end, effective preservation is much more than a vague notion of "proper" building form and detailing. It entails an in-depth understanding of how seemingly incongruent building components and design elements come together to create harmonious historic structures. Part of this effort involves collecting information on a structure's age, architect, building materials, and construction methods. But, this is only half the story. Restoration in the United States' competitive real-estate market also includes an understanding of how historic structures relate to their built environment, both in the past and in the present.

Knowing architectural style is essential in restoration; in its simplest form, it differentiates building types. On a more sophisticated level, it reflects construction technology, craftsmanship, and traditions at crucial historic junctures. Unfortunately, many property owners still fail to fully understand the importance of style. Modern-day preservationists are responsible for working with these property owners. Those preservationists who are able to successfully restore a historic structure without sacrificing its original architectural integrity will continue to enjoy a decided advantage over those who do not.

Colonial Period

Early British settlers in the Northeast lived in wigwams.[7] First developed by the Algonquin and Iroquois nations, these conical shaped shelters were often built just below ground level. Rafter beams five to eight feet long were fastened to a center roof ridge and then attached to two parallel anchored bases to construct these durable dugouts. Animal skins, tree bark, and cattails secured tightly against these rafter beams formed a watertight covering. Flooring consisted of corn silk, tree bark, and animal hides stitched together.[8] A central fireplace and open flue served both cooking and heating purposes.

Sixteenth-century French pioneers in the Mississippi River Valley constructed wood frame dwellings with nogging wall fill. A mixture of dried twigs, straw, and mud, nogging was layered between wood poles and support beams. Over time, these walls dried and hardened. These very durable French colonial dwellings boasted large second-story porches and verandas, hipped roofs with prominent overhangs, and gable dormers. Casement windows, wood shutters, French doors, and small chimneys provided further charm. This remained a popular residential style in the Mississippi delta into the 1850s.[9]

Sixteenth-century Spanish conquistadors in the Southwest developed their own unique building traditions. Relying on indigenous construction materials and techniques, they perfected the Pueblo style.[10] It featured thick adobe walls; flat roofs; exposed, hewn roof rafters; and small, deep-set door and window openings. A beautiful and highly versatile design, Pueblo homes have remained popular for over five hundred years. Two factors account for its longevity. First, it provides excellent protection against the harsh climate. Second, it resembles Spanish baroque styling.

Devastating wars, economic uncertainty, and religious persecution forced many seventeenth-century Europeans to migrate to the New World. Many settled on the East Coast in Portsmouth, Boston, Newport,

New York City, Charleston, and Savannah. With their practical knowledge and useful skills, these early settlers quickly transformed these fledgling outposts into modern cities.

Ingenuity abounded in the construction industry. Practical building techniques enabled colonists to erect durable dwellings inexpensively. Although many of them resembled medieval English cottages, they were still uniquely American.[11] Nowhere was this more evident than in New England. As early as 1635, New Englanders had developed their own special one- and two-story houses. These well-built Garrison colonials featured unpainted clapboard siding; large, central brick fireplaces; small, diamond-shaped casement windows; and massive hand-hewn wood shutters. Other design characteristics included prominent second-story overhangs with pendants, steeply pitched gabled roofs, and an enclosed passageway linking the main house to the barn.[12] Five houses—the Whitfield House, Guilford, Connecticut (1639); the Paul Revere House, Boston, Massachusetts (1676); the Parson Capen House, Topsfield, Massachusetts (1683); the John Ward

Garrison Colonial style, the Henry Whitfield House, Guilford, Conn., 1639.

Pennsylvania Dutch Colonial style, Graeme Park, Horsham, Pa., 1721–22.

House, Salem, Massachusetts (1684); and the Benjamin Abbott Farm in An-
dover, Massachusetts (1685)—exemplified this new, highly resilient style.

Dutch Colonial homes found throughout the Hudson and Delaware
Valleys, Staten Island, and Long Island were noted for their brick, clapboard, or rubble-fieldstone veneers, sweeping, canopied gambrel roofs and
shed roof dormers. Gabled roof parapets, exposed decorative wall anchors,
and matching end fireplaces added further charm to these picturesque one-
and-a-half–story cottages.[13] Two New York homes, the Pieter Wyckoff
House, Brooklyn (1639) and the Pieter Bronck Cottage in West Coxsockie
(1663, 1738) typified this new, innovative motif.

High-pitched gambrel roofs, rubble-fieldstone exteriors, large pediment entrances, and unique English details distinguished Pennsylvania
Dutch farmhouses from other contemporary colonials. Fine Pennsylvania
examples of these homes included the Darby House, Darby (1683) and the
Sir William Keith House, called "Graeme Park," Horsham (1721–22).

Elizabethan and Jacobean houses featured exposed end chimneys, enlarged Flemish gables, and arched door and window openings. Loosely
based on sixteenth-century English squire homes, these picturesque dwellings predominated the colonial South. Skilled artisans used the abundant
local clay and lime deposits to erect durable plantation houses for the newly
established landed gentry. Plans ran the gamut from simple single-story

grand halls to elaborate two-and-a-half–story mansions with magnificent reception halls, large hallways, and private living quarters.

The Adam Thoroughgood House, Norfolk (1636–40) and the Arthur Allen House, Surrey County (1665), both in Virginia, exemplified these new styles. Originally the manor house for a sprawling estate, the one-and-a-half–story Adam Thoroughgood House reflected the best in medieval building traditions. Its cross-mullioned casement windows; small, diamond windowpanes; and heavy wooden front door with decorative wrought-iron hinges closely resembled contemporary cottages in England or Wales.[14] In contrast, the Arthur Allen House, also known as Bacon's Castle, was a more sophisticated structure. This cruciform designed two-story brick dwelling featured a large, projecting front gable; hand-hewn beams; a prominent ceiling, and triple chimneys.[15] Simple or sophisticated, Elizabethan and Jacobean plantation houses successfully incorporated modern construction technology with traditional styling to create beautiful homes.

The growing sophistication of American colonial society in the early eighteenth century encouraged many builders to set aside medieval construction traditions and embrace the new Georgian style.[16] Relying on English pattern books by Colin Campbell, Inigo Jones, William Kent, Batty Langley, William Salmon, and John Webb, colonial artisans, such as Peter Harrison, William

Elizabethan Jacobean style, Adam Thoroughgood House, Norfolk, Va., 1636–40.

Georgian style, Jeremiah Lee Mansion, Marblehead, Mass., 1768.

Buckland, and John Ariss, produced some of the finest Georgian structures ever built. The McPhedris-Warner House, Portsmouth, New Hampshire (1718–23); "Stratford," Westmoreland County, Virginia (1725–30); "Westover," Charles City County, Virginia (1730–34); the Isaac Royall House, Medford, Massachusetts (1733–50); the Redwood Library, Newport, Rhode Island (1748–50); and the Wentworth-Gardner House, Portsmouth, New Hampshire (1760–65); exemplified this new design excellence.

Easily recognized by their straightforward brick, stone, or wood exterior veneers, Georgian structures featured either hipped or Dutch-styled roofs. Other design characteristics included raised basements, protruding front pavilions, corner pilasters, quoins, dentilated cornices, central Palladian windows, stone water tables, and roof balustrades. Government and religious buildings also reflected Georgian styling traditions, on a much grander scale. Large bell towers, impressive spires, and enlarged cupolas added prominence to these structures.

Early Republic

Following the Revolutionary War, U.S. designers began to modify Georgian styling. This resulted in two new motifs: the Federal style in New England and the Neoclassical style in the mid-Atlantic and Southern states. The Federal style, also called the Adam or the American Federal style, was primarily a residential form. Red brick or clapboard exteriors, bowed bays, raised basements; low pitched roofs, keystone lintels, and recessed arches distinguished this new highly formal design. Additional special touches included Palladian entry windows, paneled front doors with vertical sidelights and elliptical fanlights.[17]

Popular Massachusetts designers such as Asher Benjamin, Charles Bulfinch, and Samuel McIntire received much of their inspiration from the works of contemporary European architects, including Robert Adam and William Chambers. Charles Bulfinch's Tontine Crescent and Franklin Place (1794), Massachusetts State House, (1804–6), and First Harrison Gray Otis House (1796–97), all in Boston, and Samuel McIntire's Gardiner-Pingree House, in Salem (1804–5), reflected this new design.

The versatility of Neoclassical styling, or Roman classicism, set it apart from the more traditional Federal structures.[18] First used by Thomas Jefferson on the Virginia State Capitol, Richmond, Virginia (1785–89), it quickly spread throughout the South and Mid-Atlantic region. The Bank of Pennsylvania, Philadelphia (1798–1800), by Benjamin Latrobe and the Fireproof Building, Charleston, South Carolina (1827), by Robert Mills exemplified this new motif. Easily recognized by their prominent temple shapes and special French, Palladian, and Roman details, neoclassical structures were noted for their raised basements, impressive podium entrances, projecting cornices, plain Roman columns, classic moldings, and smooth brick or stone wall surfaces.[19]

Federal and neoclassical designs dominated the U.S. architectural scene until the 1820s, when Greek Revival styling, inspired by the nineteenth-century Greek War for Independence, replaced them. Although numerous such civic and religious buildings dotted the landscape, its greatest appeal was residential. Greek Revival homes were mostly two-story rectangular structures, short-side facing front, flanked by one or two one-story rectangular wings, long-side facing front. The two-story main block with its attached wings formed an "L" or "T" floor plan.

Other special design characteristics included low-pitched gabled or hipped roofs, projecting cornices atop Doric columns, off-center central doorways

Federal style, 3rd Harrison Gray Otis House, Boston, Mass., 1806. Charles Bulfinch, architect.

flanked by side lights and topped by a fanlight or transom lights, and plain pilasters. Wide plain entablatures, unadorned architrave bands at the eaves, oriel windows, and large first-floor windows lent further distinction to these early nineteenth-century structures.[20] Many well-known U.S. architects such as Alexander Jackson Davis, Benjamin Latrobe, William Strickland, Ithiel Town, and Thomas Ustick Walter applied Greek Revival details to churches, schools, homes, and government buildings throughout the country.[21]

William Strickland, Second National Bank of the United States, Philadelphia, Pennsylvania (1818–25); Alexander Parris, Quincy Market, Boston, Massachusetts (1825–26); Alexander Jackson Davis, "Colonnade Row," Lafayette Street, New York City (1829–33); Jonathan Goldsmith, Dr. John Matthews House, Painesville, Ohio (1829); Ammi B. Young, Custom House and Tower, Boston, Massachusetts (1837–47, 1915); Henry Walters, the Ohio State Capitol, Columbus (1838–61); and Thomas Ustick Walter, the U.S. Capitol, additions and new dome, Washington, D.C. (1850–64), reflected this new architectural achievement.

Romantic Period

The widespread use of band, power, and scroll saws beginning in the 1830s prompted a group of U.S. designers—led by Alexander Jackson Davis, Andrew Jackson Downing, and Richard Upjohn—to develop two new residential motifs: Carpenter Gothic and Gothic Revival. Carpenter Gothic dwellings featured steep-pitched gabled roofs, bargeboards, gabled eaves, and roof cresting. Pointed door and window openings; three-sided bays; clustered chimneys; batten-board wood siding; and large, open porches provided further charm to these highly picturesque cottages. Many homes offered additional amenities, such as built-in closets and interior kitchens.[22] Carpenter Gothic styling remained popular into the 1870s.

Its versatility was evident in Hezekiah Eldredge's St. John's Episcopal Church, Cleveland, Ohio (1838), and Oak Bluff Cottages, Martha's Vineyard, Massachusetts (1840s); Andrew Jackson Downing's Henry Delameter House, Rhinebeck, New York (1844) and Henry C. Bowen Cottage, Woodstock, Connecticut (1855); and Alexander Jackson Davis's Edward W. Nicholls House, Orange, New Jersey (1858).

Gothic Revival homes represented another new residential form. A noted eighteenth-century British architect named John Chute first applied Gothic Revival detailing to "Strawberry Hill," the country home of Sir Horace Walpole in the 1770s. Unfortunately, his efforts failed, and the design was

Carpenter Gothic style, Railroad Depot, Cambridge, N.Y., c. 1860.

quickly forgotten.[23] Revived by another English architect, James Wyatt, in 1795 it was applied to Sir William Beckford's new country estate. Wyatt chose this style because his client insisted that his new mansion include "the best Gothick design elements."[24] His efforts resulted in Fonthill Abbey. A massive Gothic dwelling with a 276-foot crossing tower, it looked more like an inexpensive movie set than a prestigious new country house.

Not deterred by these unfortunate designs, Alexander Jackson Davis, James Renwick, and Richard Upjohn brought this flamboyant style to the United States' shores. It was an immediate hit. In fact, Gothic Revival villas, churches, and collegiate buildings were still being constructed throughout the United States into the 1880s. Noteworthy examples included Alexander Jackson Davis, New York University, New York City (1832–37), Alexander Jackson Davis, "Glen Ellen," Towson, Maryland (1832–34); Richard Upjohn, Trinity Church, New York City (1839–47); and James Renwick, the Smithsonian Museum, Washington, D.C. (1846–55).

Easily identified by its symmetrical exteriors, smooth-cut ashlar walls, decorative leaded windows with hood moldings, step-gabled dormers, high-pitched roofs, and cross-gables, Gothic Revival dwellings seemed to embody the chivalry of medieval Europe as first depicted in Sir Walter Scott's

Ivanhoe (1819). Large porches and prominent central towers crowned by battlements, parapets, and finials lent further distinction to this new highly romantic design.

Mid-nineteenth-century U.S. architects developed three new Venetian inspired designs: Italianate, Italian Villa, and Renaissance Revival. Partially derived from sixteenth-century Renaissance villas, Italianate homes generally fell into two categories. They were either free flowing two- to three-story country homes or spacious townhouses. Large Corinthian-columned front porches with ornate bracketed cornices, low-slung pyramidal roofs, enlarged bays, and square-shaped cupolas distinguished Italianate structures from other contemporary residential structures. Enriched moldings, exaggerated balustrades, and rounded window and door openings with hoods afforded further prestige to these grand homes.

Many new midcentury commercial blocks, department stores, and warehouses were done in the Italianate motif. In this instance, prefabricated cast iron exterior wall surfaces with embossed "Italian" accents produced breathtaking facades.[25] Henry Austin, James Dwight Dana House, New Haven, Connecticut (1849); John B. Corlies and James Bogardus, Harper and Brothers Building, New York City (1854); John P. Gaynor and Daniel Badger, Haughwaut Building, New York City (1857–59); and Samuel Sloan, the Tallman House, Janesville, Wisconsin (1857) epitomized this exciting new design.

Italian Villa and Renaissance Revival were the other two highly acclaimed new Venetian variations. Andrew Jackson Downing first described the former in *Cottage Residences* (1842). Distinguished by their "L" and "T" floor plans, Italian Villa residences blended in well with their surroundings. These picturesque dwellings featured square-shaped central towers, extended bracketed eaves; narrow windows with rounded hoods, and low-slung roofs. Richard Upjohn, Edward King House, Newport, Rhode Island (1845–47); Henry Austin, the John P. Norton House, New Haven, Connecticut (1848–49); Richard Upjohn, Ely House, West Springfield, Massachusetts (1852–54); and Henry Austin, Morse-Libby House, Portland, Maine (1859–61), exemplified this very popular motif.

A well-known U.S. architect named John Notman first applied Renaissance Revival detailing to the Philadelphia Athenaeum (1845–47).[26] Loosely based on sixteenth-century Palladian Villas, this highly formal symmetrical design boasted smooth-cut exterior walls, quoins, triangular door and window pediments, and projecting roof cornices crowned by enlarged balustrades. These structures remained popular until the early twentieth century,

Italian Villa style, Mansion Westchester County, N.Y., 1853, derived from Andrew
Jackson Dowing pattern books.

when Beaux-Arts and neoclassical designs replaced it. Noteworthy examples included Richard Upjohn, Pierrepont Residence, Brooklyn, New York
(1856–58); McKim, Mead, and White, Henry Villard House, New York
City (1882–85); and Charles Schweinfurth, Union Club, Cleveland, Ohio
(1901–5).

United States architects in the 1850s were greatly excited about the new
additions to the Louvre Museum in Paris. Designed by Lodovico Visconti
and Hector Martin Lefuel, these wings featured exaggerated, excessive details and massive scale. In their eagerness to glorify past French, classic architectural traditions, these innovative designers had developed an entirely
new motif. This new regal form, Second Empire style, soon gained acclaim
throughout Europe.

Several prominent U.S. designers—led by John McArthur Jr., Alfred
Mullett, and John P. Snook—first experimented with Second Empire design on public buildings in the late 1850s. Flamboyant French detailing,
enlarged central pavilions, elongated wings, enormous corner pavilions,
and imposing Mansard roofs distinguished it from other classic-inspired
buildings of that era.[27] Second Empire houses also reflected French detail.

Three- and four-story residences, with their elaborate grand rooms, decorative hallways, and large open staircases, reflected the opulent lifestyles of many wealthy Americans at the time of the Civil War.

Other special design elements included prominent raised basements, enlarged entrance podiums, paired columns, projecting central pavilions, and massive polychrome Mansard roofs crowned by wrought-iron cresting. Elaborate Second Empire buildings graced the best residential neighborhoods during the Civil War. John B. Snook, Grand Central Railroad Depot, New York City (1869–71); the Flavius Hart House, Oberlin, Ohio (1875, architect unknown); John McArthur, Philadelphia City Hall, Philadelphia, Pennsylvania (1871–1900); Alfred Mullett, State, War, and Navy Building, Washington, D.C. (1871–75); and Levi Scofield, the Rufus K. Winslow House, Cleveland, Ohio (1878) epitomized this ostentatious new style.

However, its popularity proved short-lived. Deluges of negative publicity led to its demise, which began when Mark Twain, Thomas Nast, and Artemus Ward satirized it. They thought it epitomized the foolish decadence of the Gilded Age. Their light-hearted joking turned serious when several prominent public leaders were indicted for accepting bribes from building contractors.

These allegations prompted critics to question the value of this highly pretentious style, especially for public buildings. Many felt that perhaps more modestly designed buildings would better reflect traditional American values. In retrospect, much of this criticism seems unwarranted, since most of the accused were exonerated. Yet, it persisted, and in the end, the public agreed; the Second Empire style all but disappeared by the early 1880s.

French Normandy styling originated with historic French estates and farmhouses.[28] Its inclusion of Gothic and Renaissance details, massive masonry walls, conical towers, and rounded turrets set it apart from other contemporary residential motifs. Other prominent elements included stepped gabled or hipped roofs; protruding dormers with pinnacles; highly ornate, tall chimneys; and wrought-iron roof cresting. Additional details such as large, ornate entrance portals; large, round window and door headers; hood moldings with lapel stops; and cross gables evoked a medieval quality in these dwellings.

The well-respected New York architect Richard Morris Hunt applied French Normandy detailing to two Vanderbilt estates: Belcourt Castle, Newport, Rhode Island (1891) and the Biltmore, Asheville, North Carolina (1895). Custom homebuilders continued to promote this popular design well into the 1950s. Ernest May, private residence, Indian Hills Estates,

Wilmette, Illinois (1927); Joseph H. Bristol, private residence, Wilmette, Illinois (1929); and Ernest Brauder, private residence, Madison, Wisconsin (1930) epitomized this versatile style.

Many late-nineteenth-century U.S. architects believed that High Victorian Gothic styling was ideal for civic and government buildings. Derived in part from the writings of John Ruskin, it was an amalgamation of historic English, French, and Italian Gothic architectural traditions. Vertical massing, polychrome stone finishes, decorative horizontal banding, and wide foliated columns gave it a unique picturesque quality. Exaggerated arches, gabled front porches, bays, turrets, and compound rounded entrance porticos added depth. Large, truncated pyramid-shaped prominent towers; crockets; and finials provided the crowning touch to this very grand design form.

First used by Edward T. Potter, a well-known upstate New York architect, on the Nott Memorial Library at Union College, Schenectady, New York (1856), it gained national attention when Peter Bonnett Wight applied it to the National Academy of Design Building in New York City (1863–65).[29] Impressed by its splendor, two noted Boston architects Henry Van Brunt and William R. Ware, adapted it for Memorial Hall at Harvard University (1870–78).

Frank Furness also used it, on the Pennsylvania Academy of Fine Arts, Philadelphia (1871–76), as did Charles A. Cummings, on the New Old South Church, Boston, Massachusetts (1874–75) and James Lyman Silsbee on the Syracuse Savings Bank, Syracuse, New York (1876).[30] A great many High Victorian Gothic townhouses and mansions were built in Boston, New York City, and Philadelphia from the 1870s to the 1890s.

Richard Norman Shaw, a highly respected British architect, first introduced Queen Anne styling to U.S. audiences at the 1876 Centennial Celebration held in Philadelphia.[31] Loosely based on designs derived from the era of Queen Anne's reign (1702–14), this highly decorative residential motif remained fashionable for nearly forty years. Brightly colored exterior trim placed against clapboard, tile, or brick background made it unique.

Additional highlights included prominent front pavilions and bays; wrap around porches; conical towers and turrets; gabled roofs; fluted columns, angled bays, oriel windows, and stained-glass windows.[32] Prime examples of Queen Anne residences included Henry Hobson Richardson, Williams Watts Sherman House, Newport, Rhode Island (1874–76); William Ralph Emerson, Desert Estate, Mount Desert, Maine (1879); and Charles Schweinfurth, Wilson B. Chisholm House, Cleveland, Ohio (1900).

Modifications to traditional Queen Anne design elements in the 1880s

Queen Anne style, Desert Estate, Mount Desert, Maine, 1879. William Ralph Emerson, architect.

by Henry Hobson Richardson, Robert Swain Peabody, John Goddard Stearns Jr., James Folsom McKim, William Rutherford Mead, and Stanford White resulted in another charming residential design. Named "Shingle style" in the 1950s by Vincent Scully, a well-known architectural historian and professor, this new, free-flowing form was originally intended for New England summer homes.[33] However, other architects thought differently: Shingle-style clubhouses, hotels, restaurants, and homes were built throughout the country from the 1880s through the 1920s.[34]

Its free-flowing interior spaces and various wall surfaces emulated Queen Anne structures. Shingle style differed from the earlier motif, however, in its exclusive use of naturally weathered wood shingles, highlighted by brightly painted trim. Sweeping rooflines, wide verandas, massive horizontal planes, asymmetrical massing, and multiple gables lent further charm to these picturesque structures. Other unique elements included hipped dormers, rounded window and door openings, and raised rubble stone basements.

The Shingle style received national acclaim. Noteworthy examples included McKim, Mead, and White, Newport Casino, Newport, Rhode Island (1879–80); Henry Hobson Richardson, Mrs. M. F. Stoughton House, Cambridge, Massachusetts (1882–84); Peabody and Stearns, the G. N. Black House, "Kragsyde," Manchester-by-the-Sea, Massachusetts (1882–84); and McKim, Mead, and White, William G. Low House, Bristol, Rhode Island (1886–87).[35]

Vincent Scully also coined the term "Stick style" to describe another highly versatile residential design. Initially called American Gothic or Gothic English, Stick style first gained national attention due to the efforts of two well-known architects, Richard Morris Hunt and Dudley Newton. Their J. N. A. Griswold House in Newport (1862) and Jacob Cram House in Middletown (1875), both in Rhode Island, reflected the best in Stick-style design traditions. In fact, these homes set the standard for others to follow. By the mid-1880s, Stick-style homes, railroad depots, clubhouses, and bathhouses were found throughout the Northeast and Midwest.

Its asymmetrical design, exposed beams, and square bays distinguished it from other contemporary styles.[36] Additional touches included large front porches and verandas, steep pitched gable roofs, cross gables, and conical shaped towers. Wide cross braces and exposed studs arranged in fanciful patterns placed against a background of horizontal wood siding provided further character and depth. Both the Edward T. Potter, Mark Twain House, Hartford Connecticut (1873–74) and the Franklin W. Caulkins House (1882), Buffalo, New York exemplified this new multifaceted design.

Stick style, J. N. A. Griswold House, Newport, R.I., 1862. Richard Morris Hunt, architect.

Folk Victorian was another very popular late-nineteenth-century residential motif. A combination of classical, Gothic, and Italianate details, it gained favor with midwestern and western homeowners. Distinguished by its "I," "L," and "T" plans, this design boasted low-slung pyramidal roofs, bracketed eaves, and standard clapboard or shingle veneers. Prominent front and side gables; ornate cross gables, and standardized wood scroll trim marked this style. Other notable elements included extended curved front porches with decorative wood bracketed strips and lattice.

Henry Hobson Richardson often is credited with introducing French Romanesque Revival styling to the United States.[37] In reality, however, he was one of several designers to experiment with it. Easily identified by its bold asymmetrical massing and rough-cut granite or brownstone veneers, French Romanesque Revival commercial, government, and religious buildings were found throughout the United States. This also was a very popular residential style for the wealthy: prominent features included uniform facades, ornate belt courses, and protruding hipped roofs. Deep-set dormers; large segmented Syrian arches, deep-set bands of large double-hung windows, turrets, short chimneys, and conical-shaped towers provided additional bold detailing.[38] Henry Hobson Richardson epitomized this new design especially in his New York State Capitol, Albany (1876); Ames Building, Boston, Massachusetts (1882); and Marshall Field Wholesale Store, Chicago, Illinois (1883–87).[39]

Collegiate Gothic was developed specifically for U.S. campus settings. A well-known British designer, Henry Vaughan, first applied Collegiate Gothic design to the Main Chapel at St. Paul's School in Concord, New Hampshire (1886–94).[40] The style was refined by Walter Cope and John Stewardson at Bryn Mawr College in Denbigh (1891), Pembroke (1894), and Rockefeller (1904) halls and by Ralph Adam Cram at Princeton University in Campbell (1909) and McCormack (1911) halls and the Chapel (1918).[41] In the 1920s, two nationally renowned New York architects, John Russell Pope and James Gamble Rogers, included Collegiate Gothic buildings in their refurbishing plans for Yale University. This remained the design-of-choice for most U.S. campuses through World War II.

Rusticated English brick wall surfaces, bay windows, wall buttresses, pointed windows, and deeply recessed arched doorways symbolized this new romantic style. Large, squared-off central towers crowned by crenellated cornices, gargoyles, finials, and crockets added further distinction. Prime examples of Collegiate Gothic styling in the United States included Henry Ives Cobb, University of Chicago campus plan, Chicago, Illinois (1895–1915); Charles Weber Bolton, Hogg Hall, Lafayette College, Easton, Pennsylvania (1905); Maginnis and Walsh, Boston College campus site, Boston, Massachusetts (1909–1928); M. F. Cummings and Sons, Emma Willard School campus site, Troy, New York (1910), and Delano and Aldrich, John Russell Pope, and James Gamble Rogers, Yale University campus plan, New Haven, Connecticut (1917–35).

Significant advances in construction and engineering technology following the Civil War led a well-respected Chicago architect named William Le Baron Jenney to design that city's first structural steel-framed skyscraper in 1883. This French Romanesque Revival office building, known as the Home Insurance Building, closely resembled other load-bearing structures of that era. Jenney's design choice was intentional; he wanted the public to focus on his building's engineering achievement, not its style.

It took a group of prominent U.S. architects led by Dankmar Adler, Louis Sullivan, Daniel Burnham, John Wellborn Root, William Holabird, and Martin Roche to devise a new skyscraper design, which became known as the Chicago school of design. Buildings in this style closely resembled an ancient Roman column: the ground level, middle level, and upper attic level represented the base, shaft, and cornice; belt courses separated the floors.[42] Narrow vertical piers placed between decorative belt courses and topped by crowned cornices provided an illusion of height. Finally, large, three-part Chicago windows all but eliminated the fortress-like quality of earlier load-bearing structures.[43]

A broad cross-section of buildings epitomized this new dynamic form: Adler and Sullivan, the Wainwright Building, St. Louis, Missouri (1890–91); Adler and Sullivan, Schlesinger and Meyer Store (Carson, Pirie, Scott, and Company), Chicago, Illinois (1899–1904); Burnham and Root, the Reliance Building, Chicago, Illinois (1894–95); George H. Smith, the Rose Building, Cleveland, Ohio (1900); F. S. Barnum and Company, the Park Building, Cleveland, Ohio (1903); and D. S. Burnham and Company, the May Company Department Store, Cleveland, Ohio (1914).

Classical Period

An outgrowth of l'École des Beaux Arts in Paris, Beaux-Arts design first received national attention at the 1893 Columbian Exposition in Chicago. Readily identified by their symmetrical design and exaggerated proportion and scale, Beaux-Arts structures boasted tall parapets, enlarged balustrades, domes, and smooth-cut stone veneers. Massive projecting pavilions, paired Roman columns, prominent raised podium entrances, and ornate cornices and entablatures with fully enriched balustrades lent further distinction. Other notable design elements included enlarged quoins, floral swags, and deep-set moldings.[44]

Both the National Mall in Washington, D.C. (1901) and the Cleveland Group Plan, in Cleveland, Ohio (1903) contain noteworthy examples of this monumental style. The National Mall features Rankin, Kellogg, and Crane, U.S. Department of Agriculture Building (1905); Henry Bacon, Lincoln Memorial (1910); Hornblower and Marshall, National Museum of Natural History (1911); Delano and Aldrich, New Post Office (1931); and John Russell Pope, National Gallery of Art (1941).[45] The Cleveland Group Plan contains Arnold Brunner, Federal Court House and Post Office (1905–11); Lehman and Schmidt, Cuyahoga County Courthouse (1911); J. Milton Dyer, Cleveland City Hall (1916); J. H. MacDowell, Public Auditorium (1922); Walker and Weeks, Federal Reserve Bank (1923); Walker and Weeks, Cleveland Public Library (1925); and Walker and Weeks, Cleveland Board of Education Building (1930).[46]

The 1893 Columbian Exposition also introduced the classical revival style to U.S. audiences. Sometimes referred to as neoclassicism, this new

Beaux Arts structure, c. 1890s.

and highly impressive motif drew its inspiration from ancient Greek structures. Its colossal freestanding columns; pediment porticos; and large, unadorned attic levels made it unique. Graham, Anderson, Probst, and White, Terminal Tower Complex, Cleveland, Ohio (1923) exemplified this form.[47] Classical revival's popularity peaked in the mid-1930s when a prominent U.S. designer, John Russell Pope, applied classical revival detailing to the new Internal Revenue Service Building in Washington, D.C.

Eclectic

Several prominent U.S. architects—among them Frank Lloyd Wright, George G. Elmslie, George Feick Jr., Walter Burley Griffin, George Washington Maher, and William Gray Purcell—began to experiment with the Prairie style of design in 1905. It represented an amalgamation of earlier midwestern residential designs.[48]

Inclusion of free-flowing floor plans; large, open central hallways; and massive stone fireplaces typified these picturesque dwellings. Brick, stucco, or wood-shingle exteriors; horizontal bands of casement windows; low-slung hipped roofs; horizontal roof planes with projecting flattened eaves; and short, wide chimneys lent further charm to these residences.

Examples abounded throughout the United States. These included Frank Lloyd Wright, the William Winslow House, River Forest, Illinois (1893); William Gray Purcell and George Feick Jr., the Catherine Gray Home, Minneapolis, Minnesota (1907); Walter Burley Griffin, the Frederick B. Carter House, Evanston, Illinois (1911); and William Gray Purcell and George G. Elmslie, the Harold C. Bradley House, Woods Hole, Massachusetts (1912).[49]

The New England Foursquare was another highly versatile new residential form. Sometimes called the American Foursquare, this style became popular with the middle class.[50] These two-and-a-half–story square-shaped houses featured prominent raised brick basements and uniformly sized rooms. Homeowners could easily add rooms, porches, and verandas without destroying their original design. These charming dwellings boasted painted clapboard exterior veneers, low-pitched hipped or pyramidal roofs, pronounced roof overhangs, and large roof dormers. Between 1908 and 1930, Aladdin Readi-Cut Housing Company sold thousands of preassembled New England Foursquare housing kits.[51]

An innovative Boston architect named William Gibbons Preston first applied Craftsman details to several Cape Cod cottages in the 1870s. Critically acclaimed at that time for its beauty and practicality, the style was quickly forgotten. It remained in obscurity until the 1890s when two enterprising West Coast architects and brothers, Charles Sumner Greene and Henry Mather Greene, revived it.[52] Its flexible design, ornate details, fanciful rooflines, and protruding wings all clad in warm, earth-toned colors fit in well with the surrounding California landscape. Three residences in this state—the Blacker House in Pasadena, (1907); the Gamble House in Pasadena (1909); and the Nathan Bentz House in Santa Barbara, (1911)—especially embodied this new and exciting motif.

Also known as California style, the Craftsman style embraced not only the English Arts and Crafts tradition but also Japanese and Swiss accents. Open floor plans; stone, tile, or wood exterior veneers; bay projections; low-slung gabled roofs; sun rooms, and dark wood interior trim distinguished this residential design from other contemporary forms. Decorative gabled braces and built-in cabinets and shelves provided additional uniqueness. The Greene brothers also designed special rectilinear wood furniture for these custom houses.

Gustav Stickley, a nationally recognized furniture designer, first popularized bungalow styling through his *Craftsman* magazine. In it, for a reasonable fee, subscribers could purchase working drawings of bungalow cottages. In 1910, Aladdin Readi-Cut Homes, Montgomery Ward and Company, and Sears, Roebuck, and Company capitalized on Stickley's idea and introduced their own preassembled bungalow kits, which sold very well. Over the next thirty-five years, these three retailers offered more than nine hundred different kits.

These one-and-a-half–story bungalows—whose designs included combinations of elements from India, the Adirondacks region of upstate New York, and Chicago—remained popular until the 1940s. Brick, wood, fieldstone, or stucco veneers; flexible floor plans; and low-slung hipped or gabled roofs marked these dwellings. Other key design elements included shed dormers, exposed rafter beams, and wide overhanging eaves. Double-hung windows, full brick chimneys, projecting front porches supported by massive squared-off columns, and decorative gable braces added further charm to these affordable homes.[53]

Colonial Revival, Spanish Colonial Revival, and Mediterranean Revival styles first appeared in U.S. home design at the turn of the twentieth century. Derived in part from eighteenth-century British styles, Colonial Revival dwellings were popular throughout the Northeast. These two- and three-story symmetrical houses featured freestanding, rounded front porticos; paneled front doors with sidelights and fanlights; and large Palladian windows. Double-hung sash windows, quoins, corner pilasters, porches supported by classical columns, and dentilated cornices further distinguished these structures from other contemporary designs.[54]

Integrating modern construction technology with colonial detailing, designers were able to create a whole new genre of beautiful houses with a decisive historic flavor. Horatio R. Wilson, the Frederick C. Sawyer House, Chicago, Illinois (1908); Waddy B. Wood, the Woodrow Wilson House, Washington, D.C. (1915); and Arthur G. Richardson, the Robert Mahoney House, Salem, Massachusetts (1916–17) embodied this new design excellence.

Spanish Colonial Revival homes reflected similar meticulous detailing. Introduced at the 1915 Panama-California Exposition by Betram Grosvenor Goodhue, it was an immediate hit. Sometimes called California Mission style, Spanish Colonial Revival residences offered unique "U" shaped floor plans with large flagstone central courtyards. Its inclusion of red-tiled low-slung hipped roofs; large aches; terra-cotta sculptures, and parapet dormers gave it a decidedly baroque effect. Additional special elements included patterned tile floors and smooth painted stucco exterior walls. Elaborate arched front entrances with carved wood doors, wrought iron grillwork, carved spiral columns, decorative parapets and curvilinear front gables closely resembled those of seventeenth-century Spanish haciendas. California dwellings epitomizing Spanish Colonial Revival style include Henry Harwood Hewitt, Alice Lynch House, Los Angeles (1922); George Washington Smith, Baldwin House, San Marino (1926); Lester G. Scherer, La Casa de las Campanas, Los Angeles (1928); and Lutah Maria Riggs and George Washington Smith, Ravenscroft and Robledal, Santa Barbara (1926, 1927).[55]

At first glance, Mediterranean Revival and Spanish Colonial Revival designs appear very similar. After all, both motifs were baroque inspired. However, while Mediterranean Revival homes relied on Byzantine, Italian, and Moorish accents, Spanish Colonial Revival dwellings utilized Spanish baroque details.

Noted for their massiveness, symmetrical front facades, spacious floor plans, ornately carved doors and wrought-iron window grilles, masonry and stucco exteriors, and attached open gardens, Mediterranean Revival homes first appeared in the greater Miami area during World War I. Richard Kiehnel and M. Leo Elliott, "El Jardin," Coconut Grove (1916) and F. Burrall Hoffman Jr. "Vizcaya," Coral Gables (1917) led the vanguard.

One engineer destined to leave an indelible mark on Florida's architecture in the 1920s was the Californian native Addison Mizner. Mizner introduced Mediterranean Revival styling to Palm Beach. His highly acclaimed Everglades Club (1918) and El Mira Sol estates (1923) guaranteed the style's popularity for years to come. In 1925, he unveiled an ambitious plan for Boca Raton, which called for making this Mediterranean Revival seaside community a final destination point for wealthy winter tourists. The completion of the Boca Raton Resort and Club later that year was the first phase of this plan. Unfortunately, the work stopped there: financial setbacks in the late 1920s forced Mizner into bankruptcy. Although his dream was never realized, Floridians loved Mediterranean Revival architecture. It remained the design of choice well into the 1950s.[56]

English cottage or Storybook dwellings were distinguished by their high-pitched, gabled roofs; enlarged, rounded doorways, turrets, and heavy, wood-plank doors with strap hinges. Decorative half-timber, brick, or stucco walls typified these houses. Derived in part from the English Cotswold cottages, this highly picturesque style first gained popularity in the Northeast and Midwest prior to World War I. It soon spread to southern California; by the mid-1920s English Cottage apartments were being erected throughout greater Los Angeles. Stone Henge in Alameda (1927–29) exemplifies this new romantic style. Designed by a well-known Californian architect, Walter W. Dixon, it served as the backdrop for several movies.[57]

During the Great Depression of the 1930s, Sears, Roebuck, and Company sold thousands of preassembled English cottage housing kits. Their popularity continued through the mid-1940s. Ernest Mayo, private residence, Wilmette, Illinois (1915), Ben Sherwood, Disney Court Cottages, Los Angeles, California (1931), William Raymond Yelland, Normandy Village, Berkely, California (1926–28), and Albert Kahn, Kahn-Kuper Cottage, Detroit, Michigan (1931) embodied this fanciful design.

Tudor style residences represented an amalgamation of Elizabethan, English, Jacobean, and Norman influences. Its ornate timber, masonry and stucco veneers, patterned brick and stonework, and dark walnut or mahogany interiors lent texture and depth. Steep-pitched gabled roofs and prominent cross gables set it apart from other contemporary English-inspired motifs. Narrow grouped casement windows with small diamond glass panes, and tall-stacked brick chimneys crowned by glazed pots made these homes unique.

Originally intended for the wealthy, Tudor styling was quickly adopted by the middle class. Pattern books and catalogs of the 1920s, including Robert T. Jones's *Small Houses of Architectural Distinction: A Book of Suggested Plans Designed by the Architects' Small Home Service Bureau Inc.*, popularized this motif. Specifically, they offered a wide assortment of easily adapted and reasonably priced Tudor house plans. Albert Kahn, "Fairlane," Edsel Ford House, Grosse Pointe, Michigan (1927); Solon S. Berman, private residence, Wilmette, Illinois (1928); Spitzer and Jacobson, private residence, Wilmette, Illinois (1929); Bryant Fleming, Paine House, Oshkosh, Wisconsin (1929); and Richard Philipp, Sensenbrenner House, Appleton, Wisconsin (1929) exemplified this dynamic form.[58] New Tudor homes continued to be built into the 1950s.

Another very popular early-twentieth-century residential style was Dutch Colonial Revival. Modeled after seventeenth-century Dutch farmhouses, these two-and-a-half–story homes featured unique gambrel or barn roofs, flared eaves; and extended arched central doorways with trellises. The inclusion of clapboard, shingle, or cut-stone exterior veneers; full shed dormers, and multi-paned double-hung window sashes added warmth and charm to these very picturesque dwellings. Other prominent characteristics included first-floor window boxes, oval end-gable windows, quarter-round windows in attic-level end gables, and end-gable chimneys.

Aladdin Homes first capitalized on Dutch Colonial Revival design during the first decade of the twentieth century. Sears, Roebuck, and Company introduced its own Dutch Colonial Revival preassembled housing kits in the 1920s. Sears offered more than twenty-five models, including "The Puritan," "The Amsterdam," "The Rembrandt," and "The Glen Falls."[59] It remained a popular style through the Great Depression. George Richard Mann, Fletcher Hieskell House (The Dutch Colonial Inn), Little Rock, Arkansas (1905), Leenhouts and Guthrie, private residence, Wauwatosa, Wisconsin (1924), and S. B. Hayes, private residence, Lubbock, Texas, (1937) typified well-built Dutch Colonial Revival structures.

Modern to Postmodern Period

"Art Deco" was a term first coined by the famous French historian and philosopher Michel Foucault in 1966. Bevis Hillier, noted British author, followed up and wrote a book on Art Deco in 1969. Originally called "Style Moderne" at the 1925 Paris Exposition Internationale des Arts Décoratifs et Industriels Modernes, Art Deco was a direct outgrowth of early-twentieth-century Art Nouveau styling. Unique characteristics included its overall geometric shape and abstract details. Its reliance on new construction materials such as Bakelite, ferroconcrete, and vita-glass also set it apart from other forms.

The impact of this new design did not elude U.S. architects. In fact, many embraced it, for two reasons. First, it reflected the United States' successful industrial proficiency and mass productivity. To not use Art Deco styling was to deny the United States' new-found progress. Second, its streamlined appearance satisfied recently enacted municipal building codes and zoning regulations. This resulted in Art Deco railroad stations, theatres, and residences being built throughout the United States prior to World War II.

Readily identified by its streamlined look, symmetrical and asymmetrical vertical massing, colossal setbacks, and machine-made ornamentation, Art Deco styling did indeed reflect the new industrial age. Other key architectural elements such as wide doors and window openings encircled by metal trim, white or pastel stucco walls, glazed brick or tile details, chevrons, zig-zags, parapet trim, and striking floral patterns added further distinction.[61] Decorative windows—sash-style in horizontal bands, circular, glass-block, steel-casement—curved corner walls, and octagonal shaped clocks with large Roman numerals provided the crowning touches.

William Van Alen, Chrysler Building, New York City (1930); Timothy Pflueger, Oakland Paramount Theatre, Oakland, California (1931); Henry Hohauser, Park Central Hotel, Miami Beach, Florida (1937); and L. Murray Dixon, Raleigh Hotel, Miami Beach, Florida (1940) embodied this highly original style.[60]

World-renowned architect Walter Gropius founded the Bauhaus School of Design in Weimar, Germany in 1919. With the assistance of other eminent European designers, including Ludwig Mies van der Rohe, Paul Klee, and Le Corbusier, Gropius first experimented with International styling in the early 1920s. His goal was simple and direct: to rebuild war-torn Germany with an equitable new architectural form. Rather than relying on traditional approaches to construction and style, Gropius and his colleagues emphasized function and volume. Modern building techniques and new mass-produced construction materials such as reinforced concrete, glass, and steel permitted such radical thinking.

International style first gained European acclaim at the Weissenhofsied-lung Exhibition in Stuttgart, Germany (1927). It received international recognition five years later, at a special architectural exhibition at the Museum of Modern Art in New York. First coined the International style in 1932 by Henry-Russell Hitchcock and Philip Johnson in their exhibition catalog *The International Style: Architecture since 1922*, this motif was considered both stark and efficient.[61] The rise of Adolph Hitler and the Nazi Party forced the Bauhaus school to relocate to the United States in 1937.

The country's architects largely ignored International styling in the 1920s. Perhaps they saw no intrinsic value in its stark realism; more likely, it did not meet client demands. Whatever the personal motivating factors, they shied away from it. Finally, in 1929 two young Philadelphia architects, George Howe and William Lescaze, applied it to their PSFS Bank Building (1929–33). The public praised their effort, and International styling quickly became the design-of-choice for many. To mark their achievement, Howe and Lescaze received a gold medal from the Philadelphia Chapter of the American Institute of Architects in 1938.[62]

The inclusion of streamlined main blocks, smooth facades, impressive setbacks, and thin vertical rising piers as an integral part of the International style marked a radical departure from traditional designs. Three New York City constructions—Reinhard and Hofmeister, Rockefeller Center (1927–35); Raymond Hood, McGraw-Hill Building (1929–30); and Shreve, Lamb, and Harmon, Empire State Building (1929–31)—embodied this new spirit. Other unique elements included smooth granite and limestone exterior wall surfaces, vertical bands of windows, flat roofs, and boxed eaves.

International styling also enjoyed limited success as a residential form. These custom-designed houses, like their commercial counterparts, relied on the latest construction technology and building materials. Richard Neutra, Dr. Philip Lovell House, Los Angeles, California (1927); Richard Neutra, Anna Stern House, Los Angeles, California (1934), Walter Gropius, the Gropius House, Lincoln, Massachusetts (1936); George F. Keck, private residence, Wilmette, Illinois (1936); and George F. Keck, the Morehead House, Madison, Wisconsin (1937) reflected this exciting new motif.

Art Moderne styling, like Art Deco design, originated at the 1925 Paris Exposition. However, unlike Art Deco which was primarily a design of the wealthy, Art Moderne was geared toward the middle class. Also called Moderne or Streamline Moderne, this motif appeared on numerous apartment houses, retail outlets, restaurants, bowling alleys, bus terminals, service stations, and dwellings from the 1920s to the 1950s. Its unbroken horizontal lines and smooth gentle curves closely resembled a sleek machine in motion.[63]

Narrow horizontal bands of aluminum or stainless steel casement windows, glass block, and smooth cement or white terra-cotta exterior veneers further conveyed a sense of motion and sleekness. Large, curved plate-glass doors; mirrored panels; and rounded corner edges with curved-glass windows added further distinction. Curved overhangs and flat roofs crowned by metal parapets were other special design touches.[64]

Mid-1930s architects in the South Beach District of Miami Beach, Florida, developed their own variation of Art Moderne. A reaction to the more staid Art Deco–style apartments and hotels built along the beach in the 1920s, these designers allowed their imaginations to go wild. This led to a whole new genre of fashionable hotels with streamlined setbacks and fanciful color schemes.[65] Unusual accents and details such as portholes, deck railings, racing stripes, extended overhangs, and radio-tower spires provided these structures with a marine quality.[66]

Andrew N. Rebori, private residence, Wilmette, Illinois (1936); Zimmerman, Saxe, McBride, and Ehmann, Walgreen Drug Store, Miami, Florida (1936); Munch and Saxelbye, Alfred I. duPont Building, Miami (1937–39); Wurdeman and Becket, Pan-Pacific Auditorium, Los Angeles, California(1935); Delano and Aldrich, Marine Air Terminal LaGuardia Airport, Queens, New York (1939); and William S. Arrasmith, Greyhound Bus Station, Cleveland, Ohio (1948) epitomized this design phenomenon.

A growing interest in colonial American history following World War I led to a revival of Cape Cod houses. Sears, Roebuck, and Company capitalized on this craze by offering preassembled housing kits for less than $5,000. Other design books also provided inexpensive drawings of one- and two-story Capes. The popularity of this house style continued through the Great Depression due in large measure to the efforts of a well-known Boston architect, Royal Barry Wills. Wills first experimented with Cape Cods in the late 1920s. In fact, one of his designs won the prestigious Better Homes in America Small House Competition in 1932. Wills received further acclaim in 1938 when he and Frank Lloyd Wright tied in a national house design contest. Convinced of their marketability, Wills published several Cape Cod style books, beginning with *Houses for Good Living* in 1940.[67] *Better Homes for Budgeteers* (1941), *Houses for Homemakers* (1945), and *Living on the Level* (1955) followed. Much of his success stemmed from his rare ability to explain intricate construction technology in simple terms.

Following World War II, the Cape Cod became the design of choice for many federally sponsored new houses. In fact, many GIs jokingly referred to their new cottages as government-issued houses. Identified by clapboard or shingle siding, steep gabled roofs, and protruding roof dormers, these compact one-and-a-half–story dwellings dominated suburbia for years. Other prominent characteristics included brick side chimneys, double-hung windows, handcrafted interior moldings, detailed banisters, and hardwood floors. Capes remained popular through the 1950s.

In the postwar years, many returning GIs and their families wanted to live a less formal lifestyle. The American ranch, as developed by Cliff May, Chris Choate, H. Roy Kelley, and William Wilson Wurster, suited their needs. Henry H. Saylor, editor of *American Architect*, coined the term "ranch house" to describe the new one-story bungalow, ranch, and hacienda cottages dotting greater Los Angeles at the time of World War I. Initially popularized by Californian architects including David Owen Dryden and Irving Gill, these simple one-story Spanish-inspired white and beige stucco dwellings with their bright red tile roofs set the stage for larger postwar ranches.

Cliff May designed thousands of Californian ranches over a forty-five year period beginning in 1932. His free-flowing one-story homes featured cross ventilation, numerous skylights, and large central courtyards. Much of his success emanated from his popular design book *Western Ranch Houses* (1946, 1958). This publication introduced the American ranch house to thousands. May's second demonstration house, called the Pacesetter House for 1947, further fired up the public's imagination. Increasingly, Americans in the 1950s equated this residential style with informal living, ideal weather, and glamour.[68] Its popularity reached such a fevered pitch in the late 1950s that homebuilders were unable to satisfy the demand.

Varying in size from 600 to 3,500 square feet, the American ranch successfully integrated outdoor space with indoor living quarters. Horizontal expanses; symmetrical "L" and "U" designs, informal front entrances, and low-slung hipped or gabled roofs distinguished this new motif. Wide overhangs; large picture windows; and various-sized glass windows provided further style distinction. The inclusion of sliding doors and stone or brick chimneys lent additional charm. Wood, stucco, or brick veneers; narrow bands of casement windows, two-car attached garages, enlarged modern kitchens, tiled bathrooms, and hardwood floors made these homes very desirable.[69]

Critics in the mid-1980s claimed that the American ranch was dead, a relic of the past, that would soon be forgotten. These dire predictions proved incorrect. In fact, the American ranch is enjoying a resurgence. Its retro look, durable construction, and highly flexible floor plans appeal to many budget-conscious families who want both quality and value in traditional homes.

Split-level styling represented another very popular postwar residential choice. Loosely based on Prairie School designs, split-levels effectively combined three floors into one compact dwelling by placing the garage, family room, and utility room on the basement level; the living, kitchen, and dining space on the first floor; and the bedrooms, bathrooms, and storage areas on the top floor.[70] Popular 1960s advertisements proudly proclaimed that split-levels were the way to go, because they provide more in a lot less space.

Similar in its informality to the American ranch, split-levels also complemented their sites. Designs included side-to-side, front-to-back, and one-and-a-half–story variations. Unlike earlier, more ornate houses, split-level dwellings were devoid of extraneous detail. Patterned brick, stone, and wood veneers; decorative shutters, large picture windows, and bowed bays replaced traditional historic design accents. The split-level is still popular today.

The modern or post–World War II International style first appeared in 1951, on the Lever House in New York City. Designed by Gordon Bunschaft of the architectural firm of Skidmore, Owings, and Merrill, this twenty-four-story rectangular slab featured unencumbered columns, exposed supports, dark glass walls, and minimal detail. It represented a paradigm of simplicity and sophistication.[71] Revisions to New York City building and zoning laws after World War II permitted slab construction. Prominent architects of that era such as Alvar Aalto, Pietro Belluschi, Walter Gropius, Philip Johnson, Charles Luckman, I. M. Pei, Ludwig Mies van der Rohe, and Eero Saarinen experimented with this radical style. This resulted in hundreds of super-blocks in the 1950s and 1960s.

These soaring skyscrapers relied on massive steel supports, reinforced concrete, and strategically placed floor supports. Their opaque glass wall surfaces, flat roof gardens, flexible floor plans, and movable wall partitions made these structures unique. Large central service cores housed elevators, air ducts, and mechanical equipment. These brightly illuminated towers appeared light years ahead of nearby office blocks.

Le Corbusier, United Nations Headquarters, New York City (1952); Charles Luckman, the Prudential Center, Boston, Massachusetts (1959–65); C. F. Murphy and Associates, the Civic Center, Chicago, Illinois (1965); Marcel Breuer and Hamilton Smith, Ameritrust Bank Tower, Cleveland, Ohio (1971); and I .M. Pei and Henry Cobb, John Hancock Tower, Boston, Massachusetts (1973) embodied this most innovative design.

Modern styling also appeared on postwar custom-built houses, mostly one-story free-flowing symmetrical units built with cantilevered construction methods. Smooth, unadorned exteriors; functional, open floor plans; and glass-curtain walls distinguished them from prewar streamlined dwellings. They also boasted modern household conveniences such as recessed lighting and all-electric stainless steel kitchens with built-in dishwashers, washing machines, and dryers. Other prominent details included metal framed sliding doors and windows, corner casement windows, plain doorways, concrete basements, and flat roofs with no eaves.[72]

Major architectural firms such as Moore, Lyndon, Trumbull, and Whitaker; Venturi and Rauch; and Cope and Lippincott; and leading designers including Marcel Breuer, Philip Johnson, and Richard Neutra experimented with modern design. Ludwig Mies van der Rohe, Dr. Edith Farnsworth

House, Plano, Illinois (1946–51); Philip Johnson, Glass House, New Ca-
naan, Connecticut (1946–49); and Marcel Breuer, Breuer House, New Ca-
naan, Connecticut (1946–48) exemplified this new controversial form.

Critics doubted the practical value of this style; they argued that its stark-
ness might be appropriate for commercial buildings but not for private
dwellings. This harsh criticism hit its mark. By the mid-1950s, many architects had modified their initial designs. These changes ran the gamut from
reintroducing traditional rooflines and using less obtrusive curves to stan-
dardizing window fenestrations and adopting standard entryways. Other significant alterations included increased living space and lively exterior trim.

Postmodernism first gained national attention in the mid-1960s. Dis-
enchanted with the stark realism of modern design and the idea that one
size fits all, postmodernists challenged the status quo. Robert Venturi, an
outspoken U.S. architect who had worked under Eero Saarinen and Louis
Kahn, led the vanguard. His *Complexity and Contradiction in Architecture*
(1967) started a design revolution.

Sometimes referred to as pluralism, postmodern style is still popular. Be-
lieving that all architecture should fit the site and not the other way around,
Venturi attacked the corporate image of modern architecture. He argued
that the self-interest of big business had corrupted this design. Its uniqueness
was gone. Multiplicity, not exclusivity, was the answer. Venturi also lashed
out at Mies van de Rohe's famous quote, "Less is more." He said, "Less is a
bore" and that artistic creativity had been all but silenced. Furthermore, he
deplored the lack of cultural meaning in modern architecture.

In a second book, *Learning from Las Vegas* (1972), Robert Venturi, along
with Denise Scott Brown and Steven Izenour, explored the merit of Los
Vegas architecture and billboards. They readily admitted to the complexities, inconsistencies, and imperfections of modern-day Las Vegas architecture. However, they claimed that it played an integral part in the country's
architectural scene and should not be arbitrarily altered or destroyed.

They concluded that architecture should be done with humor, wit, and
historical reference. The Vanna Venturi House (1962) and the Guild House
apartments (1960–65), both in Philadelphia, Pennsylvania, reflected this new
thinking. Many postmodernists took these ideas to heart. Specifically, they
amalgamated different details from a wide variety of historic sources to create
new hybrid forms. These hybrids generally accentuated design complexities
and contradictions rather than gloss over them with artificial syntheses.[73]

In challenging prevailing design trends they had created their own genre of architecture. Juxtaposing decorative accents, jostling space, and redefining both the proportion and scale of current styles helped them to achieve this goal. Many traditional architects and designers disapproved of such open-ended artistry.

Closer scrutiny suggests that many of these hybrids may not have been radical at all. In fact, many embodied standard design forms and style elements derived from legitimate sources. Taken out of their original context and placed within a modern setting they came alive in new and unexpected ways. Many of the buildings designed by postmodernists such as Carol Ross Barney, Frank Gehry, Michael Graves, Maya Lin, Richard Meier, Cesar Pelli, John Rauch, and Robert A. M. Stern reflected this kind of design ingenuity. Boldly reinterpreting traditional forms, styles, and techniques, they have successfully challenged long-accepted viewpoints regarding proper style and detail. At the same time, they have enriched the United States' architectural legacy.

Postmodernist architecture is found throughout the United States. Venturi and Rauch, Tucker Home, Katonah, New York (1975) and the Brant Johnson Home, Vail, Colorado (1976); Moore and Graves, Public Service Buildings, Portland, Oregon (1980–82) and Humana Tower, Louisville, Kentucky (1986); Johnson and Burgee, AT&T Building, New York City (1978–84); and Langdon and Wilson, J. Paul Getty Museum, Malibu, California (1970–75) illustrate the diversity of postmodern styling.

Preservationists must remain keenly aware of the latest design trends and how contemporary architects are applying traditional historic detailing to modern buildings in new and unexpected ways. Knowledge of the key elements comprising historical styles helps in understanding this process. Specifically, it furnishes insight into how past architects and builders successfully combined the latest construction advances with fashionable motifs to create enduring structures.

The United States' physical legacy surrounds us, even if at times it is obscured by more recent development. Preservationists must continue to promote and protect this nation's architectural legacy. One of the most effective ways to achieve this desired end is to work with local decision-makers in both the public and private sectors to institute positive, long-lasting change.

Preservationists know the importance of these alliances. Increasingly, they are working with community leaders to revitalize historic buildings and sites throughout the United States. Authentic restoration must remain at the forefront of twenty-first-century development. Understanding this country's architectural legacy and its various design components is essential in achieving that goal. Preservationists who wish to practice this profession have a number of options. They may seek employment in one of three economic sectors: the non-profit organization, the public agency, or the private firm. The following three chapters describe the role played by professional preservationists in each.

Notes

1. Joseph L. Sax, "Heritage of Preservation as a Public Duty: The Abbe Gregoire and the Origins of an Idea," *Michigan Law Review* 88 (1990): 1142–43.

2. John Ruskin, *The Seven Lamps of Architecture* (New York: Dover, 1989), 186–87.

3. J. Mordaunt Crook, *The Dilemma of Style: Architectural Ideas from the Picturesque to the Post-Modern* (Chicago: Univ. of Chicago Press, 1987), 52–53.

4. archINFORM, "Eugène Emmanuel Viollet-le-Duc," www.eng.archiform.net/arch/2677.htm.

5. Marc Nadaux, "Eugène Viollet-le-Duc," *Le XIXe siècle*, www.19e.org/personnages/france/V/violletleduc.htm.

6. Norman Tyler, *Historic Preservation: An Introduction to Its History, Principles, and Practice* (New York: Norton, 2000), 24–25, 28–29.

7. Tara Prindle, "Building Our Wigwam," *Native American Technology and Art: Scenes from the Eastern Woodlands: A Virtual Tour, circa 1550*, www.nativetech.org/scenes/buildingwigwam.html.

8. Ibid.

9. Sandra Pollock, "American Federal, 1780–1820," Real Site Designs, 2001, www.realviews.com/homes/fed.html.

10. Talbot Hamlin, *Greek Revival Architecture in America* (New York: Dover, 1944), 213–19.

11. James M. Fitch, *American Building and the Historical Forces That Shaped It* (Boston: Houghton Mifflin, 1966), 8–15.

12. William H. Pierson Jr., *American Buildings and Their Architects*, Vol. 1: *The Colonial and Neo-Classical Styles* (New York: Oxford Univ. Press, 1970), 22–23.

13. Hugh Morrison, *Early American Architecture: From the First Colonial Settlements to the National Period* (New York: Oxford Univ. Press, 1952), 120–33.

14. Leland M. Roth, *A Concise History of American Architecture* (New York: Harper and Row, 1980), 24.

15. Ibid., 24–25.

16. Ibid., 58–62.

17. Ibid., 24–27.

18. John J. G. Blumenson, *Identifying American Architecture: A Pictorial Guide to Styles and Terms, 1600–1945* (New York: Norton, 1982), 23.

19. Ibid.

20. Morrison, *Early American Architecture*, 575–76.

21. Roth, *A Concise History*, 92–100.

22. Andrew Jackson Downing, *The Architecture of Country Homes* (New York: Dover, 1969), 92, 104–5; Richard Klein and David Lipstreu, "Bargeboard Details in the Western Reserve of Ohio 1830–1860," *American Preservation Technology* 13, no. 4 (1981): 34–37.

23. Richmond Libraries, "Horace Walpole 1717–1797 and Strawberry Hill," *Local Studies Collection, Local History Notes* (2005): 1–8, www.richmond.gov.uk/local_history_h_walpole.pdf.

24. Jonathan Goldsmith, *The Natural and Artificial Wonders of the United Kingdom: With Engravings in Three Volumes*, vol. 2: *England and Wales* (London: G. B. Whittaker, 1825), 321–26, www.beckford.c18.net/wbgoldsmith1825.html.

25. Roth, *A Concise History*, 120–21.

26. "The Nott Memorial: Edward Tuckerman Potter." Union College, Schenectady, N.Y., www.union.edu/Campus/Nott_Memorial/potter.php; the Athenaeum of Philadelphia, the Athenaeum Building, www.philaathenaeum.org/building.html.

27. Blumenson, *Identifying American Architecture*, 53.

28. Roth, *A Concise History*, 120–21.

29. Ibid.

30. David Ramsey, "Drawings on Banks, Silsbee's Artful Chaos Anchors Clinton Square," Syracuse (N.Y.) *Post-Standard*, Aug. 25, 2002, final edition, H1.

31. "Richard Norman Shaw." Great Buildings Collection, Great Architects, 2006, www.greatbuildings.com/architects/Richard_Norman_Shaw.html.

32. Blumenson, *Identifying American Architecture*, 62–63; Historic Preservation Commission, Wilmette, Ill., Architectural Style, Queen Anne, www.wilmette.com/whpe.queenanne.htm.

33. Antoinette F. Downing and Vincent J. Scully Jr., *The Architectural Heritage of Newport, Rhode Island, 1640–1915* (Cambridge: Harvard Univ. Press, 1952), 97–98.

34. Vincent J. Scully Jr., *The Shingle Style and the Stick Style: Architectural Theory and Design from Richardson to the Origins of Wright* (New Haven, Conn.: Yale Univ. Press, 1971), 98–112.

35. Sandra Pollock, "Shingle Style, 1874 to 1900s: The Truly American Style," Real Site Designs, www.realviews.com/homes/shing.html.

36. Blumenson, *Identifying American Architecture*, 60–61.

37. Ibid.

38. Roth, *A Concise History*, 164–71.

39. Ibid., 164–74.

40. Robert A. M. Stern, *The Architecture of St. Paul's School and the Design of the Ohrstrom Library, Henry Vaughn Legacy* (Concord, N.H.: St. Paul's School Ohrstrom Library, 1999), www.library.sps.edu/exhibits/stern/vaughn.shtml; Ralph Adam Cram, "Good and Bad Modern Gothic," *Architectural Review* 1, no. 5 (Oct. 1899): 117–18.

41. Marianne Hansen, "Collegiate Gothic–Cope and Stewardson," Bryn Mawr

College Special Collections, Sept. 21–Dec. 20, 2001, www.brynmawr.edu/library/exhibits/thomas/gothic.html.

42. Carl W. Condit, *The Chicago School of Architecture: A History of Commercial and Public Buildings in the Chicago Area, 1875–1925* (Chicago: Univ. of Chicago Press, 1964), 16.

43. Sarah Bradford Landau and Carl W. Condit, *Rise of New York Skyscrapers, 1865–1913* (New Haven: Yale Univ. Press, 1996), 184–85, 191.

44. Chuck LaChiusa, "Beaux Arts Style," *Buffalo Architecture and History*, 2003, http://ah.bfn.org/a/DCTNRY/b/beaux.html.

45. "Washington, D.C., National Mall," www.nps.gov/nr/travel/wash/dc/70htm.

46. Arnold Brunner, "Cleveland's Group Plan" (paper presented at the Eighth National Conference on City Planning, New York, New York, June 5–7, 1916), 14–34, www.library.cornell.edu/Reps/DOCS/brunner.htm.

47. Blumenson, *Identifying American Architecture*, 68–69.

48. Historic Preservation Commission, Wilmette, Ill., Architectural Style, Prairie School, www.wilmette.com/whpe/prairieschool.htm.

49. Roth, *A Concise History*, 210–11.

50. Sandra Pollock, *American Architecture*, "American Foursquare, 1895–1930," www.realviews.com/homes/orsq.html.

51. Ronica Roth, "Built in a Day: Capturing the Era of Catalog Architecture," *The Magazine of the National Endowment for the Humanities* 19, no. 5 (Sept–Oct. 1998): 26–31, www.neh.gov/news/humanities/1998-09/aladdin.html

52. "History of the Gamble House," Univ. of Southern California, City of Pasadena, www.gamblehouse.org/history/index.html; Greene and Greene Virtual Archives Team, "Charles Sumner and Henry Mather Greene Biography." Univ. of Southern California, www.usc.edu/dept/architecture/greeneandgreene/about greenes.html; Robert Winter, ed., *Toward a Simpler Way of Life, The Arts and Crafts Architects of California* (Berkeley: Univ. of California Press, 1997), 1–6.

53. Historic Preservation Commission, Wilmette, Ill., "Architectural Style, Craftsman Style," www.wilmette.com/whpe/craftsman.htm.

54. "Antique Homes, The Sales Directory of Antique and Historic Properties, Historic Style Guide," www.antiquehomes.magazine.com/style-guide/colonial revival1.html; Historic Preservation Commission, Wilmette, Ill., "Architectural Style, Colonial Style," www.wilmette.com/whpe/colonial.htm.

55. Blumenson, *Identifying American Architecture*, 8–9; "Different Types of Bungalows-Moderne," Mid-Town Renovators, www.mid-townrenovators.com/pages/bungalow-modern.html; David Gebhard, "Founding Father: George Washington Smith," http://www.architect.com/Publish/GWS.html. "Fine Restoration of Classic Homes, Spanish Colonial Revival," Mid-Town Renovators, www.mid-townrenovators.com/pages/bungalow_spanish_col_revival.html.

56. Erick Valle, "Florida Vernacular Architecture," *Traditional Neighborhood Design, Building a Better Place to Live*, www.tndhomes.com/phd05.htm; Donald W. Curl, "The Architecture of Addison Mizner," *Spanish River Papers* (Oct. 1978): 3–5, www.bocahistory.org/pdf; Stella Suberman, "Addison Mizner and the Boca Raton House,"

Spanish River Papers 7, no. 1 (Oct. 1978): 5–6, www.bocahistory.org/boco_history/br_history_spanish_river.asp.

57. Arrol Gellner, "Storybook Master," *Inman News*, Feb. 11, 2001, 1, http://db.inman.com/inman/content/subscribers/inman/column.cfm?.

58. Robert T. Jones, ed., *Small Houses of Architectural Distinction: A Book of Suggested Plans Designed by the Architects' Small House Service Bureau, Inc* (New York: Dover, 1987). "House Style Guide," 2003–5, www.house-styles-guide.com/tudor-medieval-revival.html.

59. Mary Beth Breckenridge, "The Construction Side of Sears," *Knight Ridder Newspapers*, May 3, 2005, 1–2, www.asu.edu/stardust/documents/theconstruction sideofsears.pdf; Sears, Roebuck, and Company, *Small Houses of the Twenties: The Sears, Roebuck 1926 House Catalog*, (New York: Dover, 1991).

60. Univ. of Wisconsin, Eau Claire, "Architectural Styles," www.uwec.edu/Geography/Ivogeler/w367/styles/s4.htm.

61. Henry-Russell Hitchcock and Philip Johnson, *The International Style: Architecture since 1922* (New York: Norton, 1932), 36; Bracha Kunda, "What Is the International Style?" Art Log. www.artlog.co.il/telaviv/what.html; Historic Preservation Commission, Wilmette, Ill., Architectural Styles: International, www.wilmette.com/whpe/artmodern/international.htm.

62. Roth, *A Concise History*, 243–48.

63. Jackie Craven, "About Architecture, Periods and Styles, 1930–1945 Art Modern." architecture.about.com/od/periodstyles/ig/Home-Styles/Art-Modern.htm.

64. Ibid.

65. "Miami Beach Architecture, Art Deco District, Architectural Styles, Moderne Streamline." *Miami Beach 411. Guide: History.* www.miamibeach411.com/History/art deco.html#6.

66. City of Miami, FL., Planning Department, Historic Preservation, "Streamline and Depression Moderne (1930–42)." *Architectural Styles*, www.historicpreser vationmiami.com/streamline.html.

67. Royal Barry Wills, *Houses for Good Living* (New York: Architectural Book Publishing Company Inc., 1940); James C. Massey and Shirley Maxwell, "The Cape Cod Revival, Reinventing Vernacular Cottages for Modern Suburbs," *Old House Journal* (Mar.–Apr. 2003), 88–93, www.oldhousejournal.com/magazine/2003/April/cape_cod.shtml.

68. Cliff May, ed., *Sunset Western Ranch Houses* (San Francisco: Lane, 1947, 1958, and 1999); John Mack Faragher, "Bungalow and Ranch House: The Architectural Backwash of California," *Western Historical Quarterly* 32, no. 2 (Summer 2001): 149–50, www.usu.edu/history/whq/rasum2001.htm.

69. David Bricker, "Ranch Houses Are Not All the Same," in *Preserving the Recent Past*, vol. 2, edited by Deborah Slaton and William G. Foulks (Washington, D.C.: Historic Preservation Foundation, National Park Service and Association for Preservation Technology International, 2000).

70. Brandy Reilly, "Split Level, 1950s–1960s," "Architectural Styles," Univ. of Wisconsin, Eau Claire, www.uwec.edu/Geography/Ivogeler/w367/styles/s43.htm;

"Background of the Vernacular: The What, How, and Why of Bi-level, Split-level, and Raised Ranch Houses," www.splitlevel.net/background4–7.html; "True Splits: A Primer on Three-Level and Four-Level Homes, also Raised Splits and Split Entry Homes," www.splitlevel.net/split-level.html.

71. Roth, *A Concise History*, 278.

72. Ibid., 314–22.

73. Fil Hearn, "Implications of Robert Venturi's Theory of Architecture," *Architecture and Civil Engineering* 2, no. 5 (2003): 357–63.

Chapter Five

The Nonprofit Role in Historic Preservation

Introduction

The voluntary or independent nonprofit sector has been a part of the U.S. landscape since the nation began. Nonprofits often bridge a gap between the private and public sectors in issues related to real-estate development and, therefore, historic preservation. Because of its independent structure of this independent sector, the constraints of private-sector requirements, especially the profit in a time/money equation, need not be met. The public-sector requirements of pleasing the electorate and earning votes within a political term of office are not major concerns for the nonprofit organization (NPO) either. The nonprofit here fulfills a crucial role: to work on real estate development in a particular area over an extended period of time with regard not for private profits but only for raising support through tax-deductible donations.[1]

The following steps illustrate the role played by the nonprofit in this process:

1. A city or town government is concerned about dilapidation of the houses in a local neighborhood.
2. Its landmarks commission may seek assistance from a local preservation nonprofit in organizing a neighborhood group of property owners.
3. This group of homeowners and businesses proposes outlining an area to be designated a historic district.
4. After approval by city council, the historic district is nominated to the National Register of Historic Places.

5. Once achieving the National Register designation and its accompanying tax credits, the new district attracts private investment.

Throughout the process, the preservation organization offers preliminary architectural analysis, proposes design guidelines and promotes the new district. Additional illustrations of this important nonprofit role are described later, in the "Profiles in Preservation."

The significance of the nonprofit sector increased during the 1980s and 1990s due to the growth of the IRS code and related taxation issues. The nonprofit sector, made up of charitable organizations and other groups dedicated to the public's interest are designated as tax-exempt, meaning they are not taxed by state or local governments on property holdings, and/or tax deductible, meaning that individuals' donations to these groups result in relief from certain taxes.[2]

Tax policies influence historic preservation efforts in several ways. Chapter 7 illustrates the effect of the ITC and historic preservation or conservation easements on private-sector preservation. This chapter will demonstrate other tax influences on saving historic structures.

Nonprofits include charitable organizations, schools, religious groups, foundations, and a variety of other institutions regarded as serving the public interest. Within this group are many entities that specifically relate to preservation:

1. preservation organizations on the national, state, regional, and local level;
2. community development corporations, mostly found in large central cities;
3. related organizations, such as conservation or environmental groups; and
4. historical societies, museums, and landmarks.

This chapter elaborates on preservation organizations, those whose primary purpose is to protect historic properties. Community development will be discussed in detail later. Related organizations and societies, museums, and landmarks will also be mentioned throughout this book.

Nonprofit preservation organizations are the most obvious sources of assistance to those considering a preservation project. Many of these groups began in the early years of U.S. development, as described in chapter 2. Some no longer exist. This chapter will focus on currently active preservation organizations, their history, accomplishments, operations, and leadership profiles. The section entitled "Profiles in Preservation," will begin with the largest of them all, the National Trust for Historic Preservation and will then focus on the local and statewide groups.

Nonprofit organizations are only as effective as their leadership. The personnel carrying out preservation activities must have an inspirational leader, who is supported by a knowledgeable board of trustees. The following examples are drawn from preservation associations considered the most productive in the U.S. preservation movement. Though not an exhaustive list, the groups listed on it typify successfully run organizations. A full catalog could include hundreds of nonprofit preservation organizations, some of them already mentioned in chapter two; this section notes other important and recognized groups that have achieved the goals of saving historic resources. This is important because their methods do not conform to any particular pattern; their scale varies from large to small, and the types of historic resources reflect local differences across the United States. However, two characteristics are particularly relevant for the HPP: the leaders of these organizations have a passion for historic preservation and an ability to strategically accomplish their goals and objectives.

Profiles in Preservation

The National Scene

National Trust for Historic Preservation

The most prominent preservation organization on the national level in the United States is the National Trust for Historic Preservation. As chapter 2 indicated, the National Trust evolved out of the post–World War II era of reconstruction of the United States' cities. Although no bombing had occurred on the American continent during the 1940s, urban renewal in the 1950s and '60s, with its slum-clearance objectives, had a similar effect. The appearance of the so-called federal bulldozer led to a coalescence of preservation leaders. President Harry Truman was at the forefront of this movement in 1949 when he signed legislation creating the National Trust.[3]

The initial focus of the trust involved the acquisition of important historic properties, such as the Woodlawn Plantation in Virginia. The trust acquired many other buildings and sites during its early years. However, its vision soon expanded to embrace the broader goals of public education and assistance to local organizations and projects.

Over time, the National Trust became less reliant on federal financial support and became more representative of the country's larger preservation movement. To exemplify this last point, in 1980 it launched the Main Street program, which offered technical assistance to communities suffering the loss of their historic central business districts to highway-oriented retailing.[4] Specifically, the Main Street program stimulated viable economic development in older commercial districts. Main Streets that participate in the program are located in large cities, small towns, and rural villages. The four-point approach is the same throughout:

1. Creating a workable organization, consisting of stakeholders in the district and other volunteers, to implement plans.
2. Marketing the district through advertising and special events.
3. Promoting appropriate design using historic assets to guide decisions.
4. Assessing the economic base and initiating positive changes.

Founders of the Main Street program included Mary Means, Scott Gerloff, Clark Schoettle, and Tom Moriarty. Following a series of demonstration projects in towns around the country, the Main Street Center was established in 1980. Combining the talents of architects and designers with people who knew business economics and practices, the team set up a center to offer expertise and advice to communities throughout the country. More than 1200 programs are currently part of the Main Street network. Its founders name certain principles as defining the philosophy of the Main Street program and accounting for its success. These are:

1. Comprehensive. The approach must include all four points.
2. Incremental. Activities should occur in steps to achieve enduring change.
3. Self-help. The whole community should commit itself to help.
4. Partnerships. Change will involve public, private, and nonprofit sectors.
5. Identifying and capitalizing on assets. Each community has unique resources.
6. Emphasizing quality work over quantity. Projects should be done with attention to excellence.
7. Change. Emphasis should be on improving business practices, altering appearances, and introducing new ideas.

8. Implementation. The project must demonstrate accomplishments as it moves along.

Later the trust's Community Partners program focused on residential neighborhoods through local preservation organizations and its ability to offer technical assistance. National Trust programs encourage the creation and support of special statewide organizations in addition to the state historic preservation offices. Its highly popular national conferences bring together urban and rural preservationists from across the United States and abroad. Trust publications offer a wide array of technical manuals and well-researched books and magazines.

Since 1993, Richard Moe has brought his public administration skills to the leadership of the National Trust for Historic Preservation. Under his direction, the trust expanded its role into a number of new initiatives that include controlling urban sprawl and revitalizing urban areas. In an era of shrinking federal resources, Moe created a stronger link with state and local organizations and strengthened the country's preservation movement in a number of ways.

Expansion of the Main Street program, launching Community Partnerships and generating various publications that are geared toward educating civic leaders and preservationists on the important economic and social values of preservation are all products of Moe's creative and constructive leadership.[5]

In the *Journal of the American Planning Association* review of their book, *Changing Places: Rebuilding Community in the Age of Sprawl*, Richard Moe and Carter Wilkie were commended for offering two answers to the sprawl dilemma: growth management at the urban edge and reinventing downtown.[6] Although these ideas are not exactly original, they outline an innovative and expansive direction for the National Trust. The trust's new emphasis on informing the planning and real estate development process with an urban design focus on landscapes and places is one of Moe's important contributions to the future of historic preservation.

Statewide Organizations

Preservation North Carolina

As a statewide organization, Preservation North Carolina stands out. Founded in 1939, its purpose is to protect buildings, landscapes, and important historical sites. It makes property acquisitions and passes those properties on to preservation-sensitive buyers. Since its founding, it has saved over 450 historic properties, and as of 2007, it also owns and operates two museums. The organization has achieved broad national recognition for its work in educating the public on the importance of historic preservation.[7]

Preservation North Carolina is also acknowledged as a model for statewide organizations across the United States. It works closely with the North Carolina State Historic Preservation Office on a variety of projects, such as coordinating efforts to evaluate damage from years of hurricanes that devastated eastern North Carolina. Through its Endangered Properties program, the organization assists rural and small-town historic properties where investment is needed. In urban areas, provision of affordable housing is one of their many program objectives. In 1997, Preservation North Carolina lobbied the state legislature to provide rehabilitation tax credits, a significant accomplishment for preservation throughout the state.

Among its many awards, Preservation North Carolina is recognized for preserving historic school buildings and abandoned factories. Its projects are sensitive to environmental and cultural features while promoting the economic uses and development of important historical properties.

An organization that has thrived for more than sixty-five years may attribute its success to many outstanding leaders. While the officers of its day-to-day operations are important, the board of directors also plays a significant role. The leadership of J. Myrick Howard, in particular, proved crucial to Preservation North Carolina.

Historic Landmarks Foundation of Indiana

This statewide organization, founded in 1960 in Indiana's capital city, Indianapolis, is the largest private statewide preservation group in the United States.[8] The Indiana Foundation includes not only its headquarters in Indianapolis but also nine regional offices throughout the state that offer assistance to local preservation efforts.

Historic Landmarks Foundation of Indiana comprises an array of programs that offer intervention strategies, but, when all else fails, it will purchase threatened buildings for neighborhood revitalization. On the assumption that all preservation is local, the foundation creates local partnerships and supports grassroots efforts to save Indiana's heritage.

Through its thirty-member board of trustees, many civic leaders combined their talents to save historic structures and places of significance throughout the state. This strong partnership, led for more than forty years by community volunteers and committed members, works with local groups across Indiana. Public education plays an important role in the foundation's work: it offers a speakers bureau, historic tours, classroom activities, and field trips for interested parties. Under the direction of J. Reid Williamson, it built a robust base of future preservationists.[9]

Georgia Trust for Historic Preservation

The Georgia Trust for Historic Preservation creatively integrates education into its program with a unique venture, Talking Walls. This heritage

The Cotton Exchange, Savannah, Ga., c.1886. William Gibbons Preston, architect. Located on historic Bay Street, this very impressive brick structure with its terra cotta trim represented the first of several new commercial buildings to be built in downtown Savannah during the last two decades of the 19th century. Photo by V. Benson.

education program enhances the instruction of social studies to the emerging generation of students by incorporating historic preservation into its curriculum.[10]

Each state promotes preservation following different paths. In the Georgia Trust case, a revolving fund addresses endangered buildings and sites and assists owners in rehabilitating their properties by providing critical financial support when most needed. The organization avails itself of the expertise offered by the Main Street program of the National Trust.

The Georgia Trust operates three prominent house museums in different parts of the state. It also sponsors the Georgia Preservation Industry Council, a network of developers, property owners, architects, and artisans who carry out preservation work.

Greg Paxton, who has served the organization since 1981, is the president and CEO of the Georgia Trust. Many of the trust's initiatives can be attributed to his extensive and dedicated leadership. As a former board member of the National Trust, Paxton chaired the Statewide Partners, the national association of preservation organizations, and the Preservation Action lobbying group. In preparation for his very productive professional preservation career, Mr. Paxton received his master's degree in historic preservation from the University of Vermont.

Nonprofits with a Local and Regional Scope

Some nonprofits begin as grassroots efforts without any special assistance from statewide groups. They become regional leaders over an extended period of time. Such was the case of the Cleveland Restoration Society. The authors have closely observed the development of this organization since the early 1980s. This detailed description of its operation is intended to help the HPP better understand some of the specific elements necessary for a flourishing enterprise, as HPPs may be called on to create and develop such an organization.

Cleveland Restoration Society and Preservation Resource Center of Northeast Ohio

The Cleveland Restoration Society (CRS) originated in 1972 as the Downtown Restoration Society. With the encouragement of the George Gund Foundation in the 1980s, a new and expanded board of trustees took the organization in a more professional direction. Under the able leadership of a full-time executive director, a new agenda of advocacy activities emerged. Protests of demolitions and appearances at Cleveland's Landmarks Commission hearings exerted political pressures on city officials. Local publicity and activism achieved several major victories. It brought notice and new members to the organization.

Cleveland's downtown experienced a building boom in the 1980s. In the empty spaces left by urban renewal new office buildings appeared. Development pressures quickly targeted landmark structures. Through the 106 Review process (see chapter 3), CRS assisted in planning efforts involving the 1892 Society for Savings bank building, a Public Square anchor. One of the first skyscrapers in downtown Cleveland, it was threatened with demolition in the 1980s. The new bank, now Key Tower, altered its demolition plans and incorporated the red sandstone Romanesque building into its new fifty-five-story tower, the largest building between New York and Chicago. World-famous architect Cesar Pelli unveiled his model for Key Tower at a Restoration Society meeting, to the applause of preservationists.

A second major victory for preservation involved the downtown Playhouse Square Theater District. Slated for demolition in the 1970s, these four elaborate reflections of the Roaring Twenties—the Palace, State, Allen, and Ohio theaters—were saved from the wrecking ball by an eleventh-hour rescue. In conjunction with the Junior League of Cleveland, which intervened at this climactic moment, CRS worked diligently with the Playhouse Square Foundation to restore all four theaters to their former grandeur.

In neighborhood preservation, CRS collaborates with many community development corporations, whose efforts characterize the central city. The society propagated unique partnerships between city and county officials. Efforts by such pairings assist low-to-moderate income households to purchase affordable housing while preserving unique historic districts. Gentrification and displacement are rare occurrences in Cleveland's neighborhoods.[11]

The recent establishment of the Preservation Resource Center of Northeastern Ohio expanded the CRS scope to include several surrounding counties. The society now offers technical assistance to preservation organizations in Cleveland suburbs, Akron, and Canton, Ohio. Thus, the Restoration Society enjoys recognition as a statewide presence.

The Cleveland Restoration Society's initial purpose was to preserve central business district structures that were falling to the bulldozers. The founders, headed by real estate heiress Maxine Goodman Levin, purchased several historic buildings in the 1970s. Unfortunately, Cleveland suffered the loss of businesses and population at an alarming rate, and, by 1980 the city government defaulted on its loans. It was not a good period for any real estate development, much less historic preservation.

In the early 1980s, Kathleen Crowther, with a master's degree in urban studies from the Maxine Goodman Levin College of Urban Affairs at Cleveland State's downtown university, accepted the position of executive director of CRS. With funding from local foundations, she structured a series of new programs. These included strong preservation advocacy, publication of the *Facade* newsletter, appearances at city council and Landmarks Commission meetings and prudent development of a board of trustees made up of civic officials and business leaders.

Crowther received significant support from local foundations, government grants and individual donations. Levin, recognizing the progress unfolding, contributed a near-downtown mansion and more than a million dollars for its restoration. It became the headquarters for Cleveland Restoration Society. The third floor is leased by the Cleveland Neighborhood Development Corporation, umbrella organization for the local CDCs. It is a most propitious arrangement for both organizations.

CRS has been responsible for the restoration of many downtown buildings through its advocacy work. These include a major banking hall, a large theater district, and an important warehouse district that now houses a new downtown population. Its inner-city neighborhood program—which works with city council, county government, and community development corporations—is a model for many other preservation groups.

One of its most popular and well-known programs is the Sacred Landmarks Assistance Program (SLAP). Central city churches, temples, and other religious structures benefit from CRS architectural assessments and technical assistance. The steeple-lighting program of SLAP enhances the city's night skyline.

Crowther is considered one of the outstanding preservation leaders in the United States today.[12] Her organizational skills include the careful selection of competent staff, which numbers around fifteen full-time. Throughout the past decade, CRS expanded its reach to include the Preservation Resource Center of Northeast Ohio. This center offers assistance to many communities within this populous region. Crowther's leadership qualities are recognized by the National Trust for Historic Preservation: she chairs the trust's Partnership Program and has joined the trust's board of trustees.[12]

Pittsburgh History and Landmarks Foundation

One might argue that the Pittsburgh History and Landmarks Foundation has a regional scope. However, its strong central city focus also qualifies it as a local entity. Urban renewal programs of the 1960s brought the preservation movement to life in many cities, including Pittsburgh. As the federal government provided additional funds for demolition and slum clearance, the cities' historic cores looked bombed out. Many fine structures were lost.

In 1964, Pittsburgh citizens reacted by creating the Pittsburgh History and Landmarks Foundation (PHLF).[13] Under the direction of two of its founders, Arthur Ziegler and James Van Trump, the Landmarks Foundation began to purchase and renovate properties with its unique revolving-fund program. With foundation grants and other donations, the fund restored inner-city neighborhoods and provided housing for low-to-moderate income residents.

Over time the PHLF also restored the exceptional railroad station that became its headquarters and the anchor for a shopping complex called Station Square. With its creative adaptive reuse of historic railroad buildings and its distinctive setting on the Monongahela River across from downtown Pittsburgh, Station Square became a major tourist attraction and a valuable piece of real estate.

In 1994 the complex was sold to Forest City Enterprises of Cleveland, Ohio, a large development firm, for a considerable price ($20 million, it was reported). The money generated from the sale became an endowment fund for further neighborhood restoration and educational preservation programs throughout Pittsburgh. Art Ziegler's strong leadership is enhanced by the able assistance of James Van Trump, prolific author Walter Kidney, and neighborhood activist Stanley Lowe.

Under Ziegler's leadership, PHLF inaugurated a number of new concepts for historic preservation.[14] Shortly after its inception, the foundation established the revolving fund to preserve inner-city neighborhoods, such as the community of Manchester and the Mexican War Streets. The fund also encouraged the formation of neighborhood community development corporations; currently there are more than thirty CDCs in Pittsburgh.

PHLF commenced a countywide survey of historic buildings and landmarks, an invaluable aid to promoting the cause of preservation. Several important and popular publications by Walter Kidney and Albert Tanner fully described this survey information. In its advocacy role, PHLF campaigned to save the North Side Post Office, adaptively reused for the Pittsburgh Children's Museum. It also worked to save the Rachel Carson Homestead, birthplace and childhood home of the author of *Silent Spring*, the book often credited with launching the environmental movement in the United States.[15] PHLF also was an early proponent of protection for historic religious structures. For this particular purpose, the group provides funds for bricks-and-mortar projects throughout Allegheny County.

The transformation of Pittsburgh's Manchester neighborhood was the vision of PHLF's noted preservation leader Stanley Lowe. Lowe used the revenues from the Station Square sale for restoring this declining inner-city neighborhood. Lowe's contributions encouraging African American participation in preservation activities across the United States have been recognized by the National Trust.

San Antonio Conservation Society

San Antonio, Texas, was the first local community to produce an organization that recognized the symbiotic relationship between preservation of the natural and the built environment.[16] The impressive San Antonio Conservation Society (SACS) began in 1924 and for most of its impressive history has been led by women. From its initiation by two artists, Rena Maverick Green and Emily Edwards, the SACS has fought many battles to save the unique qualities of the Alamo; San Antonio's Riverwalk; and La Villita, the city's historic original town center. During periods of new real estate development and extensive highway expansion, the society fought for the beautification of the San Antonio River and its constant upgrading.

Throughout the Great Depression of the 1930s, the society continued to purchase land and old buildings, such as the San Jose Mission Granary. Presidents of the society's board were Amanda Cartwright Taylor, Rena Maverick Green, Elizabeth Orynski Graham, and Lee Upson Palfrey. Under the leadership of Mayor Maury Maverick, the city began restoration of La Villita, the original town center, and the Riverwalk.

In the 1940s, the SACS continued its advocacy work under the leadership of Amanda Taylor, Martha Camp, Mary Kenney, Agnes Temple, and Floy Edwards Fontaine. The 1950s began with Ethel Wilson Harris leading a frustrating period in which the society resisted new development pressures. Eleanor Freeborn Bennett, Wanda Graham Ford, Helen Bechtel, and Lois Graves guided SACS with constant vigilance through the decade. In the 1960s many court battles ensued. In spite of the inspired

The Riverwalk, San Antonio, Tx. A wedding party is about to embark on a riverboat ride. With its numerous activities and attractions, San Antonio's Riverwalk is one of that city's most popular tourist stops.

leadership of Vivian Hamlin, Lillian Maverick Padgett, Peggy Tobin, Lorraine Rainey, Lita Price, and Pinkie Martin, the group's tremendous effort failed to halt highway construction. However, it never gave up.

On the lighter side, a Night in Old San Antonio event drew the public's attention to the possibilities of historic preservation as a tourist attraction. Twenty-two buildings were saved in the World's Fair (Hemisfair) site. The San Antonio Conservation Society Foundation was formed to own and manage their many properties.

The 1970s and early 1980s saw a shift in SACS strategy from pure advocacy to negotiating real estate deals. Vivian Hamlin, Beverly Blount, Nancy Healey, Mary Ann Blocker Castleberry, and Joanna Parish oversaw the board during these transactions. At this time Pat Osborne became the first San Antonio historic preservation officer.

Peggy Penshorn, Lynn Bobbit, Bebe Canales Inkley, Janet Wheat Francis, and Liz Davis were all elected presidents of the society during this period. They helped to strengthen the city's preservation ordinance while continuing to make real estate deals. In the 1980s, Ineill Schooler, Marianne Jones, Sally Matthews Buchanan, Paula Piper, and Loyce Ince supervised the completion of a large study of San Antonio's historic schools. They also pressed the city to commit to a survey of historic structures within a thirty-six-mile boundary. In 2001 Jill Harrison Souter, elected president of the SACS, continued to promote community education through a special speakers' bureau and by raising funds for property preservation.

The San Antonio story illustrates the important role of female NPO leadership throughout the earliest years of preservation in the United States. The twenty-first century demonstrates a fresh preservation consciousness among the historically male-dominated professions of architecture, real estate development, and urban planning.[17]

In many Western states, it is difficult to separate the natural from the built environments. The desire to preserve native lands—such as the Arizona cave dwellings and national parks in Wyoming (Yellowstone, 1872) in California (Yosemite, 1890)—coalesced with saving early Catholic missions and old mining towns. In 1924, SACS, recognizing this mutually beneficial relationship, intervened in plans to destroy the San Antonio River by channeling it for flood control. Through many decades, the preservation of this beautiful river with its historic bridges and semi-tropical lushness demonstrates how environmental conservation and historic preservation may work together.

SACS also demonstrates the importance of developing expertise in cutting real estate deals. While the early years of the historic preservation movement often focused on clashes over urban renewal issues and demolition of historic properties, most modern preservation organizations have become deal-makers.

San Antonio leadership came over a long period of time, from the large number of supporters already noted. The commitment and intensity that characterized these prominent entrepreneurs is reflected in the remarkable preservation of this twenty-first century city.

Historic Seattle

The Historic Seattle Preservation and Development Authority is an NPO that was chartered by the City of Seattle in 1974. It purchased and restored at least two dozen historic properties, the best known of which are Pike Place Market and Pioneer Square.[18]

Early Seattle activists first came together in the 1960s, following the destruction of the Occidental Hotel. One of them, Victor Steinbrueck, carried out an inventory of the buildings in Pioneer Square. In the 1970s, Pike Place Market was saved from the wrecking ball. Steinbrueck and Folke Nyberg later surveyed the historic resources of the whole city.

Since 1992, John Chaney took over the helm of Historic Seattle. Chaney came to this post with a wealth of preservation experience in both public and nonprofit sectors; as an urban planner and architectural historian, he includes among his skills the organizational management ability to bring public and private projects to fruition. His work with all three sectors proved invaluable in the preservation of apartment buildings, private homes, sacred spaces, and Seattle's Olmsted Park System.

Chaney's education commenced at the University of Washington in urban planning and architectural history.[19] He launched his preservation career in 1968 when he first surveyed buildings in Seattle's Pioneer Square, with the intention of determining the potential for historic district designation. From there he started his professional career with Oregon City, Oregon, where his government work included a comprehensive plan and preservation program.

In 1982, he returned to Seattle to staff the City of Seattle Landmarks Preservation Board. His responsibilities included administering preservation programs in all of Seattle's historic districts, including Pioneer Square. In 1992 he left the city government to become executive director of the nonprofit Historic Seattle. This nonprofit leader's career path is interesting in that it lets him experience the local government processes that often frame the real estate development aspects of historic preservation. Moving from the public- or private-sector to the nonprofit organization, as in John Chaney's noteworthy example, offers the HPP indispensable dexterity.

The management of a nonprofit preservation organization such as Historic Seattle requires knowledge of real estate finance, budgeting, fundraising, and program development for each project. In addition, public relations and education are vital to persuading citizens of the value of historic and cultural resources. Chaney's career serves as a model for the aspiring HPP.

Sacred Landmark Preservation

Some nonprofit entities are involved in preservation of historic religious buildings referred to as sacred landmarks. Although, of course, congregations are interested in the preservation of their own religious structures, several nonprofit organizations focus on these buildings. Historic sacred landmarks are often important identifying and significant architectural artifacts on the landscape. The desire to preserve these aesthetic treasures generated programs throughout the United States, from New Mexico to Minnesota, from Boston to Chicago.

In 1992, Historic Boston, Incorporated, introduced its Steeples Project. This program is dedicated to building maintenance through a matching grant initiative. Faith Action in Denver, Colorado, developed in 1999 to educate the public on the importance of sacred landmarks and to help congregations evaluate their preservation needs. Chicago had its own Inspired Partnership organization, while the New York Landmarks Conservancy sponsored a Sacred Sites Program. In New Mexico, the Cornerstone Community Partnership trains volunteers to repair the adobe walls of church buildings. Prairie Churches of North Dakota focuses on helping rural communities restore their historic churches, and Minnesota's Preservation Alliance provides a networking service for all religious and sacred sites. The Pittsburgh History and Landmarks Foundation also awards small grants through its Historic Religious Properties Initiative.

Partners for Sacred Places

Acting as an umbrella for the organizations mentioned above and other such projects springing up across the United States, Partners for Sacred Places is based in Philadelphia. Long led by Diane Cohen and A. Robert Jaeger, they published a 1998 study called Sacred Places at Risk.[20] It documented the growth of the sacred landmarks movement and the important role played by these religious structures in their communities. Among other things, this study detailed the monetary contribution of religious structures to their communities through the various services offered within each.

Founded in 1989, Partners preserves and, in some cases, adaptively reuses historic religious structures. Closely associated with the National Trust for Historic Preservation, it offers technical assistance for preserving sacred structures throughout the United States. It conducts studies that emphasize the importance of these buildings on their communities and the value of preserving them for economic, cultural and social purposes. The HPP may find that significant religious structures are the identifying elements that anchor neighborhoods and offer a sense of community to historic areas. They may also serve as magnets, attracting new residents or visitors to historic districts.

Religious building restoration is in a category all its own. In cities large and small sacred landmarks are recognized as a repository of cultural and aesthetic treasures. This makes them unique architectural structures. They may, in the attention paid them by civic officials and preservation advocates, form an identity for a neighborhood or a community that is unlike that of any other building.

Center for Sacred Landmarks

Northeastern Ohio has a regional organization that also recognizes the value of historic religious structures.[21] Although its focus is not primarily preservation, it conducts research and educates the public on the exceptional value of these buildings to city neighborhoods and downtowns. The Center for Sacred Landmarks, located at Cleveland State University, works closely with the Cleveland Restoration Society to preserve these magnificent structures. The center also spawned similar programs at Kent State University, the University of Akron, and Youngstown State University.

The founding director of the Center for Sacred Landmarks is Dr. Michael Tevesz, who, although trained as a paleontologist, directs some of his energy to preparing archives and films on historic religious buildings. He also presents a special course on sacred landmarks at the Maxine Goodman Levin College of Urban Affairs at Cleveland State University.

Lessons Learned: How to Set Up and Operate a Nonprofit for Preservation

A nonprofit preservation organization follows a series of steps in its initiation and operation. Though the HPP may be hired after the organization is inaugurated, the professional must understand each one of these stages and its importance. An organization is a vehicle for moving in a certain direction; the care with which it is constructed will determine how far it will go. A clear destination is a must, periodic maintenance will be necessary, and the driver should be competent and knowledgeable about the road ahead.

Most successful nonprofits will proceed through the following steps:

1. Assess support—initiators must first survey the area for similar or related groups. Don't reinvent the wheel unless the wheel is broken beyond repair. Define the area that the nonprofit will represent (district, city, region). Studying model organizations, both local and larger, checking national and statewide organizations and developing a mailing list of interested parties will help in determining whether the organization fulfills a need or not.
2. Write a mission statement declaring the vision and goals of the organization. Preservation organizations may be of several types:
   a. those that give education only;
   b. those that extend education plus advocacy (weak or strong: weak advocates complain and write letters to public officials while strong

advocates may hold demonstrations, picket, threaten sanctions, even purchase property);

c. those that buy and sell real estate;

d. those that offer technical assistance, such as architectural or financial advice;

e. public programs linking public and private sectors to revitalize neighborhoods;

f. all of the above.

The mission statement should clearly define the organization type, with the understanding that changes may occur. Studying mission statements of other similar organizations is often helpful.

3. Develop an organizational structure. Most NPOs consist of a board of directors, a paid staff, a voting or nonvoting membership, and community advisors. Advisors may be board members who meet regularly or community leaders who may not meet at all but may be called upon for advice. Advisors often legitimize the organization in the eyes of civic officials and potential supporters. The board of directors should be chosen carefully, bringing to the task certain skills, enthusiasm for the cause, and an ability to raise funds.

4. Incorporate the organization under state laws and seek the status of a 501(c)(3) corporation under the IRS code.

5. Apply for grant funding from foundations and local government. (Grant-proposal writing will be discussed in detail in the next section.) It is very important that the board of directors and its members provide some donations that will be indicated in grant proposals to show their own commitment to the organization.

6. With initial funds in hand, hire staff. The executive director is the key to leadership in the community. Director qualifications may vary significantly. Education may include architecture, history, art, law, planning, public administration, business, or any of a number of other degrees. Experience working in the field also may be useful. The skills and abilities required for success, however, are specific: leadership, organization, salesmanship, good written and spoken communication. The director also may hire other people with specific strengths; teams may be assembled for accomplishing specific projects. The most well recognized preservation nonprofits have leaders whose careers can be studied, such as those in the preceding section.

7. Develop a set of programs reflecting the mission, goals, and objectives. The organization should be placed within a framework of

other related NPOs and political entities. For example, if the organization is located in a city or a small town, the director should
become acquainted and develop relationships with the city administration and council members and contact statewide organizations
and the National Trust for Historic Preservation and plan to attend
conferences. This is for the purpose of earning credibility; it also
furthers funding efforts.

8. Once the staff is in place, a headquarters must be set up in an appropriate location, preferably in a historic building or a historic district.

9. With the new address, design official stationery reflecting the organization's theme. It should list board members, staff, and advisory
   committee. All written materials and business cards should follow the
   same theme; a professionally designed logo is critical in establishing
   an identity for the organization. Web page design should also begin.

10. Research local ordinances, building codes, landmarks commissions,
    colleges, and preservation coursework.

11. Develop committees to oversee and implement programs and pro-
    vide staff for these committees.

12. Financial planning—a finance committee should have oversight of
    budgeting, with regular outside audits of the books.

Regular board meetings should be held, in which the staff and committees report progress. If the board is more than ten members, an executive
committee may be appointed to set the agenda for board meetings.

If the organization operates according to this model, it will function
in a manner that is understandable to both the public and private sectors.
Eventually, the rules for the organization may be codified and subject to
periodic review. The longevity and success of the organization will depend
on its adherence to its principles and the drive of its leadership.[22]

Grant-Proposal Writing

One of the most important skills a historic preservation professional should
develop is the ability to raise funds. Although this is particularly true of the
nonprofit, skills achieved in grant-writing courses may be used in both the
public- and private-sectors as well as the nonprofit organization.

Foundations and donor agencies abound throughout the United States.
HPPs should be familiarizing themselves with local foundations, statewide
grant-makers and the many government agencies that offer assistance to

preservation. Some may have access to foundation centers where they can narrow their search to those funders who have a particular interest in historic preservation. Although local centers are found in only a few cities, such as Washington, D.C. and Cleveland, Ohio, online access makes the materials available to any location.

Grant proposals are often an important source to raise funds for support.[23] Here, again, grant writers generally follow a series of steps:

1. Assess foundations in the area and examine their interests in and willingness to fund particular types of organizations. Once a foundation is located, the steps to preparing a grant proposal are straightforward. Good descriptions are available in many publications; however, the authors recommend the book by Mary Hall and Susan Howlett: *Getting Funded: The Complete Guide to Proposal Writing*. Determining the project focus is crucial to success. A nonprofit organization's focus should reflect the mission statement of the organization and the specific project for which the funds will be used. In most requests, the foundation expects that a portion, perhaps 20 percent, of the funding will go to defray the expenses of the organization itself. A careful description of the project, including its importance to the community, is critical to a well-conceived proposal.

2. Choose one or two foundations to target. Make initial contact with the program officer and discuss your proposal. Get complete instructions from that foundation and follow them carefully.

3. Assemble a package of boilerplate materials, applicable to all grant proposals, including:
   a. a mission statement;
   b. board list with short bios;
   c. executive director résumé;
   d. background (history) of the preservation organization;
   e. evidence of the IRS 501 (c)(3) designation.
   The grant proposal writer should then describe the organization: its history, leadership, board, staff, support from others—such as previous funding and individual donations. Letters of support for the project and résumés of key participants should be included in its appendix.

4. Write the request itself. Frame it in terms of a program that the funds will carry out. Include the exact funding needed. Also, make the case for who will benefit from this program. Identify who will have the responsibility for carrying out the program, their related qualifications

and experience, the time it will take to accomplish the task, how the program's goals will be evaluated when the project is completed.

5. Develop a detailed proposal budget. A carefully drawn project budget should be included, together with a budget analysis and discussion that explains each of the budget figures. A project timeline should accompany the budget analysis. Periodic reports of the project's progress may be offered to the funding agency.

6. Seek relevant support letters from outside (not the board or staff) leaders: these may include the advisory committee, city officials, those affected by the program, and other relevant groups.

For submission, package the proposal carefully, following all instructions outlined by the foundation. Also, observe the dates on which the foundation board meets and include a cover letter explaining the proposal. A table of contents is often useful, with pagination, and an executive summary of one page may also be included.

The cover letter should introduce the proposal and explain briefly its request in terms of both its purpose and exact funding requested. The cover letter is written on the organization's stationery, listing board members and community advisors, which communicates the stability of the organization. These suggestions may seem self-evident; however, they form a useful checklist for raising grant funds. Hall and Howlett list the specific components of a grant proposal: a title page, an executive summary, a purpose or needs statement, an approach to the project, an evaluation of the results and the qualifications of the personnel who will carry out the work.

Please note that each foundation or agency will have specific grant formats; these must be followed precisely. Some smaller foundations will request only a proposal letter. Others have more elaborate requirements. The format described here is a general description and should give the HPP a broad outline of what is expected.

Other methods for fund-raising include soliciting individual donations by writing letters to a comprehensive mailing list of interested parties. Some preservation organizations hold various fund-raising events, particularly in important historic buildings.

The nonprofit organization opportunities can be divided into two categories:

1. preservation organizations
2. community-development corporations

Community-Development Corporations

Community-development corporations (CDCs) are a product of the 1974 federal government effort to assist central city neighborhoods in their revitalization.[24]

In many U.S. cities and towns, government officials are not equipped to provide a long-term, intense focus on revitalization of individual districts. It was this understanding that brought about the federal government's Community Development Block Grant program to create nonprofit CDCs for city and town neighborhoods.[25] The program resulted in a thirty-year diffusion of CDCs across the country. Although local government policies may have influenced property values by providing public improvements, tax increment financing, planning, and data collection, the CDC is the grassroots organization that has transformed many inner-city real estate markets.[26]

Since older neighborhoods have the potential to become historic districts, HPPs will find employment opportunities in CDCs, organizations in residential neighborhoods with specific boundaries. They usually have local offices, directors and paid staff or volunteers who gather information about their area. They may conduct surveys of their residents to assess problems, assist in planning for new developments, arrange neighborhood events, publish local newsletters, represent their areas in community discussions, and generally keep track of activities that affect their residents. They also participate in major transportation planning, local school issues, policing, environmental issues and other factors that ultimately affect residential property values.

Similar to nonprofits that focus exclusively on preservation, each CDC is specific to one area and offers a broader array of services to local residents and businesses. Conflicts may arise over the issue of preservation of existing landscapes and buildings and developing new structures, especially in commercial centers. The HPP must have particular skills in conflict management, in employing sensitive design ideas that fit the historic context, and in convincing residents to set high standards for their area. HPPs should understand community needs as well as the cultural characteristics affecting their neighborhood. They must also represent the CDC in major community concerns—such as taxation, schools, safety and security services, and other political matters.

If HPPs are to be successful in CDC employment, a strong knowledge of the physical attributes of their area is critical. The buildings, streetscape, open spaces, and traffic patterns are all important to successful performance.

Therefore, preparation in urban planning, urban design, or urban studies will be invaluable.

From the 1960s to the 1980s, CDCs emerged in many different city and town neighborhoods. Some were favorably regarded and received additional support from local foundations and donors; others were unable to operate efficiently. The CDC program has been credited with reversing decline and beginning a transformation that has attracted investment capital and historic preservation. CDCs are active in Pittsburgh, Philadelphia, Detroit, Chicago, Milwaukee, among other cities and towns across the United States.

Publicizing Preservation in the Nonprofit Sector

Nonprofits may not have the funds to advertise the merits of historic preservation, but they have certain avenues that others often do not possess. Nonprofits may offer local information by sending newsletters and mailings, programming events, educating advocates through local schools and colleges, and expanding their outreach through their Web sites.

Newsletters and mailings are labor intensive but many nonprofits have access to large volunteer teams that often perform these tasks at little or no cost. Regular mailings keep members informed regarding endangered buildings, warn of impending demolition requests, and make announcements of upcoming meetings and rallies. Some newsletters include job announcements and other features useful to the professional. Information about board members and civic leaders sheds light on political situations not always found in the local press. Many nonprofits communicate also through the Internet.

Program events may offer important opportunities to make the case for historic preservation. They might promote individuals by giving awards for accomplishments or preservation financial support. Civic leaders may be featured in a way that promotes new support for the preservation organization as well as educates the public. Some events are held in important historic structures that have been restored or those in need. Groups of historic interest (such as preservation leaders of Underground Railroad depots, Native American sites, or Hispanic landmarks) may hold frequent public programs. Although preservation nonprofits often compete for funds with conservation groups, they should regard cooperation as an opportunity to share the expense of events while informing the public about mutual concerns.

Schools and colleges offer many occasions for educating students about the value of historic preservation. They also may recruit interested parties into membership and volunteerism. Students respond positively to messages of environmental protection, planning the landscape, protecting important landmarks, and other ways of saving cultural symbols. Presentations in educational settings are often open to the nonprofit HPP.

One of the most effective communicators of the value of historic preservation is the National Trust for Historic Preservation.[27] This organization gives members its nationally recognized magazine *Preservation*, for a low annual fee, as well as other publications (*Changing Places* by Richard Moe and Carter Wilkie, for example). The National Trust offers a well-attended national conference, support for statewide preservation organizations, partnerships with local groups and its important Main Street program, which gives small towns and neighborhoods technical help and advice. The Trust has published *Preservation* for several decades; over time this monthly periodical expanded its coverage to include articles of interest and assistance to professionals and advertisements for important historic properties for sale, technical services available to preservationists, and tours and cruises featuring historic places worldwide. It also warns of threats to landmarks, buildings, and historic sites.

The National Trust's international convention attracts thousands of visitors to different cities every year. The host city puts its valued landmarks and districts on display through well-prepared tours. These conferences present short courses and lectures that aid participants in preservation. The latest building techniques and financial strategies are presented in informative and interactive sessions.

The National Trust, in addition to promoting its own properties, encourages states to expand their preservation work through the creation of a system of statewide partners. These partners assist the state historic preservation offices in identifying historic properties and promoting preservation across the United States. Although large towns and cities have local nonprofits to publicize their efforts, preservation of farmsteads and villages may be assisted in their publications through statewide nonprofits.

The National Trust's highly innovative Main Street initiative offers technical assistance to small towns and city neighborhoods throughout the United States.[28] When this team of preservation professionals arrives in a community, free publicity often follows. Local newspapers and other publications report on their progress as they offer advice and planning to communities often leading to brick-and-mortar projects. The Main Street program allows property owners and public officials to observe a vision of their community and to discern its economic potential in an era of highway bypasses and big box retailing.

Given the U.S. tradition of private property rights, most preservation involves purchase of historic structures or some form of influence over the adaptive reuse of private property. One such form is the passing of ordinances that restrict demolition or offer design guidelines within historic districts. Historic districts attract private investors who regard usage restrictions as a reassurance of retaining values.

Small historic towns or villages that have experienced this type of investment surround many U.S. cities. Historic preservation professionals will find that nonprofit organizations often serve as the catalyst for influencing, educating and developing innovative ways to encourage these preservation investments. This kind of development will sustain the economic health of both historic city neighborhoods and small towns.

Careers in the Nonprofit Sector

The nonprofit sector is distinguished by the expanding role it plays in U.S. society. Its growth, estimated by some to have doubled in the past ten years, offers a significant opportunity for employment for HPPs. Of course, not all nonprofits are dealing with historic real estate, but a great number are doing just that.

In many institutions of higher learning, organizational or nonprofit management is a popular innovation. It usually introduces the student to budgeting, proposal and grant writing, board development, program planning, and other, business related, courses. The HPP may take such a program or combine it with a number of related fields, such as art history or urban planning, to prepare for work in the nonprofit sector. A background in architecture is useful for historic preservation, but an architecture degree is not essential. All of the skills mentioned for private real estate development would be helpful, depending on the mission of the nonprofit organization. A broad understanding of the political climate and an ability to connect with local networks are equally important in nonprofit employment.

Nonprofits generally prosper based on their expertise in fund-raising. Research and writing of excellent proposals to convince donors and foundations to support the organization is a key skill for the HPP in nonprofit employment.

Notes

1. Virginia Benson, "The Rise of the Independent Sector in Urban Land Development," *Growth and Change* 16, no. 3 (July 1985): 26.

2. "U.S. Internal Revenue Code, Sec. 501 (c)(3)," www.Fourmilab.ch/ustax/www/+26-A-1-F-I-SO1.html.

3. Norman Tyler, *Historic Preservation: An Introduction to Its History, Principles and Practice* (New York: Norton, 2000): 42.

4. "The Four-Point Main Street Approach to Commercial District Revitalization," www.mainstreet.org/content.aspx?page=38section=2.

5. Richard Moe and Carter Wilkie, *Changing Places: Rebuilding Community in the Age of Sprawl* (New York: Henry Holt, 1997).

6. Virginia Benson, review of *Changing Places. Journal of the American Planning Association* 65, no. 1 (Winter 1999): 124–25.

7. Angela M. Greenfield, "What Is Preservation North Carolina?" press kit (June 2006), www.presnc.org/learnmore/presskit_what_is_pnc.html.

8. Historic Landmarks Foundation of Indiana, "About Us," www.historicland marks.org/aboutus/aboutus.html.

9. Editorial, "J. Reid Williamson," *Preservation* 57, no. 6 (Nov.–Dec. 2005): 8.

10. Georgia Trust, "Missions and Goals," www.georgiatrust.org/aboutus/mission_goals.htm.

11. Cleveland Restoration Society, "A Brief History of the Cleveland Restoration Society," www.clevelandrestoration.org/AboutUs/history.htm.

12. Moe and Wilkie, *Changing Places*, 241.

13. Arthur Ziegler, "Implications of Urban Social Policy: The Quest for Community Self-Determination," in *Readings in Historic Preservation*, ed. Norman Williams Jr., Edmund H. Kellogg, and Frank Gilbert (New Brunswick, N.J.: Rutgers Univ. Press, 1983), 305–8.

14. Arthur Ziegler, Leopold Adler II, and Walter Kidney, *Revolving Funds for Historic Preservation* (Pittsburgh, Pa.: Ober Park Association, 1975).

15. Rachel Carson, *Silent Spring* (New York: Houghton-Mifflin, 1962).

16. Lewis F. Fisher, "Saving San Antonio: The Precarious Preservation of a Heritage," www.saconservation.org/about/milestone_6.htm.

17. Eugenie Birch and Douglas Roby, "The Planner and the Preservationist: An Uneasy Alliance," *Journal of the American Planning Association* 50, no. 2 (Spring 1984): 194–207.

18. Historic Seattle: "Dedicated to Architectural Preservation," www.historic seattle.org/about/ourhistory.aspx.

19. Heather MacIntosh, "History of Historic Preservation in Seattle," www.historicseattle.org/projects/historyofpreservation.aspx.

20. Diane Cohen, and A. Robert Jaeger. *Sacred Places at Risk*, (Philadelphia, Pa.: Partners for Sacred Places, 1997), 50.

21. Michael Tevesz and Harvey Newman, "The City Worships," in *Introduction to Urban Studies*, ed. Roberta Steinbacher and Virginia Benson, 3d. ed. (Dubuque, Iowa: Kendall-Hunt Publishing, 2006), 105–21.

22. Richard T. Ingram, *Ten Basic Responsibilities of Nonprofit Boards* (Washington, D.C.: National Center of Nonprofit Boards, 1996).

23. Mary Hall and Susan Howlett, *Getting Funded: A Complete Guide to Proposal Writing* (Portland, Ore.: Continuing Education Publications, Portland State Univ. Press, 2003).

24. W. Dennis Keating, Norman Krumholz, and Philip Starr, eds. *Revitalizing Urban Neighborhoods: Studies in Government and Public Policy* (Lawrence: Univ. Press of Kansas, 1996), 2–5.

25. David Rusk, *Inside Game, Outside Game: Winning Strategies for Saving Urban America* (Washington, D.C.: Brookings Institution Press, 1999), 13.

26. Peter Levavi, "Citywide CDCs: Chicago CDCs Increase Efficiency," paper presented at Sacred Landmarks Conference, Maxine Goodman Levin College of Urban Affairs, Cleveland State University (May–June 1996); Enterprise Foundation, "Unique Public-Private Parnership Commits Half-Billion Dollars Over Next Decade to Spark Inner-City Revitalization," press release, Aug. 2002; OMG Center for Collaborative Learning, "A Decade of Development: An Assessment of Neighborhood Progress, Inc.," research report (Jan. 2001): 1–24.

27. National Trust for Historic Preservation, www.nationaltrust.org.

28. National Trust Main Street Center, www.mainstreet.org/content.aspx?page=28section-1.

Chapter Six

The Public-Sector Role in Historic Preservation

Introduction

The role of government at all levels is essential to both historic preservation and environmental conservation: government policies stimulate the private and nonprofit sectors; and public-private partnerships enable the HPP's work by providing initial investments, management assistance with projects, citizen support, and many other benefits.

Chapter 3 outlined the federal legislation that governs preservation activity that takes place on the state and local level. An important federal preservation task is designation of properties to the National Register of Historic Places. The National Park Service in the Department of the Interior determines whether properties meet the criteria for this designation. This decision may qualify owners for an investment tax credit (ITC) on their income-producing properties. Each state has a federally designated state historic preservation office and a governor-appointed citizen/professional advisory board that reviews all nominations to the register.

Steps in the National Register Process

The local public sector plays an important, although often indirect, role in this process. The tax incentives' stimulation of real estate development and especially urban revitalization impels the public sector to encourage several related activities:

1. structuring community-development corporations in neighborhoods,
2. designating urban historic districts,

3. promoting historic preservation tourism,
4. endorsing National Register nominations.

Thus, the HPP employed in the public sector should study the criteria carefully.

The process for designation of properties to the register begins at the local level with the preparation of a nomination. The nomination format includes a very detailed description of the property, its location on a USGS map, architectural drawings of buildings and landscapes. The property is nominated for its appropriateness in one or more of four categories that are detailed in chapter 7. To review briefly, the criteria are the following:

- Criterion A—Properties can be eligible for the National Register if they are associated with events that have made a significant contribution to the broad patterns of our history.[1]
- Criterion B—Properties may be eligible for the National Register if they are associated with the lives of persons significant in our past.[2]
- Criterion C—Properties may be eligible for the National Register if they embody the distinctive characteristics of a type, period, or method of construction, or that represent the work of a master, or that possess high artistic value, represent a significant and distinguishable entity whose components may lack individual distinction.[3]
- Criterion D—Properties may be eligible for the National Register if they have yielded, or may be likely to yield, information important in prehistory or history.[4]

The nomination form requires an explicit historical account of the property's owners, architects, and any important features and events relevant to the rationale for Register consideration. The nominator should obtain the approval of the property owner, who may wish to get the listing in order to access the IRS tax benefits for historic preservation. Support letters from public officials often accompany the nomination.

The nominator contacts the state historic preservation office and usually receives help and guidance from the staff in preparing the nomination. Normally, the local government is notified and expresses approval or disapproval. If the governmental entity disapproves, the SHPO is inclined to accept their opinion. However, that is not often the case, and the nomination usually proceeds through a process of approvals, first by an advisory board at the state level, then to the district office of the National Park Service, then and ultimately to the Office of the Secretary of the Interior. Occasionally, the nomination will be rejected and returned to the state officer, but that is rare once the other approvals are given.

Once the property has received the National Register listing, it is the responsibility of the public sector to monitor it and to see that the Secretary of the Interior's Standards for Rehabilitation are followed. The National Register designation exemplifies the importance of the public sector in encouraging and regulating historic preservation projects.

Local Government Preservation

The balance of this chapter focuses on local government input into the preservation process. Local governments may be found in cities, counties, regional agencies, small towns and even rural areas. Most opportunities for HPP careers will be located in urban areas; however, other local jurisdictions should not be overlooked.

Most U.S. cities developed around a historic core frequently located on a body of water.[5] Urban settlements emerged along rivers, lakes, or oceanfronts

Memorial Park, River Front, Cleveland, Ohio. Gracing the historic Cuyahoga River, this green space, a tribute to Cleveland poet Hart Crane, provides solace for its visitors. Photo by Philip Leiter.

for cargo dockage, waterpower, milling, fishing, and water supply for industry or household use. Recreational use of the water began much later. In many cities, waterfront land is owned or controlled by local public port authorities; the fate of historic port structures is in their hands.

As cities evolved, grew, and spread, the intensive building development at the center was considered obsolete. Early in the twentieth century, small buildings were replaced with taller structures, roadways expanded, and zoning laws divided the land by use. Although some cities were able to retain historic neighborhoods, the emerging city-planning field was imbued with slum clearance, new construction, and traffic-related projects.[6] Many important large edifices—such as landmark government halls, religious buildings and mansions—survived the wrecking ball, and the initial impetus to preserve began in places other than city halls.

Chapters 2 (history) and 4 (architecture) discussed the public sector's role at the federal and state levels. However, most preservationists agree that historic preservation generally takes place in a local jurisdiction and therefore must meet local ordinance requirements, as suggested in chapter 3 (legal issues). City governments play a very important role in deciding which buildings and landscapes are worthy of preservation.[7] To achieve public support, the following arguments favoring preservation are often expressed:

1. Aesthetic value—this decision depends upon general acceptance of ideas of beauty.[8]
2. Scarcity—uniqueness has great appeal, especially when it identifies a particular place.[9]
3. Architectural diversity or mixing of various ages and styles adds to the city's ambience.[10]
4. Diversity of scales creates interest by inserting monumental structures into smaller-scale ensembles.
5. Adaptive reuse of older buildings saves resources.[11]
6. Important cultural icons achieve a high level of public support.[12]
7. Heritage tourism is growing in importance in many U.S. city economies.
8. Education, recreation, and inspiration are outcomes of preservation.[13]

Local governments may offer incentives that encourage historic preservation. For example, several states allow tax incentives for local-level preservation projects. The following states allow local municipal or county

The Fountain of Eternal Life, Cleveland, Ohio, 1964. Marshall Fredericks, designer and sculptor. Surrounded by historic buildings and the BP America Tower, this inspiring monument is part of a larger 20th century war memorial honoring those men and women who sacrificed their lives for freedom. Photo by Philip Leiter.

governments to decide whether to allow property tax abatements: California, Delaware, Florida, Iowa, Louisiana, Maine, Maryland, Massachusetts, Mississippi, Montana, New Hampshire, New York, North Carolina, South Carolina, Texas, Virginia, and Washington.

In some places, local governments have the option of providing a property-tax freeze on income-producing landmarks (Georgia) or restrictions on historic property assessments due to preservation easements (Idaho, Iowa, Nebraska, Ohio, Tennessee, Virginia, and the District of Columbia). All of these options enable preservation professionals employed by local government to assist preservation projects.

City or town planning functions are often coordinated with landmarks commissions and their local ordinances. For historic preservation to occur, legal procedures must be followed. The public sector plays a significant role in this process through its planning, zoning, and urban design activities.

Preservation Planning

Preservation planning is an interactive aspect of each discipline. According to Eugenie Birch and Douglas Roby, planners and preservationists were at odds for much of the twentieth century.[14] Planners were interested in cleaning up crowded cities; planning transportation routes; and promoting green spaces, sewer systems, safe roadways, and new construction. Preservationists were widely regarded as sentimental amateurs who generally obstructed progress.

In recent years, urban designers and conservationists brought these disparate fields together. Urban conservation is a popular term described as "a long-term commitment to maintain a city's cultural and historic identity while also accommodating inevitable transition, growth and new uses."[15] In most cities, planners acknowledge the importance of historic landmark buildings. They also assist neighborhoods in developing design guidelines for historic districts. Planning and landmarks commissioners work together to preserve a community's unique and irreplaceable historic resources. This is also the case in small towns and rural areas in which the community has recognized the importance of its wealth of historic fabric. The first step in such protection is a local ordinance.

Ordinances

States vest communities throughout the United States with the power to establish historic preservation ordinances and to regulate real estate development that affects historic sites. As the National Trust for Historic Preservation has pointed out, "among the first lessons the preservationist learns is that the legal power to protect historic places lies chiefly with local government. The strongest protection is typically found in preservation ordinances enacted by local government."[16]

These ordinances restrict demolition or at least delay the demolition permit until a new preservation-sensitive buyer may be found to purchase the property. The ordinance may regulate design of new construction or changes to existing buildings.

Local ordinances vary widely, but they generally reflect the following principles:

1. They should be in the public's interest.
2. They should respect private property ownership.
3. They should respect the "due process" clause of the U.S. Constitution.
4. They should comply with state laws.
5. They should offer "equal protection" to all.

The second principle has raised the controversial question of the right of eminent domain that is discussed in other chapters of this book. The National Trust enumerated basic elements of the typical preservation ordinance as the following:

1. Statement of Purpose
2. Definition of Terms
3. Preservation Commission membership
4. Commission Powers and Duties
5. Criteria for Designating Properties
6. Procedures for Designating Historic Landmarks and Districts
7. Review Procedures
8. Economic Hardship
9. Interim Protection
10. Demolition by Neglect
11. Penalties
12. Appeals

Each of these elements is explained in some depth on the National Trust's *Citizen's Guide*.[17] The HPP should review these elements carefully and be prepared to assess and comment upon the effectiveness of their local government's particular ordinance since they carry such great weight over the preservation decision.

Since preservation ordinances reflect local situations, they may add other diverse elements, such as limiting automobiles in districts, drawing district boundaries, designing guidelines, limiting parking lots, and controlling business uses of historic buildings.

Landmarks Commissions

The landmarks, or historic preservation, commission is generally given the charge of implementing the ordinance. Members often are political appointees with training in architecture, planning, or real estate; their duties are spelled out in the ordinance. The preservation commission may conduct surveys and maintain inventories of historic properties. Depending on the strength of the ordinance, the commissioners may assert authority over how historic properties are altered or they may have merely advisory powers. Landmarks commissions in U.S. cities developed for the purpose of identifying important buildings. Regulating demolition and protecting historic structures followed the passage by city councils of the local landmark ordinance.

Landmarks commissions recommend designation of individual structures, areas, or historic districts to appropriate government bodies. Such commissions are established in communities where citizens have an interest in planning and preservation. As has been pointed out already, depending on the issues involved, these two functions of city government may or may not cooperate: preservationists can be viewed as obstructionists when planners are pressured to respond to traffic engineering or new construction opportunities.

Designation of local landmarks may apply to sites, structures, or objects that have historical, cultural, or aesthetic value. Local landmark designation may protect the property from demolition for a period of time and thus carries weight that National Register designation does not. National Register properties, however, carry the IRS tax incentives that the local landmark ones do not. It is important for the HPP to distinguish between these two designations.

Within cities across the nation, the landmarks commissions have varying relationships with city planners. Sometimes they are closely linked; in other instances they are independent and in constant conflict.[18] Some cities, such as St. Augustine, Florida, also have official historic architectural review boards. These boards review all proposed changes and, if approved, Certificates of Appropriateness stating that the specified work has been approved.

They advise both property owners and government officials concerning maintenance, protection, enhancement, and preservation of historic resources and may designate historic landmarks, thus replacing the landmarks commission. These bodies generally hold regular public meetings that allow for decisions in a timely manner.

Historic Districts

Historic districting is an outgrowth of the local landmark ordinance and usually develops around an urban design concept. The neighborhood residents follow a common process in this often grassroots effort: first, they agree on boundaries for a proposed district; second, they adopt a set of principles for the exterior alterations of the buildings in the district; third, they appoint a design review committee to monitor the potential changes proposed by building owners; and fourth, the enforcement of the guidelines for neighborhood design then passes from the committee to the elected city officials for their approval.

In the 1980s, Benson and Klein carried out a study, published in the *Appraisal Journal*, that examined the effect on property values of historic designation.[19] They focused on two Cleveland districts, Ohio City and Shaker Square, and concluded that district designation positively affected the property values surrounding the district more than those within the district. Property values, of course, are dynamic measures, and the two districts mentioned have been the subjects of a great deal of investment and change since the study was published. It appears that in the long run the designation was a significant boon to these neighborhoods, which became the focal points of a back-to-the-city migration in recent years.

As a type of land-use zoning, historic districting provides controls on a variety of changes that are proposed in the district. These range from altering appearances of buildings to regulating their demolition. A number of studies show that such districting influences property values. Donovan Rypkema performed a study of how Indiana property values are affected by historic districting. In 1997, under the presidency of J. Reid Williamson Jr., a longtime and well-known preservation leader in the state, the Historic Landmarks Foundation funded the study of five communities. Rypkema concluded that property values within districts generally increased faster than those in the city as a whole.[20] He also observed that districting promotes stability through homeownership.

Traditional Development

New Urbanism is an important concept that has gained popularity across the United States. Its precepts combine conservation of natural resources and traditional neighborhood development, both of which employ familiar historic patterns.[21]

Postmodern architecture styles swept through new housing and commercial complexes in every city in the United States in the late twentieth century, when urban designers attempted a renaissance of traditional neighborhood styles by adding landscaping, sidewalks, detached garages, and alleys. Two new Florida communities, Seaside and Celebration, show New Urbanist planning ideas, as does Kentlands in Maryland.

In larger cities, historic districts that already possess traditional characteristics, in addition to large, mature trees and shady streets, are being rediscovered. CDCs often promote these traditional neighborhood developments as an economic tool generating growth. Historic districts, whether officially designated or not, frequently contain the characteristics New Urbanists seek, such as social interaction, sense of community, neighborhood identity, and social balance.[22] Front porches, so popular in new subdivisions, are actually used in historic areas, where sidewalks afford pedestrians the chance for a friendly greeting.

The sense of character and identity grows more meaningful through "time-thickened" experience, according to Matthew Carmona and his colleagues.[23] The idea of social balance evolves as historic areas become mixed over time; large and small houses, corner stores, churches, local schools, and other institutions flavor the neighborhood with interactions that simply fail to occur in the homogeneous subdivision. Residents choose between inner-city districts and suburban subdivisions based on a number of criteria that have tipped the balance in favor of suburbs. The most often mentioned of these are schools, security, and green space.

The HPP should promote preservation as, among other things, a way to clean up and improve the appearance and appeal of city neighborhoods. Neglect and poor maintenance (i.e., the broken windows theory) lead to further decline and antisocial behaviors that make residents wish to abandon the area.[24] Civic officials, of course, generally do not wish to lose the populations that have put them into office.

Social Effects

One of the social issues raised by those supporting historic preservation is that of segregation versus integration. As suburban development continues to sprawl across the metropolitan landscape, the trend is toward increasingly segregated patterns; large-scale subdivisions separate housing types and thus income levels. The problems connected with social segregation will not be reiterated here, but suffice it to say historic neighborhoods tend to accommodate a wide range of incomes, age categories, and other measures of diversity. Rather than alienate and divide, the historic district embraces heterogeneous populations and mixed-use development.

Historic preservation offsets the deterioration of city neighborhoods and has a positive effect on its surroundings. Social research indicates that repairs of property, fixing broken windows, removing graffiti, and other maintenance tasks positively change the social behavior of the public.[25]

Historic preservation overlaps with some concepts of urban design that are experiencing renewed interest. Those in the making-places tradition have produced numerous guidelines for desirable urban designs. Carmona and his colleagues review several of these, among them the British Commission for Architecture and the Built Environment (CABE), which enumerated seven objectives in defining places.[26] A few of these include character, unique identity and diversity, and variety and choice.[27]

Allan Jacobs and Donald Appleyard produced an urban design manifesto in which they listed the following goals:

1. livability—emphasizing relative comfort;
2. identity and control—sense of ownership;
3. access to opportunities, imagination and joy;
4. authenticity and meaning;
5. community and public life;
6. urban self-reliance; and
7. an environment for all.[28]

Although none of these guidelines appear directly related to historic preservation, they indicate dissatisfaction with new suburban subdivision planning. As Jacobs and Appleyard extended the meaning of the guidelines to specific physical characteristics, they identified five prerequisites for a sound urban environment:

1. livable streets and neighborhoods;
2. a minimum density of residential development and intensity of land use;
3. integrated activities—living, working, shopping in reasonable proximity;
4. a man-made environment that defines public space, particularly by its buildings; and
5. many separate, distinct buildings with complex arrangements rather than megastructures.[29]

This list sounds very much like the description of a historic district.

Bentley and colleagues at Oxford Polytechnic formulated a list of seven key issues for desirable environments: permeability, variety, legibility, robustness, visual appropriateness, richness, and personalization. To these they added resource efficiency, cleanliness, and biotic support. Here again, the HPP can see the connections between historic preservation, environmental conservation, and urban design.[30]

In an era in which Americans have learned the price of everything but have forgotten the values of a humane environment, historic preservation offers a countervailing force. Many communities are resisting big-box retailing in favor of smaller shops and appealing pedestrian environments. Neighborhoods that preserve a historic commercial core become magnets for investment. Examples of this are found in cities and towns across the United States: old mill villages in New England; city neighborhoods in Chicago, Pittsburgh, and Cleveland; mining towns in the Rocky Mountains; and Spanish mission centers in the Southwest.

Adaptive Reuse

Certain central city structures are often converted to functions different from their original purposes. For the HPP who works in the public sector, creative recycling of historic buildings requires an understanding of building-type markets, zoning requirements, building codes, and some of the problems and issues that may follow from such conversions. Some examples of commonly converted historic properties are train stations, warehouses, bus stations, port buildings, utility buildings, religious structures, department stores, and civic buildings.

Train Stations

Because of a mandate from the Federal Railway Administration in 1917, cities across the United States built large, central-city railroad stations to draw all the conflicting rail lines into one location.[31] Though many of these large structures have fallen to the wrecking ball, such as Penn Central Station in New York City (see chapter 2), others were rehabilitated in ways that are considered adaptive reuse.

Washington, D.C., restored its Union Station as a downtown shopping center and public attraction. Cleveland's Terminal Tower experienced a similar adaptation, as did St. Louis's Union Station. These grand structures accommodate shops, restaurants, and large open areas that offer a variety of public functions. The expense for converting such immense buildings was a difficulty; such large costs are often problematic, at least in the short run. For central cities in the United States, however, such structures may reinforce other decisions to invest in traditional downtowns.

Warehouses

Central cities often retain groups of buildings that once serviced downtown businesses and industries but no longer do. Among these clusters of buildings are warehouse districts, which, given their convenient proximity to city centers, may be converted to mixed-use neighborhoods. Warehousing is becoming a popular adaptive reuse target for loft apartments, offices, restaurants and bars.

LaClede's Landing in St. Louis, though separated from downtown by the interstate highway system, performs these new purposes. The warehouses often have the advantage of being located near a waterfront, which adds to their appeal. LaClede's Landing is only a few blocks from the Mississippi River and the landmark Gateway Arch. Other important warehouse conversions are found in Minneapolis, Seattle, Chicago, and numerous other cities. Pioneer Square in Seattle and Lowertown in St. Paul are some of the best-known examples.

Bus Stations

Though not as prevalent as the train stations, the Greyhound Bus Company built a number of Art Moderne–style stations in the 1930s, which have been converted to other uses, although some still function in their original roles. The Washington, D.C., station became the lobby of a large housing complex located directly behind it. Although many such buildings are suitable for adaptive reuse, it is important to note that certain structures are afflicted with soil pollution from oil and other pollutants having been emptied into the area surrounding them. Bus stations and automobile service stations are among these; cleaning up such polluted lands called brownfields, adds to the costs of adaptively reusing the buildings that sit on them.[32]

Port Buildings

Most U.S. cities were built along waterfronts. Whether on rivers, lakes, or oceans, shipping activities have left discarded structures in their wake. Many of the pier buildings are gone; remaining ones are occasionally modified to new uses: Boston's wharves, Toronto's quays, and Seattle's Pike Place Market are illustrations of this trend. Recent interest in waterfront development has often focused on redundant buildings left in the back-wash of new port technologies, containerization, and the introduction of immense ships.

The Fall Line on the East Coast became the location of early colonial ports that located somewhat inland to take advantage of rivers' waterpower and protected harbors. Examples are Baltimore, Maryland; Wilmington, North Carolina; Charleston, South Carolina; and Savannah, Georgia. Many cities and small towns have significant architectural structures on their waterfronts; these buildings are available for various adaptations and enjoy the waterfront views and the attractions of boating and other water-related activities.

Utility Buildings

Following the introduction of the steam engine, powerhouses were often built in classical styles that now attract new uses. Cleveland's Flats area is graced with a powerhouse whose exterior is preserved while developer Jeff Jacobs constructed a new building inside its traditionally styled brick outer walls. It houses restaurants and shops that open onto a riverfront board-walk. Baltimore recycled Power Plant Live, an even larger powerhouse, for an indoor entertainment complex along its harbor front.

Religious Buildings

Many historic churches and other sacred landmarks have new uses.[33] Jewish temples have become historical museums; churches are serving as libraries, architectural offices, and even condominiums. Large churches are sometimes preserved for public performance productions, both secular and sacred.

Restoration of religious buildings has important effects beyond simply adaptive reuse. In large cities, these sacred landmarks are recognized as unique repositories of cultural and aesthetic treasures. Such a building may, in the attention given it by civic officials and preservation advocates, provide an identity for a neighborhood in a way other buildings cannot (see chapter 5).

Other Adaptive Reuses

Many other buildings are commonly preserved through adaptive reuse. Department stores are often converted to office space. Toledo, Ohio's large Macy's Department Store building now serves as residential units. Historic hotels and office buildings become downtown housing. The YMCA Building in Akron, Ohio, for example, now serves as downtown condominium housing; the former YMCA in Cleveland houses university students and provides recreational facilities.

As new technologies entered cities, they brought with them buildings designed for specific functions; over time, for example, sailing ships, steam engines, trains, trucks, and cars filled the landscape with redundant building types. Since World War II, highway development has caused a large number of buildings to become vacant. Creative adaptations are ways of preserving these landmarks.

Leadership

The National Trust for Historic Preservation has developed a program of leadership training precisely because its members understand this essential component of preservation achievement. In their program, they broadly describe certain attributes of preservation leaders:

1. competence to manage a nonprofit organization;
2. courage to carry out tasks that lead to conflict;

3. ability to work with local elected and appointed officials;
4. skill in making the case for preservation;
5. understanding of how to build support from the community;
6. proficiency at recruiting, screening, placing, evaluating, and recognizing staff and volunteers; and
7. aptitude for managing board and staff relationships.

Preservation leadership combines knowledge of:

1. the community and how it operates,
2. who the preservation advocates are,
3. how to manage personnel,
4. programming preservation,
5. financial and economic aspects of preservation,
6. legal facets of preservation,
7. design of buildings and districts, and
8. how to communicate the message.

Leadership is about interacting with people. If the preservation advocate does not work well with others, he or she will not accomplish the task. This position requires intensive interaction and understanding of a variety of people in an array of roles with diverse agendas, of which historic preservation may be but one.

The preservation leader must understand the preservation message and communicate it in a convincing manner. Passion for preservation is a prerequisite for success. The following city profiles describe accomplishments of preservationists with the above qualities.

Certain city leaders provide excellent illustrations for others to follow. Some cities got a head start simply because of their age characteristics or their locations. Others' unique history greatly affects preservation efforts. For example, some of the early colonial ports along the Atlantic coast were ignored during the building booms that other cities experienced following World War II; demolition and new construction passed them by. Such is the providential fortune of the city of Charleston, South Carolina.

Profiles in Local Public-Sector Preservation

Charleston, South Carolina

The public-sector efforts in Charleston, South Carolina, are impelled by two grassroots organizations, the Preservation Society of Charleston, established in 1920, and the Historic Charleston Foundation, in 1957. Thus, when longtime mayor Joseph P. Riley Jr. came into office in 1975, he was met with a strong preservation community supported by the public. The Preservation Society laid the groundwork with its advocacy and education activities, and the Historic Charleston Foundation continued the work by instituting a program of purchase, restoration, and sale with its innovative revolving fund, the nation's first. Together, these two nonprofits laid the foundation for Mayor Riley's widely acclaimed achievements.

Riley combined an interest in city design with the protection of its historic resources into a program of restoration and expansion that has achieved impressive results.[34] He demonstrated that historic preservation could be an important economic development tool when applied to an entire city. The preservation in Charleston includes not just landmark buildings but also streetscapes, affordable neighborhoods, and waterfront parks. Nostalgia for times past is sensitively mixed with adaptive reuse and new infill construction. The human scale of Charleston's urban design is an important feature that retains uniqueness in a growing city.

Savannah, Georgia

Savannah has been widely admired by city planners since James Oglethorpe first laid it out in 1733. Its urban design of public squares is as important to preservationists as the historic buildings that surround them. Savannah's downtown, which emerged along its riverfront, has been the object of struggle between preservationists and some public officials who wish to provide tourist facilities. In some instances, the pro-tourism officials have won: for instance, a large hotel slices through the distinctive historic curve of Factor's Row along the Savannah River, and a new convention center was built on the other side of the river.

Nevertheless, preservationists have also accomplished a great deal with the help of public officials. A proposed federal highway that would have destroyed many of its unique squares was diverted thus saving historic buildings and squares but also the beautiful live oaks hanging with Spanish moss that give Savannah its exceptional character. For many decades Savannah has appreciated its unique historic squares. The inventory was a critical decision by city officials.[35]

St. Augustine, Florida

St. Augustine, Florida, is the oldest colonial city in the United States.[36] The city government is working to preserve its many historic structures, including the mission grounds, the fort, the bridges, and the downtown center. The unique collection of Flagler College buildings is a remnant of the impact of industrialist Henry Flagler on the eastern coast of Florida in the early twentieth century. These structures help protect the historic streets of St. Augustine.

Former mayor George Gardner expressed his thoughts on this most important city in his February 2004 Web message.

> Our Old City has a long history of dramatic change.
>
> Four hundred and thirty eight years ago, the native population was stunned by arrival of tall ships and people speaking in strange tongues. About the time this shock wave got sorted out—200 years later—our entire Spanish population was displaced as the British moved in. Twenty years later, out went the British, back came the Spanish who, after another forty years, became an American territory, and a new breed called northern tourists descended upon the continent.
>
> Another twenty years later came something called statehood, and the original grand Spanish colonial empire, spanning a continent, was reduced to the peninsula we know today. In the late 1800s our sleepy town was invaded by a man with a vision—and money—to create an American Riviera for wealthy northerners. This singular event set the standard of a second discovery of the Oldest City which remains today in the architectural splendor of Flagler College, the Alcazar Hotel, Memorial Presbyterian and numerous other churches.
>
> Much of what is happening today—all at once—might have been started years ago. But it wasn't. We can only hope that we will proceed with ample community input and understanding of the needs.
>
> Beyond that, we must share the bewilderment of those early Indians, Spaniards, British, and the townsfolk of the late 1800s, and have faith that, as Henry Flagler commented when asked about the mas-

sive foundation of his Ponce de Leon Hotel, "I think it more likely I am spending an unnecessary amount of money in the foundation walls, but I comfort myself in the reflection that a hundred years hence it will be all the same to me and the building the better because of my extravagance."[37]

Atlanta, Georgia

The City of Atlanta was established in 1836 as a terminus for the Western and Atlantic Railroad. Following the Civil War, it emerged as a leading banking and railroad center. In 1870, it became the new state capital of Georgia. A leading late-nineteenth-century economic and governmental center, Atlanta quickly became one of the fastest-growing cities in the United States.

In response to its phenomenal growth after World War I, city officials constructed a series of concrete viaducts in the Alabama–Union Street area. Further development topside included Plaza Park in the 1940s and Peachtree Fountains Plaza in the 1960s. The area underneath these viaducts was referred to as the Underground.[38]

Underground Atlanta is an early example of a partnership forged between the public and private sectors. First designated a historic district in 1968, this six-block downtown district was hidden from view by a series of early-twentieth-century viaducts and railroad tracks. However, its location did not preclude the City of Atlanta from engaging the Urban Festival Development Company (a subsidiary of the Rouse Corporation) and Cooper, Carey, and Associates Architects from fully redeveloping this site. By the early 1970s the business community proclaimed the project a huge success. Preservationists and archaeologists were impressed with the careful way in which developers preserved the original marble, granite, cast iron, brick, and wood storefronts.

Unfortunately, initial optimism soon turned to pessimism as this historic district plummeted from its 1971 place as the city's number one tourist attraction, becoming by 1978 a second-rate spot for visitors. City aldermen were reluctant to rescind outdated alcohol consumption laws, which made it impossible for nightclubs and restaurants to survive. Many did not renew their leases. They were soon followed by local retailers. The closing of the Underground occurred in the wake of a Metropolitan Atlanta Rapid Transit Authority (MARTA) announcement that it would build a new rapid line through the heart of the historic district. Preservationists were devastated by this news.

However, a group called Friends of the Underground worked with preservationists to have the Underground placed on the National Register, opening opportunities for investors to take advantage of the investment tax credit. A $142 million renovation was completed in 1989. The facility offers restaurants, entertainment venues, and retail experiences for the entire family. Hundreds of thousands of tourists are now attracted to the Underground each year.

Underground Atlanta illustrates how a public-private partnership, formed by the city officials with the assistance of the business community and civic leaders, together with preservationists can successfully transform a historic downtown district into an economically viable city center.

Baltimore, Maryland

Baltimore was founded in 1729 as a market center, and it played a crucial role in the Revolutionary War and the War of 1812.[39] International trade accounted for much of its growth and prosperity during the antebellum years. The wealthy city suffered a downturn, however, when the economic and social devastation of the Great Depression undermined its vibrant economy.

Following a resurgence after World War II, suburbanization to surrounding counties further weakened the city's central core. The downward spiral of poverty, deterioration, and abandoned properties continued into the 1950s. City government initiated a redevelopment plan with a group of businesspeople, the Greater Baltimore Committee, in 1955. Their plans included a new civic center in the 1960s, Charles Center and the Inner Harbor in the 1970s, the National Aquarium in the 1980s, and the Camden Yards downtown stadium in the 1990s. Fifty historic districts benefited from the historic preservation program instigated by the Greater Baltimore Committee.

Butcher's Hill was one neighborhood preserved by these efforts. Located in East Baltimore, Butcher's Hill emerged after the Civil War as a collection of grand Victorian residences and graceful row houses. Adjacent to Baltimore's cultural and entertainment center, the neighborhood features specialty shops and art galleries and houses more than two thousand residents.

The City of Baltimore offers special incentive programs, among them American Dream Down Payment Initiatives, loan plans, Section 8 certificates, and lead-paint abatements. Valuable tax incentives consist of city property tax credits, federal tax credits and Maryland Rehabilitation Tax Credits. Recognizing the importance of sustaining community pride through home ownership, preservation leaders have partnered with other professional, business and civic groups to promote programs for low-to-moderate-income residents.

City officials, including, particularly, Donald Schaefer—the mayor who later became governor of Maryland—were instrumental in pulling together James Rouse and all the members of the Greater Baltimore Committee and steering this challenging effort.

St. Paul, Minnesota

St. Paul is another city in which public officials are dedicated to support-ing historic preservation.[40] Located on a bluff above the Mississippi River, seven miles east of Minneapolis, St. Paul was founded by Reverend Lucien Galthier in 1841. It gained political significance in 1858, when it became the state capital. The city grew as a railway center and as a hub for the Great Northern Railroad in the 1890s. In addition to state government, St. Paul's economy includes manufacture of computers, electronics, machin-ery, and beer. It is a nationally recognized center of arts and culture with an appreciation of architectural excellence. The Minnesota State Capitol Building was designed by architect Cass Gilbert.

Lowertown in St. Paul is an excellent example of an exciting historic district proud of its architectural legacy. Some of the finest late-nineteenth- and early-twentieth-century factories and warehouses are found in this eigh-teen-block area. When deterioration began to occur in the 1970s, Mayor George Latimer teamed up with preservation activists Norman Mears and Weiming Lu to reverse the trend. A $10 million grant from the McKnight Foundation helped establish a public-private partnership, the Lowertown Redevelopment Corporation (LRC), in 1978.

The ensuing years saw the conversion of the neighborhood into a district that featured offices, stores, galleries, green space, residences, restaurants, service industries, and theaters. Using the latest preservation technologies, LRC leaders transformed Lowertown into a new regional Cyber Village by integrating fiber-optic networks and telecommunication systems into a pleasant historic environment, encouraging several leading biotech and medical companies to locate there.

As mentioned, the public-private partnership of the city officials and knowledgeable business leaders joined with preservationists to create a viable historic district. Mayor George Latimer, Norman Mears, and Weiming Lu are credited with initiating the project, but many others joined in once the vision was established.

Portland, Oregon

Located in a West Coast state, Portland represents another example of the public sector transforming its central city through the use of historic preservation.[41] Founded in 1843, Portland remained a small outpost until after the Civil War. Its prime location on the Columbia River made it a leader in shipbuilding, logging, and lumbering as early as the 1870s. As many resource-based cities, Portland felt economic booms and busts. The city, which hosted the Lewis and Clark Exposition in 1905, is currently a tourist attraction in the scenic Pacific Northwest.

Portland's attractiveness is partly attributable to the powerful Portland Metro Council (PMC), a regional planning agency that offers an array of public services. It protects parks and green spaces, manages regional growth, evaluates transportation needs, and regulates garbage collection and recycling. The PMC operates the zoo, the Oregon Convention Center and the Performing Arts Center.

The city of Portland, through its Portland Development Council (PDC), enthusiastically supports preservation in nine historic districts, which emerged from the twenty-five-year vision the city produced in the 1970s. Old Town Chinatown is an example of civic commitment to preservation of culture, architecture, and historical identity. The neighborhood group, Old Town Chinatown Neighborhood Association (OTCNA), with strong support from the PDC, encourages new, widespread foreign investment. The district is well-known for its art galleries, museums, and cultural organizations, as well as the usual array of boutique shops, nightclubs, restaurants, and theaters. The PMC and PDC deserve accolades for their ability to work with the city and other planning and neighborhood groups and to take the lead in creating a desirable place to live and work.

Heritage Tourism

In the 1990s, the concept of heritage tourism has spread across the United States. Cities and towns are recognizing the economic benefits of drawing visitors to their historic cores and districts. As one travels the nation's highways, especially the Interstate system, signs that promote local historic districts abound. The National Park Service has identified local historic attractions in their park signage and the benefits to local communities are significant. Nearly every small town in the United States seems to be graced with a notable courthouse, civic center, house of worship, war memorial, or other feature that draws visitors. Even the nineteenth-century row of commercial establishments offers the weary traveler a pleasing alternative to strip malls and fast food architecture.

Cities and towns have long used self-promotion in their efforts to attract business and investment. Civic boosterism, however, has only recently focused on the attributes of historic resources. With the exception of planned "museum towns" such as Williamsburg, Virginia, and Dearborn, Michigan, which emerged after they were restored, most communities awakened to their historic potential in the late twentieth century. Often the public sector seemed to be last to realize this opportunity, and many historic structures were sacrificed to calls for slum clearance and urban renewal.

The desire to reinvent cities has come as the competition between cities and their suburbs evolved into struggles between U.S. cities and globalization of their industries. The new service centers where the city residents' focus on "quality of life" is the U.S. metropolitan image many desire. Historic preservation plays a significant role in providing unique and comfortable pedestrian environments for community centers and neighborhoods. With suburbanization emptying out city neighborhoods, civic promotion has turned to offering historic districts as an attraction for new or returning residents. Ethnic neighborhoods of the past often become the theme for promoting such areas: Little Italy, German Village, Little Havana, Slavic Village, and Irishtown are names that inundate the country's cities with historic nostalgia and opportunities for civic boosterism.

Public-Sector Preservation Publicity

Although public officials may defer preservation projects to the private or nonprofit sectors, some city leaders are inspired to initiate and publicize historic preservation to revitalize their central cores. St. Augustine, Savannah, and Charleston are notable for their public/private partnerships.

Cities may insert historic preservation into their government structure by appointing official bodies to regulate and plan for protection of resources. These government entities publicize their work through such venues as newspaper announcements and, in recent years, the Internet. Here, real estate developers and other interested parties are notified about the rules, application forms, public meetings, and other information that encourages preservation or may discourage demolition.

Wilmington, North Carolina, promotes its history on its Web page. Along with the usual advertisements for hotels and other attractions, the city includes a fascinating and well-documented history that harkens back to its 1739 incorporation. Throughout the rough-and-tumble years of the American Revolution, Wilmington produced several patriots who formed the Sons of Liberty and played a vital role in the new nation's independence. Because of its distance from the ocean, the small port declined after the Revolutionary War. It grew later with navigational improvements and entered a new phase as the lifeline of the Confederacy shipping naval stores, rice, cotton, peanuts, and, more importantly, military armaments during the Civil War.[42]

Following the Civil War, Wilmington suffered during Reconstruction when the number of newly freed slaves who began to advance in the growing economy was eclipsed by the white leaders who took over city government.

As many towns along the Atlantic coast's Low Country languished, growth was occurring on the Piedmont, especially Georgia and the Carolinas. Wilmington, however, did not experience a growth surge until, in preparation for the Second World War, the government invested in military installations in the area.

By the 1960s, the City of Wilmington had become inspired by its treasure of historic resources and began in earnest to preserve its many antebellum houses and its commercial district on the Cape Fear River. Today, the city attracts tourists and retirees who appreciate its old-fashioned pedestrian streets as well as its unique collection of landmark buildings.

Like Wilmington, many other cities have greatly enhanced communication regarding the value of historic preservation through the use of electronic media and the Internet. Public service programming and paid advertising on television promotes the cause as well as myriads of pages on the World Wide Web. Creative ideas using these media are open opportunities for the HPP who chooses a public-sector position.

Careers in the Public Sector

Opportunities for HPP careers in government may be found at a number of levels. Following are suggestions for government units that offer such positions. This is by no means an exhaustive listing.

Federal Level

As described in chapter 3, since the 1966 National Historic Preservation Act, preservation laws and public policies on the national level have been implemented by many entities. Those familiar with the public processes will find employment through the appropriate departments, such as the Department of the Interior, the National Park Service, and many related agencies. Those with an understanding of the Section 106 review process will find that all connections to land use across the United States—including the Departments of Transportation, Housing and Urban Development, and others— will be interested in the HPP's qualifications.

State Level

State historic preservation offices vary from state to state, but the states' need for trained HPPs is broadly understood. Working from local to state to federal government positions is a common path for career professionals. Since state governments differ in size, the opportunities found in each also differ. In states where advanced programs exist, breaking into the field may be more competitive than in those states just beginning their programs; however, ambitious HPPs may find themselves instituting new ideas and programs in this growing field. State governments also promote heritage tourism and may offer travel and tourism positions in the preservation field.

Local Level

Cities and counties are discovering the importance of historic preservation to the revitalization of urban neighborhoods, inner-ring suburbs, and small towns. City agencies will include planning positions in downtowns and neighborhoods, as well as economic-development and other related positions. The creative HPP must be able to identify links among historic preservation, environmental conservation, and many other related fields.

City and county governments are often places where personnel freely move among private-, nonprofit-, and public-sector positions. The well-trained HPP will certainly find these opportunities.

Notes

1. Andres Duany, Elizabeth Plater-Zyberk, and Jeff Speck, *Suburban Nation: The Rise of Sprawl and the Decline of the American Dream* (New York: North Point, 2000), 253–61.

2. Matthew Carmona, Tim Heath, Taner Oc, and Steve Tiesdell, *Public Places: Urban Spaces* (New York: Architectural Press, 2003), 114.

3. Ibid., 115.

4. James Q. Wilson and G. L. Kelling, "Broken Windows" *Atlantic Monthly* 249, no. 3 (Mar. 1982): 29–36.

5. L. Azeo Torre, *Waterfront Development* (New York: Van Nostrand Reinhold, 1989); Douglas Wrenn, *Urban Waterfront Development* (Washington, D.C.: Urban Land Institute, 1983); Ann Breen and Richard Rigby, *The New Waterfront: A Worldwide Urban Success Story* (London: Thames and Hudson, 1996).

6. Martin Anderson, "Fiasco of Urban Renewal" in *Urban Renewal: The Record and the Controversy*, ed. J. Q. Wilson (Cambridge, Mass.: MIT Press, 1966).

7. Donavan D. Rypkema, *The Economics of Historic Preservation: A Community Leader's Guide* (Washington, D.C.: National Trust for Historic Preservation, 1994).

8. Robert E. Stipe and Antoinette J. Lee, *The American Mosaic: Preserving a Nation's Heritage* (Washington, D.C.: Preservation Press, 1987).

9. Kevin Lynch, *What Time Is This Place?* (Cambridge, Mass.: MIT Press, 1972), 235.

10. Robert E. Stipe, "Why Preserve Historic Resources?" in *Readings in Historic Preservation: Why? What? How?*, ed. Norman Williams Jr., Edmund H. Kellogg, and Frank Gilbert (New Brunswick, N.J.: Rutgers Univ. Press, 1983), 59.

11. Thomas D. Bever, "Economic Benefits of Historic Preservation," in Williams, Kellogg, and Gilbert, *Readings in Historic Preservation: Why? What? How?*, 79.

12. Stanislaw Lorentz, "Reconstruction of Old Town Centers in Poland," in *Historic Preservation Today* (Charlottesville: University Press of Virginia for the Na-

tional Trust for Historic Preservation and Colonial Williamsburg, 1966): 43–50.

13. David Poinsett, "What Is Historic Preservation?" in Williams, Kellogg, and Gilbert, *Readings in Historic Preservation: Why? What? How?*, 60.

14. Eugenie Birch and Douglas Roby, "The Planner and the Preservationist," *Journal of the American Planning Association* 50, no. 2 (Spring 1984): 194–207.

15. Carmona et al., *Public Places, Urban Spaces: The Dimensions of Urban Design* (New York: Architectural Press, 2003), 114.

16. Constance C. Beaumont, *A Citizen's Guide to Protecting Historic Places: Local Preservation Ordinances*, 2; www.nationaltrust.org/smartgrowth/toolkit_citizens.pdf.

17. Ibid.

18. John Pyke, "Landmark Preservation" in Williams, Kellogg, and Gilbert, *Readings in Historic Preservation: Why? What? How?*, 135.

19. Virginia Benson and Richard Klein, "The Impact of Historic Districting on Property Values," *Appraisal Journal* 56, no. 2 (Apr. 1988): 223–32.

20. Donavan Rypkema, *Preservation and Property Values* (Indianapolis: Indiana Landmarks Foundation, 1997), 1–20.

21. Duany, Plater-Zyberk, and Speck, *Suburban Nation*, 253–61.

22. Carmona et al., *Public Places*, 114.

23. Ibid., 115.

24. Wilson and Kelling, "Broken Windows," 29–36.

25. Ibid., 30.

26. Carmona et al., *Public Places*, 115.

27. Ibid., 116.

28. Allan B. Jacobs and Donald Appleyard, "Towards an Urban Design Manifesto," *Journal of the American Planning Association* 53 (1987): 112–20.

29. Ibid., 118.

30. Ian Bentley, "Urban Design as an Anti-Profession," *Urban Design Quarterly* 65 (1998): 15.

31. George H. Drury, ed., *The Historical Guide to North American Railroads*, 2nd ed. (Waukesha, Wis.: Kalmbach, 2000), 11–12.

32. Robert A. Simons, *Turning Brownfields into Greenbacks* (Washington, D.C.: Urban Land Institute, 1998), 167.

33. Lucie K. Morisset, Luc Noppen, and Thomas Coomans, eds. *Quel Avenir Pour Quelles Églises? What Future for Which Churches?* (Montreal, Québec: Presses de l'Université du Québec, 2006).

34. Mayor Joseph P. Riley, "State of the City Address," Jan. 2006, www.charleston city.info/dept/content.aspx?nid=4468cid=4620.

35. "Preservation Strategies," Historic Savannah Foundation, www.historic savannahfoundation.org/AboutUs.asp.

36. "A Brief History of St. Augustine," www.ci.st-augustine.fl.us/visitors/history. html.

37. George Gardner, "Mayor's Web Message for February 2004," www.ci.st-augustine.fl.us/commission/from_mayor_desk/fmd2004/fmd_02_04.html.

38. "Underground Atlanta History," www.underground-atlanta.com/HTML79. phtml.

39. Gene Bracken, "About Us: Greater Baltimore Committee," www.gbc.org/AboutUs/AboutUs.aspx.

40. "St. Paul's Lowertown New Urban Village: Layers of History," www.lower town.org/LRC/heritageI.html.

41. Gary Blackmer, "Portland Historical Timeline," www.portlandonline.com/auditor/index.cfm?c=274088.

42. "Living History," City of Wilmington, N.C., www.wilmington-nc/more wilmington2.shtml.

Chapter Seven

The Private-Sector Role in Historic Preservation

Introduction

One of the founding principles of the United States is the concept of private property rights. Claiming property has historically been part of the American dream. The federal government allocated free farmland through the 1862 Homestead Act, thereby spreading population throughout the country, but well before the beginning of the twenty-first century, most U.S. citizens resided in metropolitan areas.[1] Private property rights however, remain important to Americans. Most historic preservation projects are carried out through private investment.[2]

Both the public and nonprofit sectors may assist private owners through public-private partnerships and other incentives to preserve historic structures. Private owners are, nevertheless, generally able to demolish buildings at will. To be effective, therefore, it is critically important for HPPs to understand the economics of real estate development.

Throughout the twentieth century, American preservation was justified in various ways. Sentiment for military monuments, conservation of national parks, saving cemeteries, and many other commendable motivations were cited.[3] However, in the twenty-first century, the foremost consideration is a positive financial return on the preservation investment.

This chapter considers preservation activity performed by the private sector. Because private-sector real estate markets are motivated by contemporary trends, it is essential for the HPP to recognize current situations that affect real estate activity to promote preservation.

Real Estate Development Trends

Traveling across the United States is an experience in diversity. The astute observer must note dramatic differences in historical background, race and ethnicity, physical climate, and land forms. As a result of these differences, there is great variety in the built environment. Private-sector HPPs must clearly understand local real estate markets before making preservation decisions. However, as the country's settlement patterns evolve, certain important trends emerge throughout every region: urbanization, suburbanization, highway priorities, and new construction.

Urbanization

As population flows from rural to metropolitan areas, demand for housing and commercial development increases, putting pressure on urban land.[4] The result is recycling some old buildings while demolishing others in order to build taller buildings. Meanwhile, in rural areas, population declines are creating ghost towns. In these communities, civic leaders must assess their own redundant historic buildings and sites: some small towns attempt to deal with their losses by restoring and recycling their centers; others do not.[5]

Centralization of population, a long-term trend, results in high demand for urban land on the principle that when less is available, the price is higher. Gravity models illustrate this point: The pull to the center results in higher land values, which means the investor must achieve higher rents.[6] This intensity of land use may have a negative impact on old buildings, which are regarded as obsolete and unable to offer a satisfactory return on investment (ROI) compared with new, taller buildings.

Decentralization, a second long-term urbanization trend, abandons city property for suburban green fields. For the real estate investor or developer, the outer edge of a city offers certain advantages: there are not as many brownfields requiring environmental clean-up; fewer local regulations and requirements attached to land uses; and generally large land tracts available, where mass production methods may be used for housing or commercial developments. As will be discussed in detail later, the private-sector HPP should study local land values and property appraisals to be effective in making critical preservation real estate investment decisions.

Suburbanization

Conflicts over highway-oriented sprawl and the consequent decline of older city centers are widely discussed by planners and preservationists.[7] James Conaway, editor of *Preservation* magazine, laments, "In the next 30 years, America's store of structures and roads is expected to double."[8] Marc Leepson describes the sprawl flooding the Virginia Piedmont in an article called "Holding Their Ground." He mourns Civil War battlefields, threatened by housing subdivisions and strip malls.[9] Richard Moe and Carter Wilkie began their book *Changing Places* by noting the latest Battle of Manassas, a conflict with theme park developers, in which such a threat was imminent.[10] Across the continent, Conaway's "Manifest Destination" portrayed the beautiful Napa Valley in California as endangered by a proliferation of vanity wineries.[11]

Those who are "moving up" in U.S. cities often begin to look for larger, newer houses that provide more green space. Young families abandon city neighborhoods to raise their children in environments that are perceived as safer and quieter. They are looking for good schools and for new housing that has all the amenities found in the suburbs.

However, the flip side of living where one has more space is often the long commute on crowded highways to employment centers. In many areas, suburban development means large subdivisions with few services or sidewalks and shopping malls with seas of asphalt. The automobile is essential to the lifestyle; traffic on the eight-lane highways and problems of huge megaschools may eventually take some of the luster off the shiny new suburban scene.

HPPs should also recognize inner-ring suburbs as a phenomenon of the late twentieth century. Many large cities, especially in the eastern United States, are "underbounded." Their boundaries are close to their central business districts, and the first suburbs were built just outside these boundaries in the 1920s. Often the inner-ring suburbs have large elaborate houses that are of great interest to historic preservationists who appreciate their excellent construction and fine architectural details.

The inner-ring suburbs are beginning to organize preservation planning activities, complete with preservation ordinances and landmarks commissions committed to protecting their unique neighborhoods. They are also forming historic districts, including the appropriate design guidelines. As the National Register's official age of historicity (fifty years) approaches, post–World War II districts become historic as well.

Central city neighborhoods, inner-ring suburbs, small towns swallowed up by spreading metropolitan areas, or rural communities preserving their centers, all offer opportunities for the well-trained HPP.

Highway Construction

Most scholars agree that highway construction in the United States is a priority. In spite of efforts to forestall the destruction of city neighborhoods, the National Highway Act of 1956, a military highway system that spread more than 42,500 miles of federal highways across the country, began a process of dividing city neighborhoods, isolating some of these vicinities, and preventing residents from performing their usual activities. The combination of abandonment and demolition weakened historic urban areas.[12]

Efforts by planners and civic activists to de-emphasize highway dominance have failed in most U.S. cities. Although mass transit is available, it is usually heavily subsidized and underutilized; most Americans prefer cars. Highway-oriented developments with their fast-food establishments and big-box retailers attract the price-conscious consumer. In spite of this long-term trend, there is a countervailing force leading some people to prefer historic Main Streets and walkable districts.[13]

Once again, the private-sector HPP must be prepared to understand investment decisions based on these factors, which vary considerably from region to region.

New Housing Construction

One of the most important measures of economic activity in the United States is embodied in the phrase "new housing starts." Most housing construction is taking place in suburban subdivisions. This industry employs large numbers of workers, who produce housing in mass quantities throughout the United States. Although the restoration of an older house actually requires more individual skilled labor, it does not occur on the mass scale that contemporary residential construction requires. In addition to laborers working at construction sites, the modern process often employs off-site factory workers, who produce housing components. The scale of residential production in the United States provides a variety of options and prices that attract new buyers, whose purchases are generally facilitated by banks. The HPP working in an urban neighborhood or small town must comprehend both the labor and the financing issues and be prepared to compete within this market.[14]

In light of the above trends, what will motivate the private-sector investor to attempt historic preservation? Assuming that the market forces are weak in a historic area, what incentives may be offered to offset this limitation and make a historic preservation real estate project feasible?

Through the Internal Revenue Service, the federal government developed two incentives designed to offset the limitations of market weakness: the Investment Tax Credit and Preservation or Conservation Easements. However, in order to take advantage of these incentives, the property must first be placed on the National Register of Historic Places.

National Register of Historic Places

Opinions on the kinds of properties worth saving vary greatly. Guidelines to determine whether structures are eligible for the National Register of Historic Places, though fairly straightforward, still require a great deal of interpretation by local, state, and federal officials.[15]

The following is a reiteration of these qualifications taken from the secretary of interior's National Register Criteria for Evaluation:

The quality of significance in American history, architecture, archeology, engineering, and culture is present in districts, sites, buildings, structures, and objects that possess integrity of location, design, setting, materials, workmanship, feeling, and association, and:

A. That are associated with events that have made a significant contribution to the broad patterns of our history; or
B. That are associated with the lives of persons significant in our past; or
C. That embody the distinctive characteristics of a type, period, or method of construction, or that represent the work of a master, or that possess high artistic values, or that represent a significant and distinguishable entity whose components may lack individual distinctions; or
D. That have yielded, or may be likely to yield, information important in prehistory or history.[16]

The significance of the National Register designation to the private-sector investor is that the Internal Revenue Service's investment tax credit (ITC) is provided only for those who qualify and wish to invest in the preservation of income-producing historic buildings. The tax credit often makes the difference between undertaking an economically feasible project and allowing the historic building to be demolished by neglect.

If a large development firm restores an old train station or a downtown theater complex or a local investor preserves a small building, the process is expected to make economic sense. To encourage investment in historic preservation, the federal government has devised a special tax incentive, which, unfortunately, applies only to income-producing National Register historic properties. However, some states are considering residential tax credits on state income taxes. The federal tax credit plays a critical role in preserving old buildings.

Investment Tax Credit

This chapter outlines various considerations and the process commonly used in applying the ITC to the preservation of an historic, income-producing property.

The first step for the investor is locating a property to preserve. Setting is a critical aspect of the decision; it greatly affects the potential for the National Register listing, which is necessary for receiving the ITC. Having located the property, the investor seeks professional advice on its likelihood for listing on the National Register of Historic Places. Consulting architects and preservationists may do a cursory evaluation and offer to write the application, a fairly detailed and complex process. If the property is located within a National Register district and contributes to the historic nature of the district, the opportunity for tax credits is greatly enhanced. It is important to follow carefully the secretary of the interior's Standards for Rehabilitation in performing the preservation work. For example, aluminum or vinyl siding, sandblasting of brick or wood siding, and a variety of other treatments should be avoided. Throughout the process, the economics of preserving a historic property must be evaluated. A pro forma evaluation, described in a later section of this chapter, called "How to Save: Packaging Preservation with Incentives," will guide the financial decision.

Preservation or Conservation Easements

Some states allow an added incentive to the ITC, a federal tax deduction for historic "conservation" by donating a property easement to a nonprofit organization. The easement gives the recipient the right to prevent alterations to a historic structure that may destroy its appearance and affect the

Laclede's Landing, St Louis, Mo. Named after Pierre Laclede, one of the city's founders, this rejuvenated nine-block commercial district with its fine restaurants and distinctive gift shops is a leading local tourist destination. Photo by V. Benson.

value of neighboring properties. The easement may cover the facade, in the case of commercial strips, or the entire exterior of a building. Depending on the agreement between the owner and the recipient organization, it should prevent demolition of the structure and may also cover interiors as well as exteriors. An appraiser places a value on the easement, generally 10 to 15 percent of the property's worth.[17]

The preservation/conservation easement applies to properties listed on the National Register of Historic Places or considered contributing buildings, located within a National Register district. To be considered a tax-deductable expense, the easement must be given to a nonprofit organization that is eligible to receive such donations. The recipient organization takes on, for a modest fee, the responsibility of monitoring the building and assuring its continued preservation. The owner must consult the recipient organization before making any alterations. The donated easement will be attached to the deed and should be duly recorded.

The recipient organization, which monitors changes to the property, charges the owner fees. Initial, up-front fees also include legal and appraisal costs. However, such a program often makes the preservation of the property attractive to the owner who participates.[18]

How to Save: Packaging Preservation with Incentives

Attracting investors to the market for historic preservation requires a clear understanding, on the part of the HPP, of the pros and cons of historic buildings. Several factors may be perceived by the real estate investor/developer as either obstructions or opportunities:

Prices—Mass Production v. Uniqueness

Mass production, sometimes called "Fordism," after the automaker who developed it, has helped many U.S. consumers to achieve a high standard of living.[19] The disadvantage for the real estate investor is the fairly short lifespan of mass-produced buildings, their boring, "cookie-cutter" styles and the deficient quality of their materials and assembly. However, for the developer who expects to sell a project and leave town, these factors may be irrelevant.

Unique structures cost more than mass-produced ones, and they hold their values longer and may be adapted to new uses when their original functions become obsolete. The construction expertise required to restore such places will employ more people at a higher wage than the factory-made components of new suburban development.[20] Pride in producing

Warehouses, the Strand Landmark Historic District, Galveston, Tex. Excellent examples of high quality renovation and restoration work being done in Galveston today, many of these historic structures are prized local landmarks. The trolley in the foreground transports residents and visitors throughout this district daily. Photo by V. Benson.

high-quality products may lure certain companies into historic preservation real estate, an important observation for the HPP.

Amenities—Green Space and Commuting v. Big Trees and Convenience

Most mass-produced suburban subdivisions involve clearing the land of large trees, filling in wetlands, and creating relatively flat landscapes. The addition of streets without sidewalks does not offset the settings, barren in spite of their bucolic names (Meadowbrook, Pheasant Run). Green space may be plentiful in suburban yards, but is a stark contrast to the shady sidewalks on urban neighborhood streets and well-developed city parks. City areas have utilities that are "in and paid for" and offer convenience to stores, workplaces, and even public transportation.[21] The HPP should be prepared to address these issues and make convincing arguments for preservation.

Lifestyle—Homogeneity vs. Diversity

Uniformity of residential neighborhoods will offer comfort to some homeowners, while dissimilar populations and cultures attract others. Varying lifestyles, as might be found in large cities, create interesting contrasts in some districts, although they occasionally threaten the stability of those who live there. Ethnic and racial differences may affect residential property values in U.S. cities, although these assumptions should be assessed carefully.[22] For those who wish to occupy fairly dense neighborhoods, historic districting may provide a distinctive lifestyle. Also, in some cases, surrounding property values are positively affected by the process of creating an historic district.[23]

An additional location factor that greatly affects land valuation throughout the United States is proximity to waterfronts. Many historic areas are located on rivers, lakes, or seacoasts. This very desirable location exerts additional pressure on land values and may result in destruction of historic buildings in favor of gold coast high-rise development.[24] Understanding these and other real estate variables that affect property valuation is critical for the HPP.

According to Vincent Barrett and John P. Blair, 80 percent of all land-development planning in the United States is performed by architecture, engineering, and planning (AE&P) firms.[25] HPPs should note that most residential historic preservation is on a small or individual scale that may not be of interest to the AE&P firm. Therefore, CDCs or other nonprofit preservation organizations may offer important assistance in such a project, as detailed below.

Preservation Project Implementation

Feasibility Analysis

There are generally two situations that result in the desire for an analysis of real estate feasibility: first, vacant properties that offer development opportunity (sites), leading to proposals for new development by AE&Ps, and second, investors or developers, such as a real estate investment trust (REIT) looking for a building project, an investment that leads to purchase or options. A third possibility is a historic building in need of investment and redevelopment. Usually before historic preservation takes place, ownership control of the building or buildings is critical. In securing the property, the preservation real estate investor will take the following steps:

Step One: Control the Property through Purchase or Option

The investor in a historic property may be an active participant in its purchase and renovation or, in the case of a large project, may be part of a group of passive investors who do not want active roles in the construction or operation but rather look to achieve returns on their investment. Passive investors may represent institutional funds, such as pension funds or REITs. The investor may wish to hold the property at a specific price for a specified time period while he further assesses the project's feasibility. This is called an option agreement and should be in writing.

Step Two: Hire a Preservation-Sensitive AE&P Firm

This step involves a preliminary architectural assessment of the project, an opinion on its potential for National Register listing and tax incentives, and a preliminary pro forma. At this stage a yes or no decision may be made.

The field of historic preservation has become of increasing interest to architecture firms. Although the study of architecture in many colleges focuses on design of new construction, the competition is very intense. The appearance of so-called design-build firms, in which non-architects carry out construction, have added to the competitive environment. Restorative development and historic preservation were joined together by those who wish to conserve natural environments as well as protect the built environments. More preservation education programs are springing up across the United States. For the HPP seeking it, the information on local firms abounds through advertising and online sources.

Step Three: Evaluate the Feasibility of Rehabilitation through
Market Research and Building Analysis

The discussion presented here is intended to be a general overview of the real estate development process involved in historic preservation. It will not explain the detailed analysis that should underlie a final development decision. For such information, the HPP should consult real estate feasibility and financial textbooks.[26]

Within the market analyses are normally included both direct and indirect forces that affect the preservation project. Direct forces are the familiar supply and demand factors. Indirect ones are the social, political, and environmental factors. These all must be assessed in the market study.

Step Four: Sketch a Rehabilitation Plan of Pre-Construction Drawings

The AE&P firm will produce a preliminary assessment that may involve general drawings. These will indicate interior and exterior considerations. All of the steps up to this point may occur simultaneously before a decision is made.

Step Five: Conduct an Initial Pro Forma Analysis.

The pro forma will contain data from the assessment and will lead to the ultimate question: Does this project make economic sense or not?

The HPP employed by a private development firm will quickly learn the process of assessing project feasibility. The experienced developer often will bypass the market study on the assumption that the HPP already knows the following:

1. demographics of the area,
2. existing rental market,
3. sales demand by building type and unit size,
4. absorption rate, and
5. construction costs.

The HPP must fully understand these factors before he or she can produce a pro forma. The bank may require a market study before offering a mortgage for the project but it may be done later in the process, after the initial pro forma.

Demographics of the Area

These data may be obtained from government census, local universities, or real estate firms that collect such demographic information as age, household income, educational attainment, and racial and ethnic backgrounds. Census data are collected periodically, and relevant population characteristics may change rapidly depending on local conditions. Thus, migration of populations and industries in the United States is widely analyzed.

The study of demographics is generally considered to directly influence supply and demand, particularly in the area of residential land use. Therefore, the ability to predict these factors is of great interest to historic preservation professionals as well as city planners, government officials, and various businesspeople.

Existing Rental Market

Surveys of properties similar to the proposed historic structure will indicate realistic rental prices and also reveal vacancy rates for particular commercial buildings and areas. The HPP should develop a good sense of these variations throughout a metropolitan region.

When one narrows the supply and demand relationship to the local area, the examination of current market supply can be achieved by assessing local research. Such studies are often produced by the public sector, area colleges and universities, and real estate organizations. The HPP may be called on to examine buildings within historic districts that are of various functions: commercial, residential, industrial conversions, among others. Each building type will have a different current market supply and demand.

Sales Demand by Building Type and Unit Size

Further narrowing the scope of analysis, the HPP must address particular local conditions. In the real estate field, buildings are often described in terms of square footage or gross leasable area (GLA). Construction costs and rents per square foot can both be assessed through general indexes or catalogs of the industry. Regions across the United States vary greatly with regard to these criteria, so close inspection of sales demand, building architecture, and spatial configurations of the local area can be critical to implementing a preservation project that meets local demand.[27]

Absorption Rate

This principle is further elaborated in many real estate finance textbooks and forms the basis for the pro forma and for the cash flow statement described in the following sections. That is the reason that supply and demand predictions are so critical to the success of any real estate project, but particularly the historic preservation venture.

The preservation project, by virtue of its unique characteristics, generally makes the market assessment more difficult. New construction, with its bland replications, sometimes called a cookie-cutter approach, has the advantage of easier predictability.

The HPP should be aware of this when collecting data that help to make the case for bank loans, investor confidence and developer interest in a historic project and be prepared to assemble extensive data to demonstrate market demand. Another important principle for the HPP to understand is that real estate is a time/money one. Delays in either construction or rehabilitation can make a project infeasible, but a long delay in leasing or selling a property is also a critical problem for the investor.[28]

Construction Costs and Estimating

Finally, the estimation of preservation costs is more difficult than those of new construction. HPPs must understand the competition (new construction v. historic preservation) if they are to be effective in performing these tasks. They may familiarize themselves with contemporary rules of thumb for their area (such as $100 per square foot for new construction). Cost estimating confirms the importance of engaging a preservation-sensitive and experienced AE&P firm. Detailed cost estimates for labor and materials are available in technical manuals and catalogs or through local unions.

Cost estimates for the pro forma analysis may vary considerably depending on how carefully the preservation process is done. If one expects a 20 percent tax credit for the project, which must be a depreciating income-producer, the secretary of the interior's standards must be followed and may increase the costs. If a 10 percent tax credit is sought, the work done has certain flexibility but still must meet building code requirements.

The HPP must learn to ask the developer the right questions, such as the following:

1. What are the economic constraints?
2. What is the market for this project? Prices, sizes, types of units?
3. What amenities should be provided?
4. What is the leasing market for commercial projects?
5. What types of retail will locate at the site?

Pro Forma Analysis

The pro forma projects income and expenses for preserving an income-producing property. It requires estimates for the costs incurred as well as the expected return on the investment. It is essential for the private investor to achieve his or her stated financial goals. For some investors, the cash flow must produce a regular income; for others, the return may be delayed until reversion or sale of the property. Some investors are interested primarily in the tax consequences.

For most projects, the developer provides some equity capital and a bank or another group will hold a mortgage on the balance. Following is an example of the components of a pro forma analysis.[29]

To begin an historic preservation project of a particular structure, one must measure the gross area of the building. The gross leasable area (GLA) is what is left after deducting approximately 30 percent of the gross area for service areas and circulation corridors. If the building has several stories, the upper floors will probably lease for a lower price per square foot than the ground floor. This is especially true if the ground floor is leased for commercial use and the upper floors are occupied by offices or apartments. The rent per square foot of GLA, minus any vacancies, determines the annual gross income (AGI).

The AGI is then adjusted by subtracting the total expenses of operating the building and the real estate taxes, which gives the net operating income (NOI). This is sometimes referred to as triple-net, the income "netting out" the operating costs and taxes.

The economic value of the project is determined by dividing the net income by the capitalization rate (the capitalization rate is based on the real estate value related to net income). The economic value is multiplied by the mortgage loan percentage to achieve the actual loan amount, which then is multiplied by the debt service constant, to give the annual debt service (the debt service constant is a method of computation that expresses the payment in terms of the percentage of the total loan). When this debt service is subtracted from the NOI, the annual cash flow is achieved. This cash flow may also be seen as the profit before taxes.

Once the costs for the building and land are added to the rehabilitation costs, the replacement costs are obtained. This figure minus the mortgage loan reveals the investor cash required. The before-tax profit divided by the cash required indicates the return realized by the investor. The cost of the land, which is not considered to depreciate in value, is subtracted from the replacement cost of the building to arrive at the depreciable value of the project. Depreciation allowed by the U.S. Treasury 1993 guidelines covers what is determined to be the useful life of the building. A newly rehabilitated building starts the clock again, and the schedule for straight-line depreciation is 27.5 years for residential buildings and 39 years for non-residential.

The annual NOI minus the annual interest payment and the annual depreciation will show whether there is taxable income or loss. The NOI multiplied by the investor's tax rate will reveal his or her federal tax liability. The annual cash flow minus this liability shows the net consequence that, divided by the cash investment required shows the investors percentage of return on equity.

Table 7.1: Typical Project Pro Forma/ Cash Flow

Gross area of building   _____ square feet
–10% for service area   _____
–20% for circulation   _____
Total leasable area   _____
X annual rent/square foot   _____

Annual gross income   _____
Annual operating expenses   _____ (rule of thumb)

Annual gross income   _____
–Real estate taxes   _____
–Operating expenses   _____

Net operating income (NOI)   _____
÷ capitalization rate (based on interest rate)   _____

Economic value of project   _____
X mortgage loan percentage   _____

Mortgage loan   _____
X Debt service constant   _____

Annual debt service   _____
Annual NOI   _____
–Annual debt service   _____

Annual cash flow   _____
(or pretax profit)

Economic value of project   _____
X mortgage loan percentage   _____

Mortgage loan   _____
X debt service constant   _____

Annual debt service   _____
Annual NOI   _____
–Debt service   _____
Annual cash flow or Pretax profit   _____
Gross area of building   _____ square feet
X Estimated construction cost   _____

Construction/development cost   _____
–Cost of land and building   _____

Replacement cost of project   ═══════════════
–Mortgage loan   _____

Cash investment   ═══════════════

Annual Cash Flow   _____
(pretax profit)
÷ cash investment   _____

Return on cash investment   _____ percent
(before taxes)
Replacement cost of project   _____
–Cost of land   _____

Total depreciable value of project   ═══════════════
Divided by useful life of building   _____
(U.S. Treasury Guidelines)

Annual allowable depreciation   ═══════════════
(straight-line method)
Annual NOI   _____
–Annual interest payment   _____
–Annual allowable depreciation   _____

Taxable income or loss   ═══════════════
(Compute for each year for life of mortgage, taxable income or loss, varies annually)
X Federal income tax rate   _____
Federal income tax liability   _____

Annual cash flow   ═══════════════
–Tax liability   _____

Net consequence   ═══════════════
÷ Cash investment required   _____

Percentage of return on equity   ═══════════════

This feasibility analysis section covers the very general process that HPPs will confront if they practice in the private sector, most likely working for real estate developers or AE&P firms. Each aspect of the process should be thoroughly explored, and the HPP should add current methods and information to his/her arsenal of tools to be effective in this challenging career.

Case Study of Preservation Project

A case study of a preservation project is also useful for the HPP to begin to see the important financial aspects. The project described below, for example, has a final development cost of $10.2 million, and the building described has a square footage of 200,000. Of course, the net rentable area in which the return on the investment must be calculated may be only half of that figure. If it is assumed that 100,000 square feet is actually rentable, then the actual cost is in the range of $100 per square foot, a good rule-of-thumb number to remember, and may be considerably less than the cost of new construction. HPPs will be expected to have a grasp of such figures when they are dealing with private-sector investors.

The following description of a historic rubber factory, a typical, though fictional, private-sector project that may have the secretary of the interior may have approved for addition to the National Register of Historic Places in 1990. This meant that the project was eligible for historic tax credits. The information about the project was provided by a typical private-sector architectural firm that may have carried out the preservation and may currently occupy the building.

The historic rubber factory located near Cleveland is a landmark building constructed in 1912. By the 1930s the factory was no longer viable and was purchased for warehouse use. This occupant vacated the property in the 1980s, and it has deteriorated in the intervening years. This adaptive reuse provides a complement to the revitalization of its surrounding neighborhood.

During its lifetime, the rubber factory became a blight to its poverty-stricken neighborhood. High unemployment and deteriorating conditions led to the creation of a nonprofit organization, in the hopes of revitalizing the area. However, the organization was unable to find an economic use for this large structure. The city considered demolition of the building but found that it was too expensive to demolish such a strongly built structure.

In 2001 a real estate partnership was formed to purchase and renovate the factory and fill it with offices. The partnership bought the property at a sheriff's sale for back taxes and hired a design-build firm to carry out the preservation, following the secretary of the interior's standards. Since it was located in an enterprise zone, the city in which it was located granted it a ten-year tax abatement. Nevertheless, the combination of tax credits and tax abatement did not make the financing of this project an easy task. Banks expected pre-leasing agreements before they would make construction loans.

Finally, a Chicago bank agreed to finance the project after a business firm joined the partnership and pre-leased the top floor of the building.

Throughout the renovation process, the National Park Service, representing the secretary of the interior, closely supervised various aspects of the preservation. Although the table describes the development costs, it cannot elucidate the struggles inherent in such a project. In the final analysis, the firm that occupies the space can use the visible improvements in marketing its services, and the neighborhood is given an attractive and successful business operation.

Table 7.2: Development Cost Information

Site acquisition cost	$350,000
Site improvement costs, on- and off-site	$350,000
Grading	$65,000
Sewer/water/drainage	$100,000
Paving	$150,000
Curbs/sidewalks	$20,000
Landscaping/irrigation	$15,000
Construction costs	$6.8 million
Superstructure/restoration	$800,000
HVAC	$600,000
Electrical	$350,000
Plumbing/sprinklers	$350,000
Elevators	$250,000
Fees/general conditions	$900,000
Finishes	$1,000,000
Graphics	$50,000
Windows	$2.5 million
Soft costs	$2.7 million
Architecture/engineering	$200,000
Project management	$130,000
Leasing/marketing	$700,000
Legal/accounting	$300,000
Taxes/insurance	$100,000
Title fees	$20,000
Construction financing	$850,000
Governmental requirements	$400,000
Total development costs	$10.2 million

Publicizing Preservation in the Private Sector

Across America are widely known examples of private projects that feature preservation; among the most recognized are Station Square in Pittsburgh (now owned and operated by Forest City Enterprises, a private firm that also owns the restored Terminal Tower in Cleveland); the Brown Palace Hotel in Denver; Chicago's Navy Pier; New York City's South Street Seaport; Boston's Faneuil Hall and Quincy Market; Seattle's Pioneer Square; and St. Louis's LaClede's Landing.

Though many of those mentioned were also public/private partnerships, they are now operated as private businesses. As such, they advertise widely on television, radio, the Internet, newspapers, magazines, and tourist mailings—usually emphasizing certain specific characteristics of historic places. Because private businesses work for profit, they are generally better able to support large advertising budgets than either of the other two sectors, whose communications distinctions are noted in the previous chapters.

HPPs would do well to examine carefully these various advertising efforts as part of their communications preparation for a position in the private sector.

Preservation Careers in the Private Sector

The well-trained preservation professional will find employment in a number of the private organizations that were mentioned above. To avail themselves of the ITCs for their preservation projects, real estate development firms and AE&P firms will seek employees who are able to write nominations for the National Register of Historic Places. In the larger firms, a full-time employee may work on these applications. In smaller firms, a consultant is often hired to carry out this important work.

The construction industry is becoming more interested in those with historic preservation skills. As the demand increases for preserving historic downtowns and their many significant buildings, the preservation professional may assist in restoring old theaters, bank buildings, train stations, religious structures, and various other buildings whose owners are finding adaptive reuse to be in their best interests.

Related companies, which produce materials for historic preservation use—such as manufacturers of historic paints, wallpapers, plasters, tiles, stonework and other materials that are no longer part of modern construction supplies—also hire preservationists.

Preservationists may move from the public and nonprofit sectors into the private sector when they have learned to shepherd projects through the various necessary rules and regulations.

Notes

1. U.S. Census, 2000, www.census.gov/main/www/cen2000.html.

2. Advisory Council on Historic Preservation, *The Contribution of Historic Preservation to Urban Revitalization* (Washington, D.C.: GPO, 1979), 1–11.

3. Robert Stipe, *Legal Techniques in Historic Preservation* (Washington, D.C.: National Trust for Historic Preservation, 1972), 1–2.

4. David Rusk, *Inside Game, Outside Game: Winning Strategies for Saving Urban America* (Washington, D.C.: Brookings Institution Press, 1999).

5. Richard Moe and Carter Wilkie, "The Revival of Main Street" in *Changing Places: Rebuilding Community in an Age of Sprawl* (New York: Henry Holt, 1997): 142–77.

6. Ashish K. Sen and Tony E. Smith, *Gravity Models of Spatial Interaction Behavior: Advances in Spatial and Network Economics* (New York: Springer, 1995).

7. Andres Duany, Elizabeth Plater-Zyberk, and Jeff Speck, *Suburban Nation: The Rise of Sprawl and the Decline of the American Dream* (New York: North Point, 2000), 132; Mel Scott, *American City Planning since 1890* (Berkeley: Univ. of California Press, 1969), 45; Moe and Wilkie, "The Revival of Main Street," 63; Charles Birnbaum, "In Defense of Open Space," *Preservation* 57, no. 5 (Sept.–Oct., 2005): 38–39; Phillip Lopate, "Taking the High Line," *Preservation* 57, no. 4 (July–Aug. 2005): 30–33.

8. James Conaway, "Grounded," *Preservation* 57, no. 4 (July–Aug. 2005): 2.

9. Marc Leepson, "Holding Their Ground," *Preservation* 57, no. 4 (July–Aug. 2005): 24–29.

10. Moe and Wilkie, preface to *Changing Places*, x.

11. James Conaway, "Manifest Destination," *Preservation* 57, no. 4 (July–Aug. 2005): 39–41.

12. Rusk, *Inside Game, Outside Game*, 331.

13. Ibid., 332

14. G. Vincent Barrett and John P. Blair, *How to Conduct and Analyze Real Estate Market and Feasibility Studies*, 2nd ed. (New York: Van Nostrand Reinhold, 1988), 3.

15. U.S. Department of the Interior, National Park Service, "How to Apply the National Register Criteria for Evaluation," National Register Bulletin (1997): 1.

16. Ibid., 12–21.

17. Jonathan Sandvick, "Important Tools in Building Community through Preservation," paper presented at Cleveland Restoration Society Preservation Conference, Oberlin, Ohio, May 2003.

18. Thomas Bever, *Economic Benefits of Historic Preservation.* Heritage Conservation and Recreation Service (Washington, D.C.: U.S. Dept. of the Interior, 1978), 9.

19. Antonio Gramsci, *Selections from a Prison Notebook* (New York: International, 1971): 52.

20. Duany, Plater-Zyberk, and Speck, *Suburban Nation,* 156.

21. Ibid., 156.

22. Mittie Chandler, Virginia Benson, and Richard Klein, "The Impact of Public Housing: A New Perspective," *Real Estate Issues* 18, no. 1 (Spring 1993): 31.

23. Virginia Benson and Richard Klein, "The Impact of Historic Districting on Property Values," *Appraisal Journal* 56, no. 2 (Apr. 1988): 232.

24. John Lang, "Remains of the Bay," *Preservation* 55, no. 3 (May–June 2003): 37–41.

25. Barrett and Blair, *How to Conduct and Analyze Real Estate Market and Feasibility Studies,* 7.

26. Mike E. Miles, Gayle Berens and Marc A. Weiss, *Real Estate Development: Principles and Processes,* 2nd ed. (Washington, D.C.: Urban Land Institute, 1996), 7.

27. Ibid., 10.

28. Ibid., 11.

29. Laurence Cutler and Sherrie Stephens Cutler, *Recycling Cities for People: The Urban Design Process* (Boston, Mass.: Cahners Books International, 1976), 239–46.

Chapter Eight

Preserve American Culture

Introduction

Early-twentieth-century leaders promoted preservation by equating it with civic responsibility. This strategy remained unchallenged through the 1950s; however, economic and social changes in the 1960s and 1970s encouraged a less paternalistic approach. Preservationists at that time were asked which new strategies might best suit the United States' changing society. Cultural and environmental sustainability became the answer for many.

Culture is totality of socially transmitted behavior patterns, arts, beliefs, and institutions and all other products of human work and thought. It reflects a specific era, distinct social class, and recognized community. It also mirrors a particular mode of expression and is nurtured through education and training. The role of the contemporary preservationist is to save and maintain the United States' best cultural traditions.

Sustainability, a term promoted by the World Commission on Environment and Development in the late 1980s, had first appeared in U.S. parlance twenty-five years earlier.[1] Released in 1962, Rachel Carson's *Silent Spring* provided the movement with valuable new information concerning the degradation of the environment. Specifically, the book discussed the long-term dangers of environmental pollutants. Carson leveled much of her criticism against science and technology, which she claimed had been insulated from public scrutiny after World War II.[2]

Disgusted by urban sprawl, industrial pollution, unsafe drinking water, toxic wastes, and chemical spills, many Americans demanded the environment be cleaned immediately. Advocates saw a direct correlation between the recent destruction of the United States' natural environment, the mindless dissipation of our resources, and the obscene profits made by big business. They argued that effective legal restraints coming from the federal level would prevent this kind of destruction from happening again.

Environmentalists were not against technology or out to destroy the economy. What they wanted was extensive new federal controls and regulations. On April 22, 1970, they made their case, in the first Earth Day celebrations. Founded by Wisconsin Senator Gaylord Nelson, the celebration was intended to inspire awareness of the U.S. environment. More than 20 million participated in the first rallies.[3] The event was a major catalyst for reform. Specifically, it showed the political leadership in Washington, D.C., that there was broad support for the environmental movement. This led to the creation of environmental organizations throughout the country, which in turn pushed for federal intervention. President Richard M. Nixon responded by establishing the Environmental Protection Agency (EPA) in July 1970.[4]

The growing popularity of environmental issues in the late 1960s and early 1970s encouraged many business leaders to initiate their own clean-up campaigns. Two factors prompted these efforts. First, it would promote a healthier work environment, advantageous to business owners because a healthy environment leads to better employee performance. Second, it would facilitate the modernization of distribution and production methods.

Preservation leaders followed these developments with keen interest. They concluded that the new partnerships forged between environmentalists and related fields accounted for much of their success. Through diversity comes strength. Their response was to partner with conservationists and environmentalists. The three groups still work together on important program and policy objectives, many of which represent sensible compromises made with community leaders. These efforts augment sustainability by ensuring that future development will include the best of the past.

Establishing suitable new development in historic districts is crucial, especially in initial redevelopment stages. Ultimately, an effort's success or failure may depend on the willingness of preservationists and other related professionals to set aside their differences and work together. This is not a new idea. What is new is the strong can-do approach taken by many preservation leaders today; they recognize that traditional go-it-alone strategies no longer work. Present-day economic and social uncertainties, prompted in large measure by such things as escalating construction and real estate costs, necessitate increased cooperation. To do otherwise is counterproductive.

Partnering is a formidable challenge.[5] However, preservationists must continue to support cooperative ventures with conservationists and environmentalists.[6] This being said, what are the best ways to sustain these valuable partnerships? Culturally related programming is one viable option. The proliferation of national cultural programs illustrates their effectiveness. This chapter will examine several programs to see how they have enhanced the United States' identity. Although some of them may appear tangential to preservation, they all promote the country's heritage through realistic conservation, environmental, and restoration efforts.

Heritage Tourism: Case Studies

Heritage tourism is a viable new industry advancing cultural identity. If managed properly, it will stimulate economic expansion while enhancing cultural integrity and natural surroundings. This is important for three reasons. First, it sustains the United States' natural and cultural heritage. Second, it encourages local stakeholders to participate in both the planning and development phases. Last, it informs the public of recent developments in the tourist business.

The term "sustainability" implies permanence. Heritage tourism sanctions the full and permanent use of natural and physical resources without negatively impacting the cultural attributes of the district in question. Action such as this affords two direct benefits: it maximizes economic and social advantages district-wide without adversely affecting local cultural identity or customs, and it promotes a new sense of pride through expanded local business opportunities.

Congress sanctioned heritage tourism when it approved the National Heritage Partnership Act in 2006 (Public Law 109–338), establishing districts "where natural, cultural, historic, and recreational resources combine to form a cohesive, nationally distinctive landscape arising from patterns of human activity shaped by geography." More than twenty-five sites have received designation.[7] On these sites, physical remains illustrate distinct patterns of cultural experience and past traditions. Continuity serves to augment this legacy. Districts such as these also enhance existing partnerships among the citizenry, government agencies, nonprofit organizations, and businesses.

The National Park Service administers this program. One of its foremost objectives is to promote citizen pride, educational opportunities, and technical assistance. It also serves as a liaison between sites and federal

Street Scene, St. Augustine, Fla. Heritage tourism promotes sustained economic growth for participating communities while not adversely affecting local culture. This street is filled with tourists who are browsing in the galleries, shopping in the gift shops, and visiting the many local historical sites. Before heritage tourism many of these older districts were deteriorating slums.

agencies. In this capacity, it seeks technical assistance from outside government agencies. And it encourages districts to publicize their designation.[8]

Preservationists increasingly recognize the importance of heritage tourism. Tourists are filling streets, restaurants, hotels, and retail shops in record numbers. The U.S. tourist industry reported record profits, exceeding $495 billion in 1998, nearly half of these dollars were spent in outdoor museums.

Strawbery Banke, in Portsmouth, New Hampshire, is a small outdoor museum that has benefited directly from heritage tourism. Opened in 1965, this ten-acre site near the city's main wharf contains more than forty restored buildings and period gardens. Attendance figures in the 1990s averaged 65,000 visitors annually.[9] Tourists walk around the grounds and participate in a wide variety of hands-on activities related to the history and cultural tradition of that area.

A second example is Old Sturbridge Village. Situated on the David Wight farm in Sturbridge, Massachusetts, Old Sturbridge Village was founded by Albert B. Wells, president and later chairman of American Optical Company in Southbridge, Massachusetts, and antique collector. Wells first displayed his antiques in a small, picturesque building near the center of town. The Wells Historical Museum remained a favorite tourist destination for years. Convinced that visitors could not get enough Americana, Wells proposed creating a nineteenth-century New England village in Sturbridge. He envisioned a place where visitors could tour historic buildings and participate in hands-on activities.

With this goal in mind, he commissioned a well-respected Boston landscape architect, Arthur Shurcliff, to design Old Sturbridge Village.[10] Opened to the public in 1946, this 200-acre site hosts more than 270,000 visitors annually. With assets exceeding $22.5 million, Old Sturbridge Village employs 260 full-time staff members. Although recent attendance figures have dropped in the aftermath of 9/11 and a local recession, the village remains a popular tourist destination. Responding to requests for more hands-on experiences, program coordinators have introduced a number of new activities. They include such things as crafts shows, nature walks, daily demonstrations, and special exhibitions. Samson's Children's Museum was added in 2006.

Shaker Village in Canterbury, New Hampshire, is another popular outdoor site. Known for their communal living and celibacy, the Shakers emigrated from England to America in 1774. The Village of Canterbury was founded in 1792. With twenty-five historic and three reconstructed structures nestled in a 694-acre rural setting, this nonprofit village opened to tourists in 1969. Visitors enjoy touring its buildings, botanical gardens, nature trails, meadows, and ponds.[11] Canterbury flourished during the first half of the nineteenth century. In fact, by 1850, this utopian society contained more than 300 people. Unfortunately, outside economic and social pressures immediately following the Civil War all but destroyed its tranquility. By the early twentieth century, only a handful of Shakers remained, and the village's last resident died in 1992. More than 60,000 tourists visit this site annually; its unique hands-on demonstrations bring many repeat visitors. Guests also eat award-winning Shaker inspired lunches and dinners in a historic dining room, visit the bakery and museum shop, and explore the gardens and trails.

Greenfield Village in Dearborn, Michigan, and Colonial Williamsburg in Williamsburg, Virginia, are two other outstanding heritage tourism destinations. A part of the Henry Ford, a nonprofit educational institution dedicated to celebrating yesterday's traditions and today's innovation, Greenfield Village provides tourists the opportunity of participating in numerous historic events, reenactments, and hands-on demonstrations. These activities occur within historic buildings, farm sites, and workshops on a more than ninety-acre campuslike setting. Over two million people visited this site in 2003.[12]

Colonial Williamsburg is the United States' oldest and largest outdoor museum. More than 100 million tourists have visited this 301-acre site from 1932 to 2006. Like Canterbury Village, Williamsburg was a real community. Once a major cultural and political center, it served as the capital of colonial Virginia. It languished, however, once the state legislature relocated to Richmond in 1780. For the next 150 years, Williamsburg remained a backwater town. However, this changed in the 1920s when Reverend Dr. W. A. R. Goodwin of Bruton Parish Church convinced John D. Rockefeller Jr. to restore several historic structures. From this modest beginning, Williamsburg would become one of the nation's premier tourist destinations.

The Colonial Williamsburg Foundation guides all restoration efforts. This nonprofit organization serves three functions. First, it supervises the main site and nearby landmarks, including the Abby Aldrich Rockefeller Folk Art Museum and Carter's Grove Plantation. Second, the foundation oversees the restoration of historic art, crafts, and paintings. These art pieces often are displayed in various buildings. Last, it offers educational and training programs for history teachers. The Colonial Williamsburg Foundation affords visitors the unique opportunity of experiencing life in a major eighteenth-century city.[13]

Other popular museums in the United States include Plimoth Plantation, Plymouth, Massachusetts; Historic Deerfield, Deerfield, Massachusetts; Hancock Shaker Village, Pittsfield, Massachusetts; Shelburne Museum, Shelburne, Vermont; Mystic Seaport, Mystic, Connecticut; Historic St. Mary's City, St. Mary's City, Maryland; Old Salem, Winston-Salem, North Carolina; Hale Farm and Village, Bath, Ohio; Connor Prairie, Fishers, Indiana; Old World Wisconsin, Eagle, Wisconsin; Living History Farms, Urbandale, Iowa; Stuhr Museum of the Prairie Pioneer, Grand Island, Nebraska; and George Ranch, Richmond, Texas.[14] Although each site has unique cultural and historical traditions, they share one major characteristic: tourists enjoy them all.

Their success is not by chance; they rely on well-trained leaders and staff. John F. Folk and Beverly K. Sheppard, two outspoken leaders in this field, are very much aware of the problems facing heritage museum directors and their staff today. Folk and Sheppard offer several new business and program strategies.[15] These approaches are intended to help these leaders meet the economic and social challenges of the twenty-first century.

One suggestion involves reevaluating museum goals and programs to see whether they really benefit visitors. Recent economic shortfalls have led some site coordinators to emphasize the importance of goods and services, often at the expense of cultural enrichment and public education programs. They believe a happy balance can be maintained between business and tourist needs.

Folk and Sheppard also recommend a more open-ended work environment, in which tourists are welcomed to participate in decision making. Encouraging visitors to become stakeholders will inevitably ensure repeat visits. They further suggest that museum directors and coordinators downplay tourist numbers and instead concentrate on offering a wider variety of quality new experiences. They also propose the adoption of more stringent methods to measure both the quality of programming and the efficiency of delivery services. Present methods often fall short.

Preservationists play an important role in this field. Career opportunities for preservationists will increase significantly as existing museums enlarge and as new ones open. These sites will continue to educate the public about how best to maintain the United States' environmental and physical legacy. The interdisciplinary nature of the preservation field complements these efforts directly. Those preservationists with backgrounds in environmental science and history will enjoy a decided advantage in this emerging job market.

Heritage and Ecotourism

Ecotourism is responsible traveling through natural areas with the expressed idea of conserving the environment while also improving the well being of local residents.[16] It has gained many followers over the past twenty years. Supporters generally subscribe to the following guidelines: minimize environmental impact; respect the built environment; provide positive experiences for host communities and visitors; and offer financial assistance for conservation.[17] Some advocates suggest expanding ecotourism to include participation by all stakeholders. In this instance, participation may give stakeholders the right to refuse cultural tourism if it in any way impinges on their environment or established cultural values.

Two government programs promoting ecotourism are the Transportation Enhancement Program and the National Scenic Byways Program. The former is a direct outgrowth of the Intermodal Surface Transportation Efficiency Act (ISTEA) of 1991 (Public Law 102–240), which finances the majority of highway infrastructure improvements. Unlike earlier legislation which focused on resolving current problems, this program encourages municipalities to experiment with mass transportation, walking paths, bicycle trails, and other systems intended to enhance the public's traveling experience. Since 1992, ISTEA has approved more than 17,000 such projects.[18]

Approved by Congress in 1991, the National Scenic Byways Program is under the auspices of the U.S. Department of Transportation, Federal Highway Administration. Its purpose is simply to preserve historic roads, often in rural areas, and promote tourism on them.[19] Any highway may qualify. The program received a major boost in 2002 when Congress passed the Transportation Equity Act for the Twenty-first Century (TEA-21). This bill provided nearly $25.5 million for the beautification and expansion of scenic roadways. More than 130 highways have received this designation.

These byways possess intrinsic values and features not readily available on other roads.[20] Often, they connect outlying districts and landmarks. Highway sites may range from battlefields and bridges to monuments and canals. Whatever the case, they afford an exceptional travel experience. They also have the advantage of being rated the best by the U.S. secretary of transportation.[21]

Federal officials also encourage the states to promote their own highways. Some emphasize beauty, and others publicize cultural and historic importance. Some advertise the driving adventure, and others promote unique sites. Whatever the approach, state promotions have paid off well: thousands of tourists travel these byways annually.

Ohio has taken full advantage of this exciting program. The Ohio Department of Transportation (ODOT) says it best: "These roads deserve special recognition based on their scenic beauty, natural qualities, historic significance, recreational, or archeological importance."[22] The Buckeye State has designated more than twenty highways.

The Lake Erie Coastal Trail is the latest approved byway. This 293-mile shoreline route runs between Ashtabula, Ohio, and Toledo, Ohio. It boasts numerous historic landmarks and picturesque sites and received national designation in 2005.[23]

Ohio has four other nationally recognized highways: the Amish Country

Byway, the Canal Way Ohio Byway, the Historic National Road, and the Ohio River Scenic Byway. Each offers its own unique history and scenery. The 160-mile Amish Country Byway explores the many charming Amish and Appalachian towns and villages located in rural Holmes County.

The 110-mile Canal Way Ohio Byway affords a very different adventure. It twists and turns through historic Cleveland; the Mill Creek Falls district; the Cleveland Metroparks Zoo; and the Cuyahoga Valley National Park, one of two nationally recognized urban parks. (The other is Golden Gate Park in San Francisco, California.)

The scenic 225-mile Historic National Road (US 40) crosses the entire state. Also known as the Cumberland Road, this nineteenth-century stagecoach route ran from Baltimore, Maryland, to Vandalia, Illinois. Major tourist sites along it include the National Road Museum in Zanesville, the 170-year old Blaine Hill Bridge, Camp Chase Cemetery, and an aptly named statue of a pioneer mother with child, the *Madonna of the Trail.*

The 452-mile Ohio River Scenic Byway weaves through fourteen counties along the Ohio River. Many of its landmarks are related to the Underground Railroad, such as the National Underground Railroad Center, in Cincinnati. Other prominent sites on this scenic byway include the Burriss Store in Mt. Pleasant; and the Rankin House in Ripley.[24]

Maryland is another state dedicated to cultural and historic tourism. Since 1992, the Old Line State has designated more than thirty byways. The Old Ocean City Road, the Underground Railroad Trail, and the Civil War Battlefields Road are three prime examples.

The thirty-two-mile Old Ocean City Road transports travelers back in time, meandering through peaceful pastures, quiet woods, and picturesque villages. With its rambling farm houses, beautiful historic churches, and charming roadside stands, it reminds the tourist of rural life in early-nineteenth-century Maryland.

The Underground Railroad Trail is a far different experience. Running between Dorchester County and Goldsboro, this sixty-four-mile byway served as a major escape route for African Americans prior to the Civil War. Important landmarks include the Bethel African Methodist Church in Cambridge (1870), the Dorchester County Courthouse (1853), and the Underground Railroad Museum and Gift Shop in Cambridge. The old country store located in Bucktown and the historic site of Linchester, one of the oldest settlements in Carolina County, are two other favorite destinations.

The Civil War Battlefields Road is another popular roadway. Winding through Maryland's historic Frederick and Washington counties, this ninety-five-mile trail takes visitors by legendary battle sites such as Emmitsburg, Thurmont, Frederick, Brunswick, Sharpsburg, and Boonsboro. Harpers Ferry National Historic Park and Antietam National Battlefield are other popular nearby tourist destinations.[25]

The Rocky Mountain states also have benefited from this program. For example, New Mexico has more than twenty-five designated byways, among them the Billy the Kid Trail, El Camino Real, Historic Route 66, Jemez Mountain Trail, Santa Fe Trail, and the Turquoise Trail.

The Billy the Kid Trail, for example, is the same path once used by the notorious outlaw to cross the Lincoln National Forest. El Camino Real has the distinction of being the first trail blazed by sixteenth-century Spanish conquistadores as they searched for gold and riches. Crossing hundreds of miles of dangerous and rugged terrain, this picturesque byway connected Old Santa Fe to Mexico City.

Historic Route 66 is a slice of Americana. Once called "America's Main Street," this two-lane road passes adobe ruins, geological sites, mining camps, and glitzy tourist attractions. Cutting through the foothills north of Albuquerque, the Jemez Mountain Trail is an equally impressive adventure. Sightseers travel by Native American ruins, a Pueblo, logging and mining camps, and cattle ranches.

The Santa Fe and Turquoise Trails are the last two of New Mexico's nationally designated byways. The Santa Fe Trail was a major route for nineteenth-century cattle drives, and the Turquoise Trail connected outlying mining camps. Western towns such as Golden, Madrid, and Cerrillos owed their initial economic success to these roadways. Unfortunately, mine closings and new highway bypasses in the 1920s turned these boomtowns into ghost towns. They might have remained in obscurity had it not been for the National Scenic Highway designation, which attracted not only tourists but local artists.[26]

Other states also sustain ecotourism. For example, Massachusetts sponsors canoe trips on Cape Cod, and its northern neighbor New Hampshire advertises hiking adventures in the White Mountains. Arizona, Colorado, Idaho, and Vermont offer skating and cross-country and downhill skiing vacation packages. Florida and Texas promote deep-water fishing excursions and whale-watching trips.

Successful byway programs and state sponsored vacation packages such as these illustrate the growing popularity of ecotourism throughout the United States. Most important, these activities help sustain the United States' physical legacy and natural environment. Both preservation and environmental leaders openly acknowledge their effectiveness.[27]

Increasingly, preservationists are embracing cooperative partnerships with other allied disciplines; these new ventures promote versatile and effective programming for all groups involved, and they help soften the economic blow resulting from recent governmental and philanthropic financial cutbacks. Combining efforts enables participating organizations to accomplish more with less. For example, archeologists have partnered with preservationists; because they study human behavior by examining material remains from previous societies, their work provides preservationists with valuable information. Rural archeological partnerships with the U.S. National Park Service reflect this new cooperative spirit.

Rural Archeology: Case Studies

Protecting the United States' rural heritage through archeology began when Congress approved the American Antiquities Act of 1906 (16 U.S. C431–433). This bill made it a felony to desecrate any national landmark or monument. The creation of the National Park Service in 1916 guaranteed additional protection.[28]

However, the Park Service did not receive any significant federal assistance until 1935. That particular funding package was directed toward archeological digs in the Navajo National Monument in northeast Arizona. Unfortunately, funding was cut off with the outbreak of World War II. It took additional federal support through the Mission 66 program, followed by the National Preservation Act in 1966, the National Environmental Policy Act of 1969 (Public Law 91–190), the Archaeological Resources Protection Act of 1979 (Public Law 96–95), and the Native American Graves and Repatriation Act in 1990 (Public Law 101–601) before archeologists successfully restabilized these sites.[29]

The National Park Service sponsored three rural archeological studies at the Navajo National Monument in the 1950s. Two of them involved the Keet Seel and Betatakin pueblos, and the third investigated the Inscription House wall. All three of these endeavors were part of Mission 66, which began in 1956. With a budget of more than $1 billion, it protected endangered sites throughout the national park system, built park employee housing, and erected new, environmentally friendly visitor centers. It also funded redevelopment at the Navajo Monument.[30]

The end of Mission 66 in 1966 did not stop site activities. In fact, the 1970s witnessed significant advancements in rural archeology at this park. A new breed of well-educated archeologists and park managers pursued three specific goals. First, they sought site preservation and stabilization by minimizing outside destruction, which led to tighter security, stiffer fines, and mandatory prosecution of individuals caught desecrating sites. Second, they rigorously maintained the Inscription House wall and the Keet Seel and Betatakin pueblos. Third, they initiated a major beautification program.

Rural archeology received another major boost when Congress passed the Native American Graves Protection and Repatriation Act of 1990.[31] This bill addressed mounting tribal council concerns over vandalism occurring within sacred burial grounds. The Act gave these councils the authority to secure human remains, sacred funeral objects, and other items illegally seized by federal agencies, museums, or other institutions. It also created a thirty-day moratorium after unearthing sacred artifacts for those groups to determine how they would like to dispose of these items.

Prompted by Federal cutbacks in the 1990s, and bowing to pressure from archeological and preservation groups, the National Park System secured additional funding to stabilize endangered sites. Park officials responded by enforcing the collection of duties owed for mineral, crude oil, and natural gas leasing rights. All duties were set aside to protect sites.

The favorable publicity the park system received for these actions proved invaluable for several reasons. It reinforced in the minds of archeologists the federal commitment to stabilize these sites. It also fostered new pride and respect among Native American tribes. And it established a new management model that other agencies emulated.[32]

At the turn of the twenty-first century, three other Native American heritage programs were introduced: Vision 2020 in Santa Rosa, California; Preservation of Grandmother's Hill in the Poverty Hill district of Tukwila, Washington; and development of the Yellowstone region in Montana, North Dakota, and Wyoming. Vision 2020, a five-year initiative begun in 1996, called for a three-prong approach targeted toward saving their community's cultural and physical legacy. First, city planners divided Santa Rosa and its suburbs into six historic districts. Next, they recorded all the prehistoric and Native American artifacts found in those areas. Finally, they encouraged local property owners to restore their own sites.[33] Generous tax credits and technical services expedited this last step. Vision 2020 proved highly successful. Updated in 2002, it is still one of the most respected preservation programs in the United States today.

In 2001, a group of property owners in Tukwila, Washington, formed a grassroots organization called Friends of the Hill. Its purpose was to save a very popular local tribal site known as Grandmother's Hill. In less than six months, the Friends had received the support of Tukwila city officials, the King County Landmarks Commission, the Duwamish and Muckeshoot Tribes, and the Cascade Land Conservancy.

The alliance with the Cascade Land Conservancy proved especially valuable. In the fall of 2001, the conservancy embarked on a three-year campaign to purchase Grandmother's Hill. Its campaign proved highly successful: it purchased the site and turned it over to the Tukwila City Parks and Recreational Department in 2004. What distinguishes this site from other similarly endangered local landmarks is that it is still mostly wilderness. Local tribal councils are building a cultural enrichment center, hiking trails, and nature stops.[34]

The Yellowstone Heritage Partnership also relied on cultural tourism to promote rural preservation and conservation in its eighteen-county region. It conducted an extensive study in the mid-1990s to discover new ways to improve on existing cultural tourism programs. The resulting fact-finding report was a major breakthrough for this group and led to its present programming.

The study began by offering three reasons why the Yellowstone partnership should embrace cultural tourism more directly: such activity would stimulate local economic growth; second, it would succeed because other similar federally sponsored efforts had worked, and, it would help preserve Native American traditions. It then focused on economic growth potential. The report determined that cultural tourism was essential if the area intended to remain a popular tourist destination in the future. One way to ensure its future growth and success was to include local tribes directly in the decision-making process. Failure to do so would be less than cost-efficient.

The Yellowstone group followed all these recommendations. First, it invited local tribal leaders to join its board as voting members. Second, it hosted a cultural tourism workshop in 1998, during which participants discussed various new ways to expand cultural tourism.[35] Last, it established its own Web site, which provides information and promotional literature worldwide. Positive actions such as these have revitalized cultural tourism throughout North Dakota, Wyoming, and Montana.

Urban Archeology: Case Studies

Archeology also plays a pivotal role in sustaining cultural tourism. No longer confined to excavations of ancient ruins in the Southwest, burial grounds in the West, ceremonial sites in the Northwest, or heritage districts in the North Central United States, archeological digs are occurring

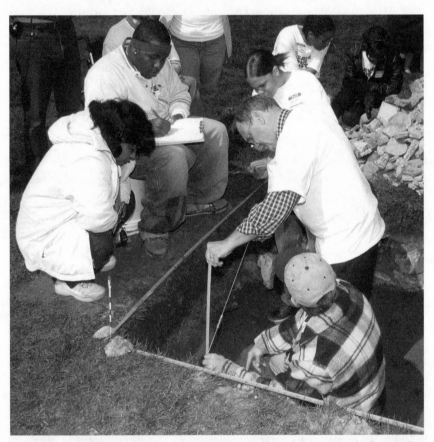

Urban Archeology Dig. Urban archeology is no longer the pastime of a few professionals in remote areas. It appeals to many different groups throughout the nation. Case in point, high school students are excavating a site in their neighborhood as part of a cultural enrichment program.

regularly in major cities throughout the country. Although at first glance urban sites may appear to bear little resemblance to rural areas, their yields are equally significant for two reasons. First, they help explain the evolution of local society by showing how people actually lived. Second, they illustrate past mores, consumer patterns, and personal preferences. Their importance as primary resources has not eluded modern-day preservationists. In fact, as mentioned, preservation advocates are increasingly partnering with archeologists, conservationists, and environmentalists to save the United States' physical legacy.

New York City, Philadelphia, and Detroit have embraced urban archeology since the 1980s. New Yorkers first became interested in archeology when sites in Harlem and the Bronx yielded a wide assortment of pre–Revolutionary War artifacts. Subsequent digs in lower Manhattan unearthed equally significant eighteenth- and nineteenth-century relics. Another excavation conducted at the seventeenth-century Governor Lovelace Tavern site proved especially valuable: household items discovered there including reading glasses, glass stemware, and wine bottles to crockery, smoking pipes, and dishware.

Recent government regulations requiring excavations before major new construction also unearthed important artifacts from old New York City. For example, a freshly discovered African American burial ground provided valuable clues as to how colonial people lived and died. Another dig in the Lower East Side uncovered artifacts dating back to an eighteenth-century Jewish neighborhood. More recent excavations in the Wall Street district produced an assortment of early nineteenth-century drugs and groceries, while another dig conducted in upper Harlem revealed nails, tools, and stone rubble from an abandoned construction pit.[36]

Urban archeology is also active in Philadelphia. As mentioned in chapter 2, Philadelphians first became interested in preservation in the nineteenth century while saving Independence Hall. Urban archeology enhances this interest; for example, a late 1990s dig conducted in Philadelphia's historic market district unearthed valuable nineteenth-century building foundations and artifacts.[37]

Initially established as a wealthy residential neighborhood, this area soon became a leading commercial and industrial center. Its prime location near downtown guaranteed its economic importance. Gradually, however, its majestic houses and tree-lined streets gave way to unremarkable stores, warehouses, and parking lots.

All that remains of this historic market district are two small buildings and a renovated auto center. Recent excavations produced a wide variety of interesting artifacts, which ran the gamut from decorative pottery, tools, medicines, and kitchen utensils to finely crafted leather belts, clothing, jewelry, and German-style beer. They illustrate the vitality of this once proud neighborhood.

In 2002, the Michigan Department of Transportation authorized an excavation in the heart of Detroit's historic East Riverfront district. This dig did not adversely affect the neighborhood. This proved important because many of the structures in this district qualified for the National Register of Historic Places.[38] The East Riverfront site yielded many artifacts, including a number of nineteenth-century building foundations. Household items found included clothing, food remains, handmade utensils, stoneware, and tools. These findings provide us valuable insight into how nineteenth-century Detroit residents lived and worked.[39]

. . .

Preservationists are increasingly partnering with professionals in related fields, such as ecotourism and archeology. All these fields share our common objective: to preserve and sustain the United States' cultural and historic identity. Establishing amicable working relationships with archeologists, business leaders, developers, environmentalists, and government officials has enabled preservationists to attain unprecedented goals. These partnerships will continue to grow as these professions strive for more efficient management of existing resources and greater program diversity.[40]

Notes

1. U.S. Environmental Protection Agency, "What Is Sustainability?" www. epa.gov/sustainability/basicinfo.htm.

2. Stacy J. Silveira, "The American Environmental Movement: Surviving through Diversity," *Boston College Environmental Affairs Law Review* 28, nos. 2–3 (2001): 503–4.

3. Ibid., 507.

4. Reorganization Plan No. 3 of 1970, 35 F.R. 15623,84 Stat. 2086, www.access.gpo.gov/uscode/title5a/5a_4_93.html.

5. Russ Linden, "Learning to Manage Horizontally: The Promise and Challenge of Collaboration," *Public Management* 85, no. 7 (Aug. 2003): 8–11.

6. Storm Cunningham, "Restorative Development: The New Growth Strategy for Communities of All Sizes," *Public Management* 85, no. 7 (Aug. 2003): 4–7.

7. National Park Service, "What Is a National Heritage Area?" www.cr.nps. gov/history/heritageareas/FAQ/INDEX.htm.

8. Ibid.

9. Strawbery Banke Museum, Portsmouth, N.H., www.strawberybanke.org/ museum/history/history.html.

10. Jack Larkin and Mark Ashton, "Celebrating 50 Years of History," *Old Sturbridge Visitor* (Spring–Summer 1996): 4–6, 6–7, www.osv.org/education/OSVVisitors/OSVHistory.html.

11. "Canterbury Shaker Village," www.shakers.org.

12. The Henry Ford, "Greenfield Village," www.hfmgv.org/about/default.asp.

13. Colonial Williamsburg Foundation, "The History of Colonial Williamsburg," www.history.org/Foundation/cwhistory.cfm.

14. Outdoor Museum Forum, "America's Outdoor Museums," www.outdoor history.org.

15. John F. Folk and Beverly K. Sheppard. *Thriving in the Knowledge Age: New Business Models for Museums and Other Cultural Institutions* (Lanham, Md.: AltaMira, 2006).

16. International Council on Monuments and Sites, International Scientific Committee Cultural Tourism. *Eighth Draft of the International Cultural Tourism Charter,* "Managing Tourism at Places of Heritage Significance, Objectives of the Charter" (Oct. 1999), www.icomos.org/tourism/charter.html.

17. International Ecotourism Society, "Ecotourism Definition and Principles" (Washington D.C.: International Ecotourism Society, 2004), 1, www.ecotourism. org/webmodules/webartdesnet/templates/?a=95+Z=2.

18. Intermodal Surface Transportation Efficiency Act of 1991, Pub. Law 102–240, 105, Stat. 1914.

19. U.S. Department of Transportation, TEA-21-Transportation Equity Act for the 21st Century, Moving Americans into the 21st Century-Fact Sheet: National Scenic Byways Program, www.fhwa.dot.gov/TEA21/factsheets/scenic.htm.

20. U.S. Department of Transportation, Federal Highway Administration, "U.S. Transportation Secretary Mineta Names Thirty-Six New National Scenic Byways All-American Roads," June 13, 2002, 1, www.dot.gov/affairs/fhwa2702.htm.

21. Sharon Hurt Davidson, "Branding America's Byways," *Public Roads* 64, no. 6 (May–June 2001): 3, www.tfrc.gov/pubrds/mayjuno1/byways.html.

22. Ohio Department of Transportation, Ohio Byways, www.ohiobyways.com.

23. Molly Kavanaugh, "State's 21st Scenic Byway Hugs Lake," *Cleveland Plain Dealer,* Apr. 20, 2005, Metro section, B3.

24. Ohio Department of Transportation, *Ohio Byways Program,* "Designated Ohio Byway, National Scenic Byway, Amish County Byway," www.ohiobyways. com/AmishCounty1–3.htm; "Designated Ohio Byway, National Scenic Byway, Canal Way Byway," www.ohio; byways.com/CanalWayOhio1–3.htm; "Designated Ohio Byway, National Scenic Byway, Historic National Road," www.ohiobyways.

com/Historic_National_Road_scenic_byway1–3.htm; "Designated Ohio Byway, National Scenic Byway, Ohio River Scenic Byway," www.ohiobyways.com/Ohio River/OhioRiver1–2.htm.

25. National Scenic Byways Program, "Maryland, America's Byways, www.byways. org/explore/states/MD; Maryland, America's Byways, Old Ocean City Road, Maryland, http://www.byways.org/explore/byways/2259; Underground Railroad Trail, Maryland, www.byways.org/explore/byways/2260; Civil War Battlefields, Maryland, www.byways.org/explore/byways/69085.

26. National Scenic Byways Program, "New Mexico, America's Byways," www. byways.org/explore/states/NM; Billy the Kid Trail, New Mexico, www.byways.org/ explore/byways/2062; El Camino Real, New Mexico, www.byways.org/explore/ byways/2065; Historic Route 66, New Mexico, www.byways.org/explore/byways/2489; Jemez Mountain Trail, New Mexico, www.byways.org/explore/byways/2061; Santa Fe Trail, New Mexico, www.byways.org/explore/byways/2287; Turquoise Trail, New Mexico, www.byways.org/explore/byways/2094.

27. "Real Adventures, Incredible Vacations and Great Getaways," Paddle Cape Cod, East Falmouth Massachusetts Ecotour, www.realadventures.com/listing/1021727_ Paddle_Cape_Cod; "New Hampshire Vacations and New Hampshire Travel, New Hampshire Bike Tours and Trips, Bicycling Tours in New Hampshire and Cycling Vacations," www.realadventures.com/new-hampshire.htm?mNextRecord=10.

28. Hal K. Rothman, "The Modern Era," in *Navajo National Monument: A Place and Its People: An Administrative History*. Professional Papers No. 40. Santa Fe, N.M.: National Park Service, Division of History. Southwest Cultural Resources Center, 1991. www.nps.gov/archive/nava/adhi/adhi1a.htm.

29. Rothman, "The Modern Era," National Park Service, *Navajo Administrative History* (1991), www.nps.gov/archive/nava/adhi/adhi5.htm.

30. The Recent Past Preservation Network, "Mission 66, Modern Architecture in the National Parks," www.mission66.com/mission.html.

31. Native American Graves Protection and Repatriation Act of 1990, Pub. Law 601, 101st Cong., 1st sess. (Nov. 16, 1991), www.nathpo.org/News/Sacred-Sites/NewsSacredSites.htm.

32. Rothman, "The Modern Era," and "Archeology at Navajo," in *Navajo Na-tinal Monument*, www.nps.gov/nava/adhi/adhi7e.htm.

33. City of Santa Rosa, Calif., www.ci.santarosa.ca.us/CD/pdf/1–7GP11.

34. Holly Taylor, "April 2004: The Preservation of Grandmother's Hill," *Preser-vation Seattle: Historic Seattle's Online Monthly Preservation Magazine* (Apr. 2004), www. historicseattle.org/preservationseattle/preservationenv/defaultapril2.htm [chap. 8].

35. "Feasibility Study of Cultural Tourism and Economic Development in the Yellowstone Region," Yellowstone Heritage Partnership 1999. Project No. 05–06–02944, www.ywhc.org/index.php?.

36. George Bovenizer and Vikram Sura, "Digging New York City, Dusting Off History," *New York 24 Journal* 7 (2001), www.nyc24.org/2001/issue07/story02/1html.

37. Cultural Resource Group, Louis Berger Group *Buried beneath Philadelphia: The Archaeology of North 7th and Arch Streets* (East Orange, N.J.: Louis Berger and Associates, 1998), 1–2, 4, www.culturalresourcegroup.com/pdf/philadelphia.pdf.

38. Cultural Resource Group, Louis Berger Group, "Urban Archaeology in the City of Detroit," http://culturalresourcegroup.com/projects/detroit.htm.

Chapter Nine

The Future of Historic Preservation

Trends and Careers

Introduction

The historic preservation movement is growing throughout the United States and around the world. The values of conservation and sustainability are very popular for not only their cultural significance but also their contribution to the economic activity of heritage tourism. They also play a significant role in educational advancement by protecting irreplaceable historic resources.

The future of historic preservation opportunities for the historic preservation professionals (HPPs) in the United States will depend on their ability to assess fundamental trends in society. This discussion includes several themes that were explored in previous chapters and are expected to weigh heavily on the future; thus, the authors determined to project some of their potential impacts. Among the issues to be examined are urban sprawl, changing demographics, conservation/preservation cooperation, population mobility, government planning/economic development, legal regulations, preservation organizations, and globalization.

Urban Sprawl

The spreading of metropolitan populations across the landscape is a great concern for planners and preservationists today. Problems occur both at city centers that are losing population and at so-called edge cities, where highways and suburban tracts extend into former agricultural areas.[1] Losses are experienced on both accounts. What is the net effect on historic preservation?

Many endangered landmark buildings remain in the central city, among them magnificent religious structures, unique commercial buildings, and beautiful civic edifices. Adaptive reuse for these threatened buildings must be found before it is too late. Bulldozing older buildings to create parking lots results in the loss of irreplaceable structures and sites.

Adaptation is occurring in many downtown districts throughout the United States as foresighted developers preserve historic warehouses for new offices and apartments. However, some buildings are particularly difficult to modify. Civic structures, for example, often seem inadequate to accommodate the expectations of city officials. Downtown department stores represent an important type of large building that must be reconfigured to compete with commercial big-box retailing in suburban malls. Historic religious landmarks, which populate many inner-city neighborhoods, are an even more complicated category of distressed structures.[2]

Central cities, however, offer a multitude of attractions that enable them to compete with suburbs as places to live and work. Certain civic structures, such as courthouses and government offices, continue to attract professionals who require face-to-face contact in downtown areas. Other important draws include waterfront locations, hotels, museums, theaters, and sports venues. Major historic landmark buildings and historic districts, when appropriately restored, add important components to the charm of downtowns.

Declining city neighborhoods, however, face challenges, such as those by population loss, especially when young families migrate to suburban areas. For many years, the federal government and local banks engaged in redlining poor neighborhoods, which made it difficult or impossible for ethnic minorities living in cities to secure mortgage loans. Consequently, African Americans and other minorities could secure loans only in certain neighborhoods, a practice that ultimately contributed to racial segregation and urban decay. Although redlining is now illegal, the damage has already been done. To offset the inner-city distress, federal officials have developed special programs through the Department of Housing and Urban Development, among them the Community Development Block Grant program. Together with CDBG assistance, some inner-city residents have gathered support to develop historic districts with a focus on the restoration of older homes. In these cases, the residents will generate design guidelines that establish protections for historic properties and ultimately raise property values throughout the neighborhood.[3]

In other parts of the city, absentee landlords allow their properties to deteriorate with the express purpose of paying lower property taxes. One

of the peculiarities of urban real estate property tax is its tendency to pun-
ish those who improve their properties by charging them higher tax rates.
City governments may enforce building codes, but all too often arson fires
destroy crumbling buildings. Occasionally, city officials will take the properties by eminent domain, to clear the site for new development rather
than assist homeowners in restoring their historic homes.

Most municipal leaders deplore urban sprawl. The aftermath of suburbanization may include the loss of a political power base, of economic support for public services, and of civic prestige—along with an array of other
negative consequences. On the other hand, public officials may not wish
to participate in regional planning, since this may also erode their political
power. Incorporated communities that have their own governments surround many cities. These elected officials often resist getting involved with
the city's problems. However, regional or countywide governments have
begun to gain popularity.[4]

HPPs can find opportunities in all of the above circumstances. A groundswell of support for historic preservation among public-, nonprofit-, and
even some private-sector entities may cause it to become an important solution to urban sprawl, affording the newly trained preservation professional
many employment opportunities.

A city may encourage historic districting and landmark status for its
buildings, realizing the appeal of such structures for tourists as well as
citizens. Its suburbs, conversely, may want to create a small-town identity
for themselves. This will lead them to recognize their own older historic
commercial areas and begin preservation movements for such centers. In
many metropolitan areas, urban sprawl has swallowed up small towns that
have their own historic identities, which attract residential development.
Large cities in the eastern half of the United States often encounter this
phenomenon. These small towns may offer excellent career potential for
innovative HPPs, who may apply for positions as zoning administrators
civic planners or may find other small-town leadership roles.

Trends

As long as real estate development cartel (developers, banks, real estate
agents, building contractors, and land owners) continues to support suburban subdivisions and public-sector (federal, state and local governments)
and nonprofit pressure groups are unable or unwilling to forestall it, sprawl
will continue. Although a few states intervene with growth boundaries—

such as green belts that circle the built-up urban area and prevent expansion, as in Oregon and Maryland—the HPP should be aware that most continue to push for expansion and unlimited development.

Technological advances may affect this configuration in a number of distinct ways. For example, many futurists expect that in the near future the daily commute to the city will become a thing of the past and that telecommunications will enable most people to spend their work time at home.[5] In such circumstances, cities may function as cultural artifacts and entertainment centers rather than workplaces. In contrast, the HPP should be prepared to live in a world of inertia, political pressures, face-to-face contacts, and many other personal and economic commitments. Such pressures will make it difficult to leave particular geographic areas.

The HPP also needs to understand the many motivations within the real estate development process itself and to work with those striving to achieve preservation goals both in cities and suburbs. There are at least two sides to every story: HPPs should be prepared to argue the costs and benefits of residing in the city and also to recognize the various factors that lead to suburbanization. At the same time, they should remember that some suburban or small-town officials will hire HPPs to assist them in the planning and development of identifiable centers around their own historic commercial buildings.

Demographic Changes

As most people recognize, the U.S. population is constantly changing. Major characteristics of this evolution are the following: aging of the population, changing racial and ethnic mix of the population, and increasing immigration.[6] How will these transformations affect the field of historic preservation?

The current aging of the general population indicates that more people are entering retirement. Due to greater longevity and falling birth rates, the average age of Americans is rising. The oldest baby boomers entered their seventh decade in 2006. This significant demographic shift will affect many features of U.S. society, including the real estate field and, consequently, historic preservation.

For example, retirement may lead older people to move from the Frostbelt to the Sunbelt. This trend, begun in the 1950s following the invention of air conditioning, will be further stimulated by demographic circumstances. For some, the desire to escape harsh winter weather will be encouragement to purchase second houses or condominiums in a warmer climate while maintaining their original northern residences. These decisions often correlate directly with age categories devised by demographers: young-old, medium-old or old-old.[7] Health considerations also play an important part in these decisions: older parents may move to the Sunbelt for a limited period of time only to return to the northern states and their families and friends when they are unable to care for themselves.[8]

Retirees may leave older sections of the city as they scale down their housing, moving from larger to smaller homes or opting for condominium living or retirement communities. All of these choices affect historic areas and may afford new opportunities to repopulate neighborhoods with young families or find new uses for commercial structures. Loft apartments in warehouse districts, for example, often appeal to empty nesters who want freedom from home maintenance.

A second transformation occurring within the U.S. population involves the assimilation of various ethnic and racial groups. Adjustments to new populations are occurring across the nation; increasing numbers of Latinos, Asians, Africans, and others are substantially altering the makeup of the U.S. population, which for several centuries was largely of European origin. Cultural transformations such as these change the expectations of citizens in numerous ways, among them language, dress, food, music, to name only a few. One particular example involves the variations in worship: new congregations now occupy sacred landmarks once dedicated to other religious traditions. The art and architectural manifestations of various cultures are evident in sacred landmarks throughout the United States.[9]

But not everyone respects historic structures; some find them offensive. In 2001, for example, the Taliban destroyed two statues of Buddha built during the sixth century in Afghanistan. Religious leaders said the statues were idolatrous and should be obliterated. Another example occurred in a Cleveland suburb in 1992. The suburb, once populated predominantly by whites, now had a black majority. An African American city council member said that the early-twentieth-century Georgian colonial high school reminded him of slavery. Some residents tried to save the building, but city officials ended up razing it. These scenarios illustrate part of the preservationist's problem: understanding and respecting people and cultural changes while preserving artifacts, architecture, and monuments. The HPP must remain well informed to make persuasive and rational arguments and to demonstrate that historical landmarks are worth preserving.[10]

In addition to the spreading of the metropolitan areas, this population mix has undergone other modifications. In some states, segregation of groups by age and income has resulted in a landscape of homogeneity rather than diversity. Developers who clear large tracts of land and build housing subdivisions that include only dwellings generally in the same price level perpetuate this pattern. The argument that economies of scale produce better houses for lower prices is specious at best, particularly when housing prices are rising in most areas.

However, not everyone wants such segregation. In fact, a growing number of Americans are looking for a lifestyle that includes contact with a wide variety of people. This may lead them back to the central city or a small-town melting pot.[11] Most people wishing to live in areas free of crime are demanding defensible space.[12] Thus, historic districts in the city must be made secure; this is being achieved through community policing and block watch programs.

The HPP should be familiar with diverse populations and their preferences. Two attractions of historic districts are the intimate scale of the area and district architecture. Often this architecture is associated with some particular ethnic settlement, even after the original group that constructed it is no longer in the neighborhood. Many quality-of-life variables correspond to historic preservation and should be part of the HPP's knowledge base.[13] Just as professional real estate agents are, HPPs must be prepared to enthusiastically market historic areas and buildings.

Trends

One might expect a continuation of demographic patterns already suggested. As new retirees, for example, choose where to spend their golden years, many wish to continue living in their own homes. This may require restoration of their properties, which will cause them to seek the assistance of preservation-sensitive professionals. In some cases, state or local governments might offer tax incentives to homeowners who restore their residences.

As the ethnic and racial makeup of the United States changes, there will be new opportunities to support historic commemorations of past events. In addition to monuments and battlefields, these might include recognition of Underground Railroad stops, noted former Spanish missions, and Native American sites. Archaeology is an important allied field that is attracting new audiences through targeted media presentations.[14] Halls of fame, museums, and restored historic towns have sprung up across the United States, engendering great support from government officials as well as the general public. (Chapter 8 discusses this phenomenon in detail.) Each of these examples creates a career opportunity for the well-trained preservation professional.

Globalization means, among other things, the movement of various ethnic groups into and out of the United States. Immigration might be expected to continue unabated, since the United States is an attractive place for employment, education, and quality of life. Immigrants arrive with their own cultures and architectural styles; therefore, members of these groups who want to preserve the places where they settle will need assistance in maintaining their neighborhoods' original cultural ties and distinctions as they add their own. The Spanish and Native American societies found in the Southwest represent one example, and various Asian societies are another. The study of worldwide arts and cultures enables HPPs to reach out to these new populations.

Conservation/Preservation Cooperation

Public interest in conserving the nation's natural environment flourished throughout the twentieth century. Some high points in this phenomenon occurred concurrently with the historic preservation movement; for example, the century began with a number of national park designations (although Yellowstone and Yosemite were set aside in the late-nineteenth century). This great fascination with protecting natural wonders in the American West spread across the entire country. An expansion of historic archaeology—excavations ranging from indigenous burial mounds in Ohio and Florida to aboriginal caves in the Southwest—served to protect Native American artifacts.

By the mid-twentieth century, conservationists and preservationists were working together on San Antonio's river restoration project, various other urban waterfronts, heritage river corridors and scenic rivers.[15] The importance of cleaning the water and greening the landscape inspired environmental conservationists and preservationists alike: since most urban areas originated along waterfronts, oceans, rivers and lakes, areas adjacent to bodies of water are often sites of the earliest structures.

Over time, preservationists became aware of the damage to historic structures inflicted by air and water pollution—acid rain had a particularly deleterious effect on building materials, particularly cemetery monuments, for example. Environmentalists concurrently expressed concern about the relentless damage caused by both suburban sprawl and new highway construction through historic neighborhoods.

At the same time, these two movements possess distinct differences. Where preservationists primarily concern themselves with buildings and man-made artifacts, environmentalists usually focus on the natural landscape untouched by human habitation. In the latter case, the conservation of animal habitats often takes precedence over human occupancy of historic structures.

Sadly, the environmental movement is fragmented nationally and worldwide. Celebrating Earth Day has not brought the environmental advocates together promoting a common strategy. The movement now runs the gamut from the benevolent protection of animals (People for the Ethical Treatment of Animals) to the destructive arson protests of housing construction (Earth Liberation Front). It also includes broadly supported public policies and government programs such as the Environmental Protection Agency.[16] The historic preservation movement differs from the environmental movement in that it concentrates its attention on preserving human artifacts and cultural objects exclusively.

However, the two interest groups find much common ground, especially in metropolitan areas. The idea of green building is compatible with saving historic structures. It involves conservation of materials by efficient resource allocation and use of less-polluting fuels. All of these efforts must be understood by the HPP. Where common interests are apparent, every effort should be made to find ways to partner with groups that have similar goals.

Starting in the 1990s, the concept of sustainability has been sweeping across the United States. Since the closing of the Western frontier, many citizens have focused their careers on a society whose artifacts are disposable and which caused suburban sprawl and the ravaging of natural resources and landscapes. They are now conscious of fouling the nest where they live. An awareness of this situation has prompted a natural alliance between those wishing to preserve the nation's natural environment (conservationists) and those who wish to save the nation's built environment (historic preservationists).[17]

Sustainability is much more than a buzzword. The public increasingly commends efforts to renovate old buildings with new, green systems.[18] These projects combining all three economic sectors result in public/private partnerships often assisted by prominent nonprofit organizations. Careers that meld historic preservation and environmental sustainability are found throughout the United States. The HPP must be prepared to identify common interests. They also must find ways to support each other and work together to maintain a sustainable habitat.

Trends

Combining preservation and conservation should increase the potency of both movements and should be expected to grow in applications. Urban sprawl will continue as long as government intervention in the private real estate market is limited to such things as natural disasters. The only exceptions are in a few states that have exerted land-use controls around their largest cities. Although conservationists and preservationists alike admire the regulatory efforts in place in Maryland and Oregon, each of these states has only one dominant city, which makes implementation and enforcement easier. Most cities and states can expect to struggle with sprawl and the issues described above far into the future.

Farmland conservation, involving both land and farmsteads, is an increasing concern for preservationists and environmentalists.[19] Extension of water and sewer lines, electricity, highways and other public services will continue to consume agricultural lands and intrude on natural environments and small towns within reach of metropolitan areas. Many cities are surrounded by a ring of redundant land held in suspension by farmers awaiting offers from suburban developers.

Another current dispute in the United States concerns the situating of cell-phone towers. Both preservationists and conservationists eschew the loss of beautiful landscape vistas to the forest of towers, poles, and wires transmitting modern communication. In a similar mode, wind farms, filled with windmills, though renewable energy sources, have led to more debates among those who value scenery and worry about the bird population.[20]

Both groups also fight big-box retailing. These retailers with their oceans of asphalt cut off natural water absorption and increase runoff. At the same time, they often destroy the economic vitality of small community downtowns, leaving vacancies in historic ensembles of buildings. Many other instances of cooperative efforts can be expected to occur. HPPs should broaden their knowledge of these related fields and look for common ground in order to effectively address these problems.

Mobility

Americans are on the move.[21] In spite of the many costs involved, the popularity and freedom of the open road beckons to people across the continent Some transfer their residences frequently: the average household moves once every five years.[22]

This constant mobility affects historic preservation in a number of ways, both positively and negatively. Potential homeowners may be attracted to places with a sense of identity and seek out historic neighborhoods and towns. Currently, more historic buildings are being adapted into apartments and condos than ever before. This increases public interest. In some cases, historic structures are more appreciated by new residents than by their predecessors. For those people whose neighborhoods are being gentrified by affluent newcomers, preservation may prompt increasing property taxes and cause consequent displacement. Although this predicament is less obvious in U.S. cities where recent population declines have emptied older neighborhoods, in growing places, the problem is real.[23]

HPPs must understand and predict population mobility in their targeted areas. Comprehending population dynamics will greatly influence their ability to practice their profession. Reasons for mobility vary. Some households move based on life-cycle stages, such as marriage, children, divorce, retirement, employment, and other important phases.[24] Some households relocate due to climate, school districts, or simply for a change of scenery, and others move to flee areas with high crime rates, air pollution, noise, traffic, and a myriad of other unpleasant factors. Predicting mobility is difficult since Americans expect privacy and the right to change addresses without notifying anyone, except, perhaps, the post office.

The HPP may rely on census materials or local public records to predict mobility. Local universities and colleges often help in this pursuit. Real estate associations and chambers of commerce also may provide useful data on population movements and shifts.

Trends

Given constant improvements in mobility and in spite of widespread predictions of the "electronic cottage" (i.e., working from home via computer), the American propensity to move appears long-lasting. Innovations in transportation and in energy production are currently extremely critical issues. Predicting mobility has been a fundamental goal of scholarly research for many decades.[25] The real estate field is particularly interested in this research, since its success depends on predicting space demand.

Several macro trends have been noted, such as movement to the Sunbelt from northern states. As the U.S. population ages, this movement will continue. The attraction to coastal locations and the willingness of many to pay higher prices for waterfront locations is evident along the East, West, Gulf, and Great Lakes coasts and on many other waterfront sites. Whatever problems are associated with these sites (flooding, landslides, hurricanes, storm damage) the demand continues.

The most appealing building sites for the preservationist may be occupied by historic structures that developers are pressuring either to be moved to less desirable sites or completely demolished in favor of new high-rise buildings. Keeping landmark buildings on their original sites is always preferable, although many fine old structures have been moved to new locations. Museum towns are often the recipients of such buildings.

Suburbanization is expected to continue, as is ex-urbanization, which is occurring in many parts of the United States, the thinking being "as long as we can move, we will move." Historic preservation is an important factor in the back-to-the-city movement that is taking place in some urban areas. City planners usually favor it, in some areas promoting smart growth strategies (e.g., eliminating waste, building green structures, discovering new ways to use energy, etc.).[26]

Planning/Economic Development

City-, state-, and federal-level planners acquired many tools to perform their jobs over the past century. One such device is the regulations governing geographical zoning of land. These laws evolved over time. In the early part of the twentieth century, cities were plagued with many health problems, industrial pollution, noise, soot, and other grievances. The solution to these complaints was sectioning the landscape into categories of compatible use. However, some planners surmise that over time the zoning solution might cause unforeseen consequences that create new problems.

Zoning, for example, separates residential land from workplaces and commercial developments. This, in turn, causes additional roads to be built at great expense. Traffic problems ensue along with all the other landscape horrors outlined in Kunstler's *Geography of Nowhere*.[27]

Zoning also separates households by demographic characteristics such as race, ethnicity, age, and income. These divisions often raise sensitive issues pertaining to segregation and inequality. Schooling, community services, and property taxation are perceived as inequitably divided. Zoning variances become commonplace as communities look for other ways to plan their landscapes. Recently, with the advent of mixed-use zoning many planners have come to agree that existing categories must be modified. Historic districts, built before zoning, are conducive to this change and offer an opportunity to create a more livable landscape.

Urban design and large-scale physical planning are currently viable solutions. Rather than dividing the landscape into recognizable zones, urban design brings together a variety of human needs in one comprehensive plan, which includes transportation, open space, street furnishings, and other relevant aspects based on accepted design guidelines. These generally focus on particular goals—such as public access, setback requirements, sign limitations and building heights; unlike traditional zoning, they often favor mixed-use spaces where people may walk to work or even live above the store.

Historic preservationists can work hand-in-hand with urban designers wishing to preserve their community through New Urbanist designs. Although many examples of New Urbanism reflect new construction, such as Seaside and Celebration, both in Florida, the melding of historic districts and New Urbanist concepts is occurring in many older cities and small towns throughout the United States in traditional neighborhood developments.

In an effort to counter urban sprawl, these developments are located within built-up areas. They accommodate those wishing to walk to various locations in their neighborhoods rather than rely on automobiles or public transportation. Sidewalks, front porches, and garages in alleys behind houses often characterize this popular trend. Mixed-use zoning also allows residents to live above retail stores or offices. One argument favoring New Urbanism is that it promotes health by encouraging residents to walk or bicycle to their destinations.

While all these changes are taking place, so is another. Cities no longer unconditionally accept the plans by professional city planners. They also want input from economic development professionals, hired to attract new businesses, which will assume some of the community's tax burden and provide new jobs. Although city planners and preservationists often have similar urban design goals, economic development professionals' goals are quite different. They often conflict directly with preservationists. For example, in this era of New Urbanism and traditional neighborhood development, they may favor big-box retailing or large-scale shopping centers instead of smaller-scale retailing. They are often unconcerned about the impact of the large asphalt parking lots required by major retailing complexes.

One of the foremost weapons employed by economic developers is the right to take private property by eminent domain. It is worth noting that the impact on historic properties may be very destructive. The controversy over the use of eminent domain for the purposes of economic development persists and will continue to affect historic preservation for the foreseeable future.[28]

Lest one conclude that economic development is a spoiler, it must be noted that full employment is a worthy goal and crucial for the health of all metropolitan areas. Business and industries provide the necessary tax base to support critical services and often sustain the arts and cultural endowment of a community. Most preservation organizations depend on the contributions of these economic activities. Therefore, the critical negotiations that accompany any land-use decisions fall on those who strive to perpetuate a "quality" environment.

Trends

Zoning ordinances will change as local conditions evolve. New and growing populations also will have diverse expectations. New Urbanism is an expanding movement that encourages mixed-use zoning. Most of the initial factors behind zoning, such as noise, air pollution, odors, and other noxious conditions are no longer acceptable anywhere. Most communities welcome pristine office and industrial parks, but not the extra vehicles; however, the traffic will not be zoned out any time soon.

It is advantageous for HPPs to become familiar with local zoning regulations and variances and how to bring about needed changes in the interest of preservation. A study of New Urbanism affords practical ideas for infill development that will inevitably occur in historic districts.

Economic development will continue to be controversial, especially for the American preservation movement. "Chasing smokestacks," a popular tactic in the past, resulted in many industries moving from state to state in search of lower taxes and cheaper labor. For community leaders it is very tempting to endorse every new business proposal, often to the detriment of historic structures that get in the way of progress. Certain land uses require large tracts of land, sheets of asphalt (due to local parking regulations), and central locations with either high visibility or highway access. The HPP may need assistance from state or federal agencies or preservation organizations to prevent unwanted new projects. The competent strategist will succeed.

Legal Regulations

A significant phenomenon limiting the ability of some preservationists to perform their responsibilities is the rise in government regulations and litigation. In addition to zoning, these often well-intentioned regulations fall into several categories, which vary across the country. Health regulations, safety laws, labor contracts, and building codes are among the many official edicts to enjoin preservationists to fear personal injury litigators and to provide a morass of decrees that may halt preservation projects.[29]

While acknowledging the significance of government protections, it is also important to note their sweeping impact on historic preservation efforts. One example is the Americans with Disabilities Act, which regulates accessibility to those buildings with stairs at their entrances or that are at least two stories high. The expense of installing elevators to accommodate everyone often makes preservation economically infeasible. However, certain preservation architects are very skillful at finding ways to adapt to such regulations, and some states permit building-code adjustments that satisfy these legal obligations.

Another example of how these protections affect preservation efforts concerns the legal requirement that developers pay contractors the prevailing wage. Since preservation projects entail specialized carpentry and other skilled labor often provided by volunteers, this requirement might prevent many outstanding preservation projects from occurring. Additionally, health regulations, notably in the form of asbestos litigation, have terminated some preservation efforts. Modern ideas of public safety—including dangerous fire escapes, slippery floors, staircases, unfenced balconies and various other widely accepted risks—have become obstacles to saving many old buildings.

Trends

The United States has been called a highly litigious nation, and regulation and litigation will, in all probability, continue. For this reason, most nonprofit preservation organizations include attorneys on their boards. It is wise for HPPs to avoid legal situations that compromise their work, although sometimes it is impossible. Real estate transactions require a firm under-standing of the legal ramifications of preservation projects, hence the focus of earlier chapters. Keeping abreast of the latest court decisions favoring preservation is invaluable. At times the HPP may assist public officials in crafting legislation beneficial to historic properties. Regulations can work for preservation as well as against it.

Impact of Preservation Organizations

Chapter Five addressed the nonprofit sector and several examples of this type of preservation organization. Nonprofits in the United States and nongovernmental organizations (NGOs) worldwide address long-term issues without the concerns of either profit making or voter approval.[30] In the case of American preservation, state and local activities are greatly enhanced by such developments.

Preservation organizations require leadership training. Colleges and universities reflect this need, offering large numbers of master's degrees in business and public administration. The preservation field often involves local government officials and statewide bureaucracies in which the well-educated HPP may find a productive niche.

The impact of preservation organizations in the past century cannot be denied. This movement is growing internationally with the help of such pro-grams as UNESCO, which assembles the World Heritage List. Through the World Wide Web, the world is kept abreast of which of the valued prop-erties and sites on this list may be endangered. Also, many countries have concluded that heritage tourism is their best economic development tool. Conferences on the topic regularly take place throughout the world.[31]

Technology has vastly improved the ability to communicate the preser-vation message. The inclination to differentiate historic spaces into various districts has a new voice; Web pages and Web logs (blogs) can be used to dis-seminate the preservation message along with other real estate information.[32]

The practical value of nonprofit organizations is an asset recognized by those wishing to develop real estate, especially historic projects. Nonprof-its provide both information and public support. Their leaders successfully lobby government agencies and recommend quality contractors and archi-tects; some organizations will even provide investment capital; others offer tours of historic structures and districts.

In its ongoing role as a spokesman for preservation, the nonprofit orga-nization has access to information that others may miss. It also may serve as a repository for studies of the community, including inventories of buildings and historical research. Its staff may attend public meetings where information is exchanged. It also may have a voice in other organizational meetings or provide special access to local government and private decision-makers.

The general public usually trusts charitable nonprofits. This trust often translates into public support at the ballot box or public donations for specific projects. Well-managed nonprofit organizations also may influence local media to endorse the preservation message.

Nonprofit organizations lobby local, state, and federal government officials on behalf of historic preservation. Whatever support preservation has won, it has been the direct result of hard-fought battles successfully waged by nonprofit organizations. It is unimaginable that many twentieth-century legislative preservation accomplishments would have taken place without the important role played by such nonprofits as the National Trust for Historic Preservation and state and local organizations.

Architects, developers, and building contractors working in preservation tend to join local preservation organizations as members or become their trustees. They aid the organizations by offering voluntary assistance in preservation projects and expert advice. Their involvement often benefits both the cause and their own businesses. Making specific recommendations of contractors, however, is generally discouraged: the nonprofit must carefully avoid conflicts of interest.

Not all nonprofit preservation organizations deal with real estate. However, many preservationists participate with revolving funds, in which they buy, restore, and sell historic properties. In fact, some are major property owners who operate museum towns (such as Williamsburg, Virginia), house museums, or landmark sites. Nonprofit preservation organizations may also make deals optioning real estate to hold it for future preservation. Some preservation organizations have received neglected properties through the court system, retained these landmarks and restored them.

Nonprofit organizations also promote heritage tourism. Sponsoring historic tours offers the public, and potential investors, the occasion to identify interesting structures and sites that may reap further benefits for the community. Many preservation organizations offer a regular series of historic tours designed to educate and entertain the public, offering the community an opportunity to learn about itself and creating both community pride and social cohesion.

Trends

The nonprofit sector's ability to fill the gap between the public and private sectors is widely appreciated. Hence, it is expected that this phenomenon will continue. Historic preservation organizations are of fairly recent vintage. Small towns and city neighborhoods provide new opportunities for their creation, and many older suburbs are expressing interest in historic preservation especially as post–World War II residences qualify for the National Register's official fifty-year-old historic category. Given all the potential responsibilities mentioned here, it is expected that the nonprofit preservation organization will continue to grow, far into the future.

Historic preservation often falls into the category of arts and culture. This classification resulted from the fact that it depicts historical periods of settlement, features quality materials and excellent workmanship, and provides interesting educational opportunities. For those reasons, people who wish to leave a legacy of goodwill and philanthropy to those who follow them tend to support the preservation field. Many historic monuments and outstanding buildings are saved by such personal commitment. Searching the various local archives for historical evidence to support the National Register of Historic Places nominations makes the researcher a major contributor toward the public understanding of the history of particular places.

The Impact of Globalization

Wrapping up this discussion of historic preservation careers needs to go beyond the United States alone. Throughout the world, preservation organizations are forming and governments are discovering the importance of heritage resources in promoting their citizens' quality of life and the potential benefits to their economies. For the trained HPP, career opportunities abound in many countries.

Twenty-first century preservation has roots in a multitude of nations around the world. Given current electronic communication technology, it is possible to share the accomplishments of preservation organizations globally.

In 2001, the World Bank published a book entitled *Historic Cities and Sacred Sites: Cultural Roots for Urban Futures.*[33] This collection of essays spans the globe, describing preservation efforts from Bergen, Norway, to Tampico, Mexico. Although the focus of the book is on cultural heritage, historic structures are a critical component of cultural preservation. The book

North American Streetscape. As seen in this streetscape, a thoughtful blending of archaic and historic buildings for modern needs makes sense both aesthetically and economically. Photo by V. Benson.

emphasizes several themes mentioned in this volume, among them cultural heritage tourism, sustainable development, and sacred landmark preservation. These are worldwide concerns. The HPP may consider globalization as offering a chance to practice the profession in any sphere.

Worldwide Historic Cities

Bergen, Norway

The oldest section of this Northern European seaport city is called Bryggen. It dates from 1070 A.D. Given the great age of the historic structures around the port, the Norwegian government is actively protecting them. It is a popular tourist location in the summer, when its historic public markets bring large crowds to the waterfront site.[34]

Tampico, Mexico

Settled in the twentieth century, this gulf port town boasts several historic sites including its beautifully restored customs house. Many communities in Mexico, especially those in the Yucatán Peninsula, cater to tourists interested in Mayan artifacts and historical monuments.[35]

Quebec City, Quebec, Canada

One of the oldest cities in North America, complete with a walled city, Quebec City appeals to many visitors. Overlooking the Gulf of St. Lawrence, its Laval University was the original host of an international conference on preserving sacred landmarks. During a second conference in 2005, many European scholars described the preservation challenges in finding adaptive re-uses for these magnificent structures.[36]

Trends

As travel prospects increase, the HPP may find new career opportunities in many parts of the world. Japan, for example, is noted for its unique methods of historic building restoration.[37] Brazil has initiated a sustainable preservation strategy that educates the public on the importance of historic properties.[38] The English language is spoken in countries throughout the world. Apprehension about homogenization and cookie-cutter designs may elicit a negative reaction from influential foreign leaders who wish to retain their cultural distinctions.

Change is occurring in communities and countrysides everywhere. Urbanization, immigration and population growth positively affect many areas while decay and deterioration are evident at the same time. Desire for high economic returns on properties and a myriad of other pressures make the field of historic preservation very contentious—it is not a career for the faint of heart. However, the overpowering satisfaction of rescuing cultural heritage and patrimony, of preserving and sustaining irreplaceable works of art and architecture is a profession worth the sacrifice.

Concluding Remarks

This book is designed to fill a void. The practice of historic preservation has for too long been the private preserve of architecture and related disciplines. These authors believe that the time has come to broaden the scope of preservation and to prepare the enthusiast for a career in this essential field, a career that will have enduring consequences. Architecture and design, of course, provide a useful background. The preservationist will quickly learn that a study of those disciplines is an important component of a broad education for the HPP. However, the HPP may be able to make creative use of many other educational backgrounds, as well.

To be successful, the HPP must possess many skills and abilities. Some of these have been outlined in previous chapters. Others may wish to add to the enumeration of significant competencies. A number of leaders in the historic preservation field have been identified with various formal educational experiences. People with leadership ability bring talent from a variety of academic fields such as English, art history, urban studies, planning, geography, archaeology, law, and real estate development. Some of the most effective past leaders possessed little or no formal preservation training; however, they had great enthusiasm and enough investment resources to make their major contributions to the profession.

It is the authors' intent to recognize the valuable contributions from the past while suggesting a promising preservation passageway for the future. The book suggests certifying a new generation of historic preservation professionals who will spread the preservation message throughout the United States and abroad.

Notes

1. Joel Garreau, *Edge City: Life on the New Frontier* (New York: Anchor Books, 1991).

2. Lucie K. Morisset, Luc Noppen, and Thomas Coomans, eds., *Quel Avenir Pour Quelles Églises? What Future for Which Churches?* (Montreal, Québec: Presses de L'Université du Québec, 2006).

3. Virginia Benson and Richard Klein, "The Impact of Historic Districting on Property Values," *Appraisal Journal* 56, no. 2 (1988): 223–32.

4. David Rusk, *Inside Game, Outside Game: Winning Strategies for Saving Urban America* (Washington, D.C.: Brookings Institution Press, 1999).

5. William J. Mitchell, *City of Bits: Space, Place and the Infobahn* (Cambridge: MIT Press, 1995), 3.

6. "USA 2000: More People, More Diversity," *State Legislatures* 27, no. 5 (2001): 5, 1; Roger Daniels, *Guarding the Golden Door: American Immigration Policy and Immigrants since 1882* (New York: Hill & Wang, 2004).

7. Cary S. Kart and Jennifer McKinney, *The Realities of Aging: An Introduction to Gerontology* (New York: Allyn & Bacon, 2000).

8. Ibid., 420.

9. Stephen Steinberg, ed., *Race and Ethnicity in the United States: Issues and Debates.* (Malden, Mass.: Blackwell Pub., 2000).

10. Ismael Serageldin, Ephim Shluger, and Joan Martin-Brown, eds., *Historic Cities and Sacred Sites: Cultural Roots for Urban Futures* (Washington, D.C.: World Bank, 2000), xiv.

11. Robert Lindsey, "Middle Class Interest in Older Housing Presses Poor." *Readings in Historic Preservation: Why? What? How?* (New Brunswick, N.J.: Rutgers Univ. Press, 1983), 296.

12. Roger Daniels, Guarding the Golden Door: American Immigration Policy and Immigrants since 1882 (New York: Hill & Wand, 2004), 10; Oscar Lewis, "Defensible Space: A New Physical Planning Tool for Urban Revitalization," *Journal of the American Planning Association* 61, no. 2 (Spring 1995).

13. Mark A. Rapley, *Quality of Life Research: A Critical Introduction* (London: Sage, 2003).

14. Mark Seeman, *Cultural Variability in Context: Woodland Settlements of the Mid-Ohio Valley*, Special Paper for *Mid-Continental Journal of Archaeology*, 7 (Kent, Ohio: Kent State Univ. Press, 1992).

15. Ann Breen and Richard Rigby, *The New Waterfront: A Worldwide Urban Success Story* (London: Thames and Hudson, 1996).

16. "The Environmental Movement: Endangered Species," *Economist* (Feb. 18–24, 2006): 32–33.

17. JoAnn Kwong, "Farmland Preservation," in *Urban Land* 46 (Jan. 1987), 21–23.

18. Sanda Kaufman, "The City Protects Itself," in *Introduction to Urban Studies*, ed. Roberta Steinbacher and Virginia Benson, 3rd ed. (Dubuque, Iowa: Kendall-Hunt, 2006), 143–72.

19. Kwong, "Farmland Preservation," *Urban Land*, 21.

20. Salvatore DeLuca, "Tilting at Windmills," *Preservation* 58, no. 3 (May–June, 2006): 12–13.

21. Leszek A. Kosinski and R. Mansell Prothero, eds., *People on the Move: Studies on Internal Migration* (London: Methuen, 1975).

22. James Kunstler. *Geography of Nowhere: The Rise and Decline of America's Manmade Landscape* (New York: Touchstone, 1993).

23. W. Dennis Keating, "The City Looks Ahead," in Steinbacher and Benson, *Introduction to Urban Studies*, 89–102.

24. Peter H. Rossi, *Why Families Move* (Glencoe, Ill.: Free Press, 1955).

25. Kosinski and Prothero, *People on the Move*, 12.

26. Keating, in Steinbacher and Benson, eds., *Introduction to Urban Studies*, 89–102.

27. Kunstler, *Geography of Nowhere*, 86.

28. Sammis White, Richard Bingham, and Edward Hill, eds., *Financing Economic Development in the Twenty-first Century* (London: M. E. Sharpe, 2003); Jesse D. Siganor, "Eminent Domain and Its Use as an Economic Development Tool," PhD diss. (Cleveland State Univ., Maxine Goodman Levin College of Urban Affairs, 2006).

29. Richard Moe and Carter Wilkie, *Changing Places: Rebuilding Community in an Age of Sprawl* (New York: Henry Holt, 1997), 36–74.

30. Virginia O. Benson, "The Rise of the Independent Sector in Urban Land Development," *Growth and Change* 16, no. 3 (July 1985): 25–39.

31. "World Heritage Sites," http://whc/unesco.org.

32. National Trust for Historic Preservation, www.nationaltrust.org.

33. Serageldin, Shluger, and Martin-Brown, *Historic Cities and Sacred Sites*.

34. Siri Myrvoll, "Strategies for Preserving the Historic Identity of Bergen," in Serageldin, Shluger, and Martin-Brown, *Historic Cities and Sacred Sites*, 52–58.

35. Alfonso Gavela, "Adaptive Reuse of Mexico's Historic Architecture: Tsonpico and Tlscoltspan," in Serageldin, Shluger, and Martin-Brown, *Historic Cities and Sacred Sites*, 115–23.

36. Morisset, Noppen, and Coomans, *Quel Avenir Pour Quelles Églises? (What Future for Which Churches?)*.

37. Takeshi Nakagawa, "Heritage Surveying and Documentation in Japan," in Serageldin, Shluger, and Martin-Brown, *Historic Cities and Sacred Sites*, 258–60.

38. Francisco C. Weffort, "The Challenges of a Multiethnic and Multicultural Society," in Serageldin, Shluger, and Martin-Brown, *Historic Cities and Sacred Sites*, 35–40.

Glossary of Preservation Terms

Adaptive Use—The process of converting a building for a new use other than that for which it was originally designed, such as converting a warehouse into residential housing or converting a theater into a restaurant.

Advisory Council on Historic Preservation—A seventeen-member cabinet-level agency established to disseminate information for the president and Congress, assist preservation organizations in programming, and evaluate environmental impacts of federal projects on historic sites.

Amenity—A feature that makes a positive contribution to the environment around a structure or area.

American Antiquities Act of 1906—An act placing all landmarks under the secretary of the interior. It also mandated federal prosecution of all persons caught defacing historic sites; set up a federal system to record potential sites; and required federal agencies to protect all landmarks and sites in their jurisdiction.

American Centennial Celebration—A national fair held in Philadelphia in 1876 to commemorate the hundredth anniversary of U.S. independence and to recognize the country's cultural, industrial, and scientific advances.

Americans with Disabilities Act—Law prohibiting discrimination against persons with disabilities, requiring, among other things, that places generally open to the public, such as restaurants and hotels, be made accessible. Special rules and exemptions often apply to historic buildings and facilities.

Amortization—The writing off of the value of an asset or the periodic repayment of a debt over a specified period of time.

Appraisal—The estimated worth of a property usually substantiated by various methods of analysis, such as cost of replacement, income estimation, and market sales research.

Archaeology—Scientific study of the physical past, done through excavations and collection of artifacts from everyday life.

Bauhaus School of Design—A world-famous school of architectural design founded by Walter Gropius and Ludwig van der Rohe in 1919 in Weimar, Germany. This movement, whose name means "building house," emphasized simplicity and character in building design without extraneous detailing or applied fine art.

Building Code—Law setting minimum standards for construction and use of buildings to protect public health and safety.

Butcher's Hill—A very popular historic Baltimore neighborhood with over 1000 unique buildings and many brick row houses erected between 1850 and 1915.

Capital—Money or property invested in an asset for the creation of wealth.

Capital improvements—The investment in infrastructure such as roads, utilities, schools, bridges, and other public or private facilities.

Capitalization rate—Also known as the cap rate, the future flow of income converted into a present value, usually expressed as a percentage.

Cascade Land Conservancy—A nonprofit nature conservancy that assists land owners, local organizations, developers, and municipal governments in implementing workable conservation plans.

Cash flow statement—A financial statement that shows the actual cash available to pay salaries, expenses, and dividends; usually the after-tax profit plus depreciation.

Certificate of appropriateness—A document awarded by an official body, such as a landmarks commission or an architectural review board, that allows an applicant to proceed with any alteration, construction, or demolition according to the applicable criteria.

Certified historic structure—A structure that has been listed on the National Register of Historic Places or is located within a listed historic district and thereby is allowed certain Internal Revenue Code tax incentives for its preservation costs.

Certified rehabilitation—Any rehabilitation that meets the Secretary of the Interior's Standards for Rehabilitation and is consistent with the style of the rest of the buildings in its particular location.

City Beautiful Movement—An early-twentieth-century planning movement intended to rid U.S. cities of growing social ills and increased physical blight by promoting unprecedented business expansion and civic participation through beautification.

Columbian Exposition—The first critically acclaimed and economically successful World's Fair in the United States, this exposition, held in Chicago in 1893, celebrated the 400th anniversary of Christopher Columbus landing in the New World. Its beautiful and orderly parklike setting served as a model for many twentieth-century City Beautiful planners.

Community development block grants (CDBG)—Federal grants allocated to cities, which may be used for neighborhood or downtown projects. They offer support to community development corporations (CDCs) working to aid economically disadvantaged areas.

Community Reinvestment Act (CRA)—A federal program that directs controlling agencies to require banking institutions to provide lending in disadvantaged communities.

Conservation—An effective and systematic approach to protecting natural resources.

Culture—The totality of socially transmitted behavior patterns, arts, beliefs, and institutions related to human work and thought.

Cultural and Historic Treasures—A new game developed by the U.S. National Park Service to highlight recent historic discoveries in the United States.

Cultural Heritage Program—A program developed by the National Trust for Historic Preservation for historic communities wishing to participate in cultural tourism.

Cultural tourism—A sightseeing adventure directed toward discovering and saving of historic and natural monuments and sites.

Daughters of the American Revolution—A Washington, D.C., based private nonprofit women's service organization that promotes patriotism, history, and education.

Debt service—The payment made on a loan, usually on a periodic basis.

Deed restrictions—Conditions placed on the title of a real estate property that regulate the use of that property.

Density—As used in the real estate field, it refers to the concentration of buildings within an area, expressed as a ratio such as units per acre or floor/area ratio.

Demolition by neglect—The destruction of a building or property caused by lack of maintenance or abandonment.

Design guidelines—Strictures applied to a historic district by a design-review committee that evaluates new construction or alterations of buildings within the district for compatibility with the district's general character.

"Destroyed in '63"—A battle cry adopted by preservationists in Boston following the unpopular demolition of the John Hancock House in the summer of 1863.

Earth Day—Begun in 1970 to celebrate quality-of-life issues, this much-celebrated national event focused on the United States' environmental problems and has since expanded to include global environmental issues.

Easement (preservation or conservation)—A partial-fee interest in a building or property that has been donated to a qualified nonprofit organization offering U.S. Internal Revenue Code tax incentives for the purposes of protecting its historic character or its environmental quality.

Ecotourism—Sustainable tourism that includes participation by local stakeholders throughout the decision-making process.

Eminent Domain—A government right to take private property for public purposes after payment of just compensation to the owner, usually through a legal process.

Enabling law—Law enacted by a state setting forth the legal parameters by which local governments may operate. Source of authority for enacting local preservation ordinances.

Environmental Assessment or impact statement—Document prepared by state or federal agency to establish compliance with obligations under state or federal environmental protection laws to consider the impact of proposed actions on the environment, including historic resources.

Environmentalism—Active participation in protecting the natural world by doing away with harmful pollutants and other ecological or resource problems.

Environmental Protection Agency (EPA)—Federal agency established by President Richard Nixon in 1970 to administer laws related to controlling and reducing air and water pollution and regulating land use.

Equity—An ownership interest in real property or other assets after mortgage-loan amounts and other encumbrances have been paid.

Facadism—The preservation of the facade only of a historic building while altering or destroying the balance of the structure for a new use.

Federal Highway Act—A major transportation act passed by the U.S. Congress in 1956 calling for the construction of a modern 41,000-mile freeway system across the United States at an initial cost of $175 million.

Garden City—A movement begun by town planner Ebenezer Howard in the late-nineteenth century that countered rapid growth of industrial cities by emphasizing small-scale communities that maintained a high quality of life in a healthy planned environment.

Gentrification—The movement of the "gentry" or young urban professionals into inner-city areas that were formerly occupied by older, less-affluent residents.

Hard costs—The construction costs associated with land, labor, materials, infrastructure and fees for contractors.

Heritage tourism—Tourism that takes full advantage of natural resources without adversely affecting the same area's human culture; also, visitation of historic sites for educational and entertainment purposes.

Highest and best use—A term applied to a real estate property that reflects its ability to produce a maximum net return on the owner's investment. Preservationists might consider this a controversial concept.

Historic district—An area defined by borders that encompass buildings and other physical structures and spaces that characterize a historical period or are associated with significant events and is recognized by public officials who specify, through legislation, design review processes that control physical alterations in the area.

Homesteading—A government program in which buildings and sites are offered to the public for a minimal price if the buyer agrees to renovate the property and to occupy it for a particular period of time.

Infrastructure—The facilities usually provided by government entities; includes roads, bridges, utilities, parks, ports, and possibly schools and other public services.

Internal Rate of Return (IRR)—A real estate investment yield computed by discounting the return on an investment to its present value.

Landmark—A site or structure designated pursuant to a local preservation ordinance or other law that is worthy of preservation because of its particular historic, architectural, archeological, or cultural significance.

Lease—A contractual arrangement between a tenant and a property owner that gives the tenant a legal possession for a period of time in return for paying rent.

Leverage—Using a small investment to acquire additional capital for investment in a project.

Limited partnership—An arrangement that investors make that restricts their liability to the amount of their investment.

Loan-to-value ratio (LTV)—The mortgage loan amount divided by the appraised value of the property.

Lowertown—A highly successful St. Paul, Minnesota, historic district noted for its condos, galleries, restaurants, retail operations, and studios.

Market research—An assessment of the potential for sale of real estate within a particular area at a particular time; may include demographics, economic factors, and other relevant characteristics of the area.

Mechanic's lien—Legal claims against a real estate property owner by those who have provided labor or materials in connection with construction.

Memorandum of agreement—Document executed by consulting parties pursuant to Section 106 review process that sets forth terms for mitigating or eliminating adverse effects on historic properties resulting from agency action.

Mortgage—A legal instrument that defines the agreement between the borrower and the lender on a real estate property.

Mortgage loan constant—The percentage of the original loan balance represented by the periodic mortgage payments.

Motif—A recurring decorative theme or design element found in architecture.

Mount Vernon Ladies Association—A nonprofit organization established in 1853 by Pamela Cunningham, a wealthy Southern benefactor, to purchase and preserve the legendary home of George Washington.

Museum towns—Communities such as Williamsburg, Virginia, that have been set aside for the purpose of educating and entertaining tourists by presenting historic displays and events.

National Historic Landmark—Property included in the National Register of Historic Places that the secretary of the interior has judged to have national significance in American history, archeology, architecture, engineering, or culture.

National Historic Preservation Act—Federal law that encourages the preservation of cultural and historic resources in the United States.

National Register of Historic Places—Official inventory of districts, sites, buildings, structures, and objects significant in U.S. history, architecture, archeology, engineering, and culture.

National Scenic Byways—Federal program begun in 1991 by the U.S. Department of Transportation to preserve and promote the best historic and scenic highways in the country.

National Society of Colonial Dames of America—Private nonprofit organization that furthers the United States' heritage through preservation, patriotic service, and education.

Net operating income (NOI)—represented by the cash flow from the rent of an income real estate property after deducting the operating expenses from the gross income.

New Markets Tax Credit—Part of the Community Renewal Tax Relief Act of 2000; provides special tax credits for large scale development in low income districts.

Nonrecourse loan—A loan that limits the lender to foreclosing the mortgage and obtaining the real estate without personal liability by the borrower.

Old Town Chinatown—A downtown Portland, Oregon, historic neighborhood nationally recognized for its condos, shops, museums, galleries, restaurants, and theaters.

Operating expenses—Expenses involved in the maintenance and operation of a property, including management fees, repair costs, insurance fees, utilities, and other costs.

Opportunity cost—The return on an investment compared with the return available from other uses of that capital.

Option—A legal contract that normally gives a particular buyer the right to purchase or lease a real estate property at a specific price within a specific time period.

Outdoor historic museums—Nonprofit historic sites dedicated to promoting cultural heritage through hands-on demonstrations, event reenactments, and tours.

Paris Exposition of 1925—The Exposition Internationale des Arts Décoratifs et Industriels Modernes, which introduced the world to Bauhaus architectural design, streamlined decorative arts designs, and cubism in painting. Its impact lasted until World War II.

Passive investor—One who has no active role in the development of a real estate project but has invested capital in it.

Pattern books—Beautifully illustrated how-to books published by eighteenth-century British architects and sold to colonial American builders. Detailing every aspect of housing construction, from breaking ground to roof completion, these books determined "proper colonial architectural styling" prior to the Revolutionary War.

Present value—The estimate of the value of an income-producing asset, calculated by discounting future cash flow over the period of the loan.

Police power—the government's right to protect the public's interest by restricting the use of private property through such laws as building codes and zoning regulations.

Preservation—The act or process of applying measures to sustain the existing form, integrity, and material of a building or structure, and the existing form and vegetative cover of a site.

Preservation commission—A designation for any board that recommends to public officials the selection of historic districts or landmarks and appoints the design review committees that regulate the changes that take place in the districts or individual landmark buildings.

Real estate investment trust (REIT)—A trust created to provide real estate investors with limited liability, certain tax benefits, and liquidity.

Reconstruction Finance Corporation—A federal institution established in 1932 to provide emergency loans to banks and railroads on the brink of bankruptcy during the Great Depression.

Redlining—Drawing a line around an area on a map and, for bank loans and insurance coverage, designating it high-risk. This been outlawed in many cities.

Rehabilitation—The process of returning a property to a state of utility through repair or alteration which makes possible an efficient contemporary use.

Rehabilitation tax credit—Twenty percent federal income tax credit on expenses for the substantial rehabilitation of historic properties.

Renovation—Altering a building or property by eliminating important features, without consideration of protecting historical or aesthetic value.

Restoration—The process of accurately recovering the form and details of a property and its setting as it appeared at a particular period of time.

Revolving fund—Fund established by a public or nonprofit organization to purchase land or buildings or make grants or loans to facilitate the preservation of historic resources.

Section 106—Provision in the National Historic Preservation Act that requires federal agencies to consider effects of proposed undertakings on properties listed or eligible for listing in the National Register of Historic Places.

Section 4(f)—A provision in the Department of Transportation Act that prohibits federal approval or funding of transportation projects that require use of any historic site unless there is no feasible and prudent alternative to the project.

Setback—Distance from the street for a line of buildings, requirement usually found within zoning regulations.

Smart building—Building that incorporates certain technologies that facilitate communication networks, energy conservation and other services.

Smart growth—A movement among land-use planners that regulates development in order to offer an environmentally sound use of land around large cities, as opposed to highway-oriented suburban sprawl.

Society for the Preservation of New England Antiquities—Internationally recognized nonprofit organization established in 1910 by William Sumner Appleton to protect New England's architectural and cultural heritage, now known as Historic New England.

Soft costs—The expenses, including interest charges, appraisal fees, and other third-party charges, connected with real estate development financing.

Special taxing district—District established by local officials in which a tax is levied on property owners for public improvements that enhance the value of the property within the district. They may also be called business improvement districts (BIDS).

State Historic Preservation Officer (SHPO)—Official appointed or designated, pursuant to the National Historic Preservation Act, to administer a state's historic preservation program.

Sustainability—A term that refers to environmental design that maintains itself, thus requiring less upkeep. It also is used in conjunction with smart-growth concepts.

Sustainable tourism—Tourism that encourages the use of natural and physical resources in an area without negatively affecting its cultural preservation.

Syndication—Acquiring a number of equity investors who combine their investment in a real estate project such as a limited partnership.

Taking—Legal process of seizure of a private property by the government for the purpose of public use, following an appraisal of just compensation. A decision under a preservation ordinance may be considered a "takings" issue.

Tax credit—Dollar-for-dollar reduction of taxes owed.

Tax deduction—A subtraction from income (rather than taxes) that lowers the amount upon which taxes must be paid.

Tax increment financing—Type of financing in which the property-tax base is held level and the increase in value of the development provides the funds for capital improvements.

Tax Reform Act of 1976—Tax act that increased standard deduction percentages, delayed decreases in investment tax credits through 1980, extended general tax credits, and temporarily lowered small-business tax rates through 1977.

Tax Reform Act of 1986—Tax act that simplified the existing tax code, broadened the tax base, and eliminated many tax shelters.

Thomas Jefferson Foundation—Nonprofit organization that owns and operates Jefferson's legendary home, Monticello, the Robert H. Smith International Center for Jefferson Studies at Kenwood, and the Thomas Jefferson Center for Historic Plants.

Transferable development right (TDR)—Technique allowing landowners to transfer right to develop a specific parcel of land to another parcel.

Underground Atlanta—Opened in 1969, a downtown historic shopping and entertainment complex built below modern viaducts and utilizing a former train depot.

Urban renewal—Term to describe a partnership between government leaders and private investors to acquire and redevelop vast acreage in and around urban downtown areas in the 1950s and 1960s at low cost. Its popularity waned in the 1970s, due to lack of widespread new development in many areas where demolition took place (sometimes called "urban removal").

U.S. Department of Housing and Urban Development (HUD)—A cabinet-level federal agency that seeks to improve United States cities by promoting community development and affordable housing for low- to moderate-income residents.

Writedown—A reducing of the book value of a real estate property when changes occur in the market, such as deterioration of the property or loss of rent-contributing tenants.

Yellowstone Heritage Partnership—Nonprofit organization made up of private- and public-sector representatives from Montana, North Dakota, and Wyoming that is dedicated to preserving the natural beauty and culture of the Yellowstone National Park district through cultural tourism.

Zoning—Regulation of land use, often using density designations, by categorizing properties as industrial, commercial, residential, or mixed-use.

References

"A Brief History of St. Augustine." www.ci.st-augustine.fl.us/visitor/history.html.

"A Brief History of the Cleveland Restoration Society." www.clevelandrestoration. org/AboutUs/history.htm.

Abbot, Jacob. *The Harper Establishment or How the Story Books are Made.* New York: Harper and Brothers, 1855.

"About Us, Historic Landmarks Foundation of Indiana." www.historiclandmarks.org/aboutus/aboutus.html.

American Antiquities Act of 1906. Pub. Law 209. 59th Cong., 2nd sess., June 8, 1906.

Anderson, Martin. "Fiasco of Urban Renewal" in *Urban Renewal: The Record and the Controversy.* Edited by James Q. Wilson. Cambridge: MIT Press, 1966.

"Antique Homes, The Sales Directory of Antique and Historic Properties, Historic Style Guide." www.antiquehomes.magazine.com/style-guide/colonialrevival1.htm.

Appleton, William Sumner. "A Brief Account of the Society for the Preservation of New England Antiquities." Typewritten manuscript for Charles Messer Stowe, c. 1930. Courtesy Historic New England, Boston, Mass.

archINFORM, (2006). "Eugène Emmanuel Viollet-le-Duc." http://eng.archinform. net/arch/2677.htm.

Archpedia Architectural Encyclopedia, 2005, Styles, Post-Modern Architecture. www.archpedia.com/Styles-Post-Modern1-2.html.

Athenaeum of Philadelphia, Pa. The Athenaeum Building. www.philaathenaeum.org/building.html.

Avrami, Erica, Randall Mason, and Marta de la Torre, eds. *Values and Heritage Conservation.* Los Angeles: Getty Conservation Institute, 2000. www.getty.edu/conservation/publications/pdf.

Babcock, Richard F., and Charles L. Siemon. *The Zoning Game: Municipal Practices and Policies Revisited.* Boston: Oelgeschlageer, Gunn and Hain, 1985.

"Background of the Vernacular: The What, How, and Why of Bi-level, Split level, and Raised Ranch Houses." www.splitlevel.net/background4–7.html.

Baker, John Milnes. *American House Styles: A Concise Guide.* New York: Norton, 2002.

Barrett, G. Vincent, and John P. Blair. *How to Conduct and Analyze Real Estate Market and Feasibility Studies.* 2nd ed. New York: Van Nostrand Reinhold, 1988.

Barrington, Lewis. *Historic Restorations of the Daughters of the American Revolution.* New York: Richard R. Smith, 1941.

Beaumont, Constance C. "A Citizen's Guide to Protecting Historic Places: Local Preservation Ordinances." www.nationaltrust.org/smartgrowth/toolkit_citizens.pdf.

Bedford, Steven. *John Russell Pope, Architecture of the Empire.* New York: Rizzoli, 1998.

Bennett, Dryck. "From the Crowning Jewel to the Mistake on the Lake, The Story of the Construction of Cleveland Municipal Stadium." www.ballparks.com/baseball/american/cleve1/bennett.htm.

Benson, Virginia and Richard Klein. "The Impact of Historic Districting on Property Values." *Appraisal Journal* 56, no. 2 (Apr. 1988).

Benson, Virginia. Review of "Moe and Wilkie *Changing Places,*" *Journal of the American Planning Association* 65, no. 1 (1999).

———. "The Rise of the Independent Sector in Urban Land Development." *Growth and Change,* 16, no. 3 (July, 1985).

Bentley, Ian. "Urban Design as an Anti-Profession." *Urban Design Quarterly,* no. 65 (1998).

Berger, Louis. "Buried beneath Philadelphia, The Archaeology of North 7th and Arch Streets" (1998). http://culturalresourcegroup.com/pdf/philadelphia.pdf.

———. "Urban Archaeology in the City of Detroit" (2000). http://culturalresource group.com/projects/detroit.htm.

Berman v. Parker. 348 U.S. 26, 37 (1954).

Bever, Thomas D. "Economic Benefits of Historic Preservation, Cost of Rehabilitation vs. New Construction" in *Readings in Historic Preservation: Why? What? How?* Edited by Norman Williams Jr., Edmund H. Kellogg, and Frank Gilbert. New Brunswick, N.J.: Rutgers University Press, 1983.

———. "Heritage Conservation and Recreation Service." *The Economic Benefits of Historic Preservation.* Washington, D.C.: Department of the Interior, 1978.

Birch, Eugenie, and Douglas Roby. "The Planner and the Preservationist: An Uneasy Alliance," *Journal of the American Planning Association* 50, no. 2 (Spring 1984).

Blackmer, Gary. "Portland Historical Timeline." www.portlandonline.com/auditor/index.cfm?c=274088.

Blumenson, John J. G. *Identifying American Architecture: A Pictorial Guide to Styles and Terms, 1600–1945.* New York: Norton, 1982.

Boston City Council. *Rededication of the Old State House, Boston, July 11, 1882.* Boston: Boston City Council, 1889.

Bovenizer, George, and Vikram Sura. "Digging New York City, Dusting Off History." *New York 24 Journal* 7 (2001): 1–4. www.nyc24.org/2001/issue07/story02/page1.html.

Bracken, Gene. "About Us: Greater Baltimore Committee." www.gbc.org/AboutUs/AboutUs.aspx.

Breckenridge, Mary Beth. "The Construction Side of Sears." *Knight Ridder Newspapers,* May 3, 2005, 1–2. www.asu.edu/stardust/documents/theconstructionsideofsears.pdf.

Breen, Ann and Richard Rigby. *The New Waterfront: A Worldwide Urban Success Story.* London: Thames and Hudson, 1996.

Bricker, David. "Ranch Houses Are Not the Same," in *Preserving the Recent Past 2.* Edited by Deborah Slaton and William G. Foulks. Washington, D.C.: Historic Preservation Foundation, National Park Service and Association for Preservation Technology International, 2000.

Brunner, Arnold. "Cleveland's Group Plan," presented at the Eighth National Conference on City Planning, New York, New York, June 5–7, 1916. www.library.cornell.edu/Reps/DOCS/brunner.htm.

Burrows, Edwin G., and Mike Wallace. *Gotham, A History of New York City to 1898*. New York: Oxford Univ. Press, 1999.

"Canterbury Shaker Village." www.shakers.org.

Carmona, Matthew, Tim Heath, Taner Oc, and Steve Tiesdell. *Public Places, Urban Spaces: The Dimensions of Urban Design*. New York: Architectural Press, 2003.

Carson, Rachel. *Silent Spring*. New York: Houghton Mifflin, 1962.

Champion Tree Project International Official Website. "Mount Vernon Ladies' Association."www.championtreeproject.org/Ford%20House/Mt%20Vernon%20Ladies.htm.

Chandler, Mittie, Virginia Benson, and Richard Klein. "The Impact of Public Housing: A New Perspective." *Real Estate Issues* 18, no. 1 (Spring 1993): 31.

Churchill, Henry S. *The City Is the People*. New York: Norton, 1962.

City of Miami, Fla.: Planning Department, Historic Preservation. "Streamline and Depression Moderne (1930–42)." Architectural Styles. www.historicpreservation miami.com/streamline.html.

City of Santa Rosa, Calif. www.ci.santarosa.ca.us/CD/pdf/1–7GP11.

City of Wilmington, N.C. "Living History." www.wilmington-nc.com.

Clark, Kenneth. *The Gothic Revival: An Essay in the History of Taste*. New York: Harper and Row, 1974.

Cohen, Diane, and A. Robert Jaeger. *Sacred Places At Risk*. Philadelphia: Partners for Sacred Places, 1997.

Colonial Williamsburg Foundation. "The History of Colonial Williamsburg." www. history.org/Foundation/cwhistory.cfm.

Conaway, James. "Grounded." *Preservation* 57, no. 4 (July–Aug. 2005).

———. "Manifest Destination." *Preservation* 57, no. 4 (July–Aug. 2005).

Condit, Carl W. *The Chicago School of Architecture: A History of Commercial and Public Buildings in the Chicago Area 1875–1925*. Chicago: Univ. of Chicago Press, 1964.

Cram, Ralph Adam. "Good and Bad Modern Gothic." *Architectural Review* 1, no. 5 (Oct. 1899): 117–18.

Craven, Jackie. "About Architecture, Periods and Styles, 1930–1945 Art Modern." http://architecture.about.com/od/periodsstyles/ig/Home-Styles/Art-Modern.htm.

Crook, J. Mordaunt. *The Dilemma of Style: Architectural Ideas from the Picturesque to the Post Modern*. Chicago: Univ. of Chicago Press, 1987.

Cummings, Amos J. "A National Humiliation: A Story of Monticello." *New York Sun*, August 24, 1902, 1.

Cunningham, Ann Pamela. "Farewell Address to the Board of Regents at Mount Vernon," in *Minutes of the Council of the Mount Vernon Ladies' Association*, June 2, 1874, *Reports of the Mount Vernon Ladies's Association*, 1853–1874 (1874): 6–7.

———. "To the Ladies of the South." *Charleston Mercury*, Dec. 2, 1853.

Cunningham, Storm. *The Restoration Economy: The Greatest New Growth Frontier*. San Francisco: Berrett-Koehler, 2002, 15.

Curl, Donald W. "The Architecture of Addison Mizner." *Spanish River Papers* 7, no. 1 (Oct. 1978): 2–5. www.bocahistory.org/boca_history/br_history_spanish_river.asp.

Current, Richard N., T. Harry Williams, and Frank Freidel. *American History: A Survey*. New York: Alfred A. Knopf, 1979.

Cutler, Laurence, and Sherrie Stephens Cutler. *Recycling Cities for People: The Urban Design Process*. Boston: Cahners Books International, 1976.

Daniels, Roger. *Guarding The Golden Door: American Immigration Policy and Immigrants since 1882*. New York: Hill & Wang, 2004.

Davidson, Sharon Hurt. "Branding America's Byways." *Public Roads* 64, no. 6 (May–June 2001): 3. www.tfhrc.gov/pubrds/mayjuno1.

De la Torre, Marta, ed., *Assessing the Values of Cultural Heritage*. Los Angeles: Getty Conservation Institute, 2000. www.getty.edu/conservation/publications/pdf.

DeLuca, Salvatore. "Tilting At Windmills." *Preservation*, 58, no. 3 (May–June 2006).

Department of Transportation Act, Pub. Law 89–670, 80 Stat. 931 (1966).

"Different Types of Bungalows-Moderne." Mid-Town Renovators. www.mid-town renovators.com/pages/bungalow-modern.html.

Dix, Dorothy. "Monticello: Shrine or Bachelor's Hall?" *Good Housekeeping* (Apr. 1914): 538–41.

Domhoff, G. William. *Who Rules America Now? New Haven and Community Power Reexamined*. Englewood Cliffs, N.J.: Prentice Hall, 1983.

Dow, George F. "The Work of the Society for the Preservation of New England Antiquities." *House Beautiful* (Nov. 1925): 556–62.

Downing, Andrew Jackson. *The Architecture of Country Homes*. New York: Dover, 1969.

Downing, Antoinette F., and Vincent J. Scully Jr. *The Architectural Heritage of Newport, Rhode Island, 1640–1915*. Cambridge: Harvard Univ. Press, 1952.

Drury, George H., ed. *The Historical Guide to North American Railroads*, 2nd ed. Waukesha, Wis.: Kalmbach, 2000.

Duany, Andres, Elizabeth Plater-Zyberk and Jeff Speck. *Suburban Nation: The Rise of Sprawl and the Decline of the American Dream*. New York: North Point, 2000.

Editorial. "J. Reid Williamson," *Preservation* 57, no. 6 (Nov–Dec. 2005).

Executive Order 11593. 36 FR 8921. 3 CFR. 1971–1975 Comp.

Facca, Amy. "An Introduction to Preservation Planning." *Planning Commissioners Journal* 52 (Fall 2003): 1–5. www.planningreports.com/wfiles.w191.html.

Faragher, John Mack. "Bungalow and Ranch House: The Architectural Backwash of California." *Western Historical Quarterly* 32, no. 2 (Summer 2001): 149–50. www. usu.edu/history/whq/rasum2001.htm.

"Feasibility Study of Cultural Tourism and Economic Development in the Yellowstone Region." Yellowstone Heritage Partnership 1999. Project No. 05–06–02944. www. ywhc.org/index.php?.

Fisher, Lewis F. "Saving San Antonio: The Precarious Preservation of a Heritage." www.saconservation.org/about/milestones_6.htm.

Fitch, James M. *American Building and the Forces that Shaped It*. Boston: Houghton Mifflin, 1966.

Folk, John F., and Beverly K. Sheppard. *Thriving in the Knowledge Age: New Business Models for Museums and Other Cultural Institutions*. Lanham, Md.: AltaMira, 2006.

Gardner, George. "Mayor's Web Message for February 2004." www.ci.staugustine. com/commission/from_mayor_desk/fmd2004/fmd_02_94.html.

Garreau, Joel. *Edge City: Life on the New Frontier*. New York: Anchor Books, 1992.

Gavela, Alfonso. "Adaptive Reuse of Mexico's Historic Architecture: Tsonpico and Tlscoltspan" in *Historic Cities and Sacred Sites: Cultural Roots for Urban Futures*. Edited by Ishmael Serageldin, Ephim Shluger, and Joan Martin-Brown. Washington, D.C.: World Bank, 2001.

Gebhard, David. "Founding Father: George Washington Smith." *Santa Barbara Magazine* (1929). www.architect.com/Publish/GWS.html.

Georgia Trust. "Missions and Goals." www.georgiatrust.org/aboutus/default.htm.

Glaeser, Edward, and Claudio Goldin, eds. *Corruption and Reform Lessons from America's Economic History*. Chicago: Univ. of Chicago Press, 2006.

Goldsmith, Jonathan. *The Natural and Artificial Wonders of the United Kingdom: With Engravings in Three Volumes. Vol. 2: England and Wales.* London: G. B. Whittaker, 1825. www.beckford.c18net/wbgoldsmith1825.html.

Gramsci, Antonio. *Selections from Prison Notebooks.* New York: International Publishers, 1971.

Great Building Collection, Great Architects, 2006. www.greatbuildings.com/architects/Richard_Norman_Shaw.html.

Greene and Greene Virtual Archives Team. "Charles Summerall Henry Mather Greene Biography." Univ. of Southern California. www.usc.edu/dept/architecture/greeneandgreene/aboutgreenes.html.

———. "History of the Gable House." www.gamblehouse.org/history/index.html.

Greenfield, Angela M. "What Is Preservation North Carolina?" June 28, 2007. www.presnc.org/learnmore/presskit_what_is_pnc.html.

Hall, Mary and Susan Howlett. *Getting Funded: A Complete Guide to Proposal Writing.* Portland: Continuing Education Publications, Portland State Univ. Press, 2003.

Hamlin, Talbot. *Greek Revival Architecture in America.* New York: Dover, 1944.

Harrington, Michael. *The Other America: Poverty in the United States.* New York: Macmillan, 1962.

Hearn, Fil. "Implications of Robert Venturi's Theory of Architecture." *Architecture and Civil Engineering* 2, no. 5 (2003): 357–63.

The Henry Ford, "Greenfield Village." www.hfmgv.org/about/default.asp.

Historic Preservation Commission, Wilmette, Ill. "Architectural Styles." www.wilmette.com/whpe/colonial.htm. www.wilmette.com/whpe/craftsman.htm. www.wilmette.com/whpe/prairieschool.htm. www.wilmette.com/whpe/queenanne.htm. www.wilmette.com/whpe/artmoderne/international.htm.

———. "Indian Hills Historic District." www.wilmette.com/whpc/indianhill.htm.

"Historic Seattle: Dedicated to Architectural Preservation." www.historicseattle.org/about/ourhistory.aspx.

The History of the Gamble House, by Greene and Greene. www.gamblehouse.org/history/index.html.

Hitchcock, Henry-Russell. *The Architecture of H.H. Richardson and His Times.* Cambridge: MIT Press, 1968.

Hitchcock, Henry-Russell, and Philip Johnson. *The International Style: Architecture since 1922.* New York: Norton, 1932.

"Home and Garden, Architecture." www.architecture.about.com. www.architecture.about.com/library/blstern.htm.

Hosmer, Charles B., Jr. *Presence of the Past: A History of the Preservation Movement in the United States Before Williamsburg.* New York: G. P. Putnam's Sons, 1962.

Independence Hall Association, Philadelphia, Pa. 1999–2005. www.ushistory.org/iha.html.

Ingram, Richard T. *Ten Basic Responsibilities of Nonprofit Boards.* Washington, D.C.: National Center for Nonprofit Boards, 1996.

International Council on Monuments and Sites. *International Cultural Tourism Charter: Managing Tourism at Places of Heritage.* Los Angeles: J. Paul Getty Trust, 2003. www.nea.gov/about/Facts/Cultourism.html.

———. "ICOMOS' Mission." www.international.icomos.org/mission-eng1.htm.

International Ecotourism Society. *Ecotourism: Definitions and Principles.* Washington, D.C.: The International Ecotourism Society, 2005. www.ecotourism.org/webmodules/webarticles.net/templates.?a=95+2=2.

International World History Project. *Archeology,* 2003. www.history-world.org/ archeology.htm.

Jacobs, Allan, and Donald Appleyard. "Towards an Urban Design Manifesto." *Journal of the American Planning Association* 53, no. 1 (Winter 1987): 112–20.

Jacobs, Jane. *The Death and Life of Great American Cities.* New York: Random House, 1961.

Jones, Robert T., ed. *Small Houses of Architectural Distinction: A Book of Suggested Plans Designed by the Architect's Small Home Service Bureau.* New York: Dover, 1929.

Jordan, R. Furneaux. *A Concise History of Western Architecture.* London: Harcourt, Brace Jovanovich, 1984.

Kanof, Abram. "Uriah Phillips Levy: The Story of a Pugnacious Commodore." *Publication of the American Jewish Historical Society* 39 (Sept–June 1949–50): 1–66.

Kart, Cary S., and Jennifer M. McKinney. *The Realities of Aging: An Introduction to Gerontology.* New York: Allyn & Bacon, 2000.

Kaufman, Sanda. "The City Protects Itself." In *Introduction to Urban Studies.* Edited by Roberta Steinbacher and Virginia Benson. 3rd ed. Dubuque: Kendall-Hunt, 2006.

Kavanaugh, Molly. "State's 21st Scenic Byway Hugs Lake." *Plain Dealer,* Apr. 20, 2005, Metro section, B3.

Kayden, Jerold S. "Celebrate Penn Central: How the Supreme Court's Preservation of Grand Central Terminal helped Preserve Planning Nationwide." *Planning Magazine,* June 2003. www.planning.org/25anniversary/planning/2003jun.htm.

Keating, W. Dennis. "The City Looks Ahead." In *Introduction to Urban Studies.* Edited by Roberta Steinbacher and Virginia Benson. 3rd ed. Dubuque: Kendall-Hunt, 2006.

Keating, W. Dennis, Norman Krumholz, and Philip Star, eds. *Revitalizing Urban Neighborhoods.* Lawrence: Univ. Press of Kansas, 1996.

Kelo et al. v. City of New London et al., No. 04–108 (S.Ct. June 23, 2005). www. supremecourtus.gov/opinions/04pdf/04-108.pdf.

Klein, Richard, and David Lipstreu. "Bargeboard Details in the Western Reserve of Ohio 1830–1860." *American Preservation Technology* 13, no. 4 (1981): 34–37.

King, Thomas F. *Federal Planning and Historic Places: The Section 106 Process.* Lenham, Md.: AltaMira, 2000.

Kosinski, Leszek A., and R. Mansell Prothero, eds. *People on the Move: Studies on Internal Migration.* London: Methuen, 1975.

Kunda, Bracha. "What is the International Style?" Art Log Company. www.artlogco. il/telaviv/what.html.

Kunstler, James. *Geography of Nowhere: The Rise and Decline of America's Man-Made Landscape.* New York: Touchstone, 1993.

Kwong, JoAnn. "Farmland Preservation: The Evolution of State and Local Politics." *Urban Land* 46 (Jan. 1987): 20–23.

LaChiusa, Chuck. "Beaux Arts Style." *Buffalo Architecture and History.* 2003. http:// ah.bfn.org/a/DCTNRY/b/beaux.html.

Landau, Sarah Bradford and Carl W. Condit. *Rise of New York Skyscrapers, 1865–1913.* New Haven: Yale Univ. Press, 1996.

Lang, John. "Remains of the Bay." *Preservation* 55, no. 3 (May–June 2003).

Larkin, Jack, and Mark Ashton. "Celebrating 50 Years of History." *Old Sturbridge Visitor.* (Spring–Summer 1996): 4–6, 6–7. www.osv.org/education/OSVVisitors/ OSVHistory.html.

Laverty, Bruce, and Robert J. Hotes. "AIA Philadelphia Historic Preservation Committee."

AIA, Preservation Architect. The Newsletter of the Historic Resources Committee, July 25, 2007. www.aia.org/nwsltr-hrc1.cfm?pagename=hrc_nwsltr_20070725&archive=1.

Leepson, Marc. "Holding Their Ground." *Preservation* 57, no. 4 (July–Aug. 2005): 24–29.

Lennox, Chad, and Jennifer Revels. *Smiling Faces, Historic Places: The Economic Benefits of Historic Preservation in South Carolina.* Columbia, S.C.: South Carolina Department of Archives and History, 2002. www.state.sc.us/scdah/hpeconomic. htm.

Levavi, Peter. "Citywide CDCs: Chicago CDCs Increase Efficiency," presented at Sacred Landmarks Conference, Maxine Goodman Levin College of Urban Affairs, Cleveland State University, May–June 1996.

———. "Citywide CDCs: Chicago CDCs Increase Efficiency." *National Housing Institute, Shelterforce Online* 87 (May–June 1996). www.nhi.org/online/issues/87/ citywidecdc.html.

Linden, Russ. "Learning to Manage Horizontally: The Promise and Challenge of Collaboration." *Public Management* 85, no. 7 (Aug. 2003): 8–11.

Lindsey, Robert. "Middle-Class Interest in Older Housing Presses Poor." In *Reading in Historic Preservation: Why? What, How?* Edited by Norman Willis Jr., Edward H. Kellogg, and Frank B. Gilbert. New Brunswick, N.J.: Rutgers Univ. Press, 1983.

Listokin, Barbara and David Listokin. "Historic Preservation and Affordable Housing: Leveraging Old Resources for New Opportunities." In *Historic Facts and Findings.* Edited by James Carr. Washington, D.C.: Fannie Mae Foundation, 2005.

Littleton, Maud. *One Wish.* Pamphlet, Aug. 30, 1911, reprinted from *Congressional Record* (Washington, D.C.: GPO, 1912): 1–16.

Lopate, Phillip. "Taking the High Line, Nature and Industry Converge on an Abandoned Manhattan Railroad." *Online Preservation* (July–Aug 2005): 30–33. www. nationaltrust.org/magazine/archives/index.htm.

Lorentz, Stanislaw. "Reconstruction of Old Town Centers in Poland." *Historic Preservation Today.* Charlottesville, Va.: Univ. Press of Virginia for the National Trust for Historic Preservation and Colonial Williamsburg, 1966, 43–50.

Lynch, Kevin. *What Time is This Place?* Cambridge: MIT Press, 1972.

MacIntosh, Heather. "History of Historic Preservation in Seattle." www.historicseattle. org/projects/historyofpreservation.aspx.

The Main Street, The Four Points. www.mainstreet.org/content.aspx?page=47.

"Maryland, America's Byways." www.byways.org/explore/byways/2259–60,69085.

Massey, James C., and Shirley Maxwell. "The Cape Cod Revival, Reinventing Vernacular Cottages for Modern Suburbs. *Old House Journal* (Mar.–Apr. 2003).

May, Cliff, ed. *Sunset Western Ranch Houses.* San Francisco: Lane, 1947.

McLondon, Timothy, and JoAnn Klein. "Historic Preservation: Value Added." Univ. of Florida Center for Governmental Responsibility and the Center for Urban Policy Research at Rutgers Univ., 2002. www.rgp.ufl.edu/publications/explore/ vo8n1/historic.html.

"Mediterranean Revival." *Traditional Neighborhood Design.* www.tndhomes.3–6.com.

"Miami Beach Architecture, Art Deco District, Architectural Styles, Moderne-Streamline." *Miami Beach 411 Guide: History.* www.miamibeach411.com/History/art_deco.html.

Mid-Town Renovators. *Fine Restoration of Classic Homes, Spanish Colonial Revival.* www. mid-townrenovators.com/pages/bungalow_spanish_col_revival.html.

Miles, Mike E., Gayle Berens, and Marc A. Weiss. *Real Estate Development: Principles and Processes.* 2nd ed. Washington, D.C.: Urban Land Institute, 1996.

Mitchell, William J. *City of Bits: Space, Place and the Infobahn.* Cambridge: MIT Press, 1996.

Moe, Richard, and Carter Wilkie. *Changing Places: Rebuilding Community in an Age of Sprawl.* New York: Henry Holt, 1997.

Mohl, Raymond A. "The Interstates and the Cities: Highways, Housing, and the Freeway Revolt," Research Report, Poverty and Race Research Action Council, 2002. www.prrac.org/pdf/mohl.pdf.

Morisset, Lucie K., Luc Noppen, and Thomas Coomans, eds. *Quel Avenir Pour Quelles Églises?: What Future for Which Churches?* Montreal: Presses de l'Université du Québec, 2006.

Morrison, Hugh. *Early American Architecture: From the First Colonial Settlements to the National Period.* New York: Oxford University Press, 1952.

Nadaux, Marc. "Eugène Viollet-le-Duc," *Le XIX Siècle.* www.19e.org/personnages/france/violletleduc1.htm.

Nakagawa, Takeshi. "Heritage Surveying and Documentation in Japan." In *Historic Cities and Sacred Sites.* Edited by Ismail Serageldin, Ephim Shluger, and Joan Martin-Brown. Washington, D.C.: World Bank, 2001.

National Alliance of Preservation Commissioners. "Center for Community Design + Preservation." www.uga.edu/sed/pso/programs/napc/napc.htm

National Historic Preservation Act, Pub. Law 89–665, 80 Stat. 915 (1966).

National Housing Act of 1949, Pub. Law 89–554, 63 Stat. 413.

National Housing Act of 1954, Pub. Law 83–560, Sect. 701, 68 Stat. 590.

National Housing and Rehabilitation Association. "New Markets Credits." www.housingonline.com/TaxCredits/New Markets/tabid/40/Default.aspx.

National Park Service. Certified Local Government Program. www.nps.gov/history/hps/clg.

———. Heritage Documentation Programs. *Historic American Buildings Survey.* www.cr.nps.gov/hdp/habs/index.htm.

———. Historic American Buildings Survey (HABS), About Us. www.nps.gov/help/habs/index.htm.

———. *Historic Preservation Tax Incentives,* "Investment Tax Credit for Low Income Housing." www.cr.nps.gov/hps/tps/top/brochurex.htm.

———. *Historic Preservation Tax Incentives,* "Other Tax Provisions Affecting Use of Preservation Tax Incentives." www.2.cr.nps.gov/hps/tps/top/bro churex.htm.

———. *Historic Preservation Tax Incentives,* "What are Passive Activity Reductions?" www.cr.nps.gov/history/hps/tps/top/IRSQ_A.htm.

———. *Historic Structures Report, Part II on Independence Hall* (Apr. 1962): 81–84.

———. Independence National Historic Park. Rogers, T. Mellon. "Diary 1898." Mar. 9, 1898. Museum Collection.

———. Independence National Historic Park. *Select Committee Minutes, City of Philadelphia Pa.* (1813).

———. "National Register of Historic Places." www.cr.nps.gov/nr./publications/bulletin.com.

———. *Navajo Administrative History,* 1991. www.nps.gov/archive/nava/adhi/adhi3,5,7.htm.

———. News Release. "The National Park Service and Alliance of National Heritage Area Receive the National Trust/Advisory Council on Historic Preservation Award for Federal Partnership in Historic Preservation," Sept. 30, 2004. http://home.nps.gov/application/release/Detail.cfm.

――――. Park Net. "HABS, History." www.nps.gov/hpd/habs/index.htm.

――――. "Preservation of a Shrine, Independence Hall, Philadelphia, Pa." www.nps. gov/inde/preservation1.html.

――――. *Washington Cultural Resources, Preservation Assistance Division.* www.nps.gov/ archive/cuva/management/rmprojects/ruralus/FEISreferences.pdf.

――――. "What is a National Heritage Area?" www.cr.nps.gov/history/heritageareas// FAQ/INDEX.htm.

National Park Service and the National Trust for Historic Preservation. "America's Treasures." www.saveAmericastreasures.org/about.htm.

National Register Bulletin, National Park Service. Washington, D.C.: GPO (1998): 17–25. www.cr.nps./gov/publications/bulletins/hrb39/hrb39.pdf.

National Scenic Byways Program. "Maryland, America's Byways." www.byways.org/ explore/states/MD.

――――. "New Mexico, America's Byways." www.byways.org/explore/states/NM.

National Trust for Historic Preservation Act of 1949. Pub. Law 171. 81st Cong., 1st sess., July 15, 1949.

National Trust for Historic Preservation. "National Trust Community Investment Corporation." www.ntcicfunds.com.

Native American Graves Protection and Repatriation Act. Pub. Law 601, 101st Cong., 1st sess., Nov. 16, 1991. www.nathpo.org/News/SacredSites/NewsSacredSites102.htm.

"New Hampshire Vacations New Hampshire Travel, New Hampshire Bike Tours and Trips, Bicycling Tours in New Hampshire and Cycling Vacations." www.realadventures. com/new-hampshire.htm?m/NextRecord=10.

Newman, Oscar. "Defensible Space: A New Physical Planning Tool for Urban Re-vitalization." *Journal of the American Planning Association* 61, no. 2 (Spring 1995): 149–55.

New Market Tax Credit Initiative, National Trust for Historic Preservation NPS-IRS Connection under HP Tax Incentives. www.ntcicfunds.com/services/index.html.

"The Nott Memorial: Edward Tuckerman Potter." Union College. Schenectady, N.Y. www.union.edu?Campus/Nott_Memorial/potter.php.

Ohio Department of Transportation. *Amish County Byway.* www.ohiobyways.com/ AmishCounty1–3.htm.

――――. *Canal Way Ohio Byway.* www.ohiobyways.com/CanalWayOhio1–3.htm.

――――. *Historic National Road.* www.ohiobyways.com/Historic National-road-scenic-byways1–3.htm.

――――. *Ohio Byways Program,* "Designated Ohio Byways." www.ohiobyways.com.

――――. Ohio Byways, Website, www.ohiobyways.com/CanalWayOhio1–3.htm. www. ohiobyways.com/HolmesCounty1–3.htm. www.ohio byways.com/National-road-scenic-byways1–3.htm. www.ohiobyways.com/Ohio River1–2.htm.

――――. *Ohio River.* www.ohiobyways.com/OhioRiver OhioRiver1–2.htm.

OMG Center for Collaborative Learning. "A Decade of Development: An Assessment of Neighborhood Progress, Inc." A Research Report (Jan. 2001): 1–24. www.omg center.org/learn_rpts.shtml.

Outdoor Museum Forum. "America's Outdoor Museums," Official Website. www. outdoorhistory1–8.org.

Owsiany, David. "Ohio Court Restores Balance to Eminent Domain, Norwood Went Too Far and State Court Reels City In." *Akron Beacon Journal,* Aug. 1, 2006.

Palen, J. John. *The Urban World.* New York: McGraw-Hill, 1987.

Penn Central Transportation Co. v. City of New York, 438 U.S. 104, 98 S.C. 2646 (1978).

Pierson, William H., Jr. *American Buildings and Their Architects Vol. 1: The Colonial and Neo Classical Styles*. New York: Oxford Univ. Press, 1970.

Poch, Robert. "The Plight of Mount Vernon." *American History Magazine*, Feb. 2004. www.historynet.com/ah/blmtvernonplight.

Poinsett, David. "What is Historic Preservation?" In *Readings in Historic Preservation: Why? What? How?* Edited by Norman Williams Jr., Edmund H. Kellogg, and Frank Gilbert. New Brunswick, N.J.: Rutgers Univ. Press, 1983.

Pollock, Sandra. "American Federal, 1780–1820." *American Architecture*. www.realviews. com/homes/fed.html.

———. "American Foursquare, 1895–1930." *American Architecture*. www.realviews.com.

———. "Shingle Style, 1874 to 1900s, The Truly American Style." *American Architecture*. www.realviews.com/homes/shing.html.

"Preservation Strategies: Historic Savannah Foundation." www.historicsavannahfoun dation.org/AboutUs.asp.

"Preserve America, Explore and Enjoy our Heritage: Executive Order Report to President." http://www.preserveamerica.gov/EO.html.

Prindle, Tara. "Building Our Wigwam." *Native American Technology and Art: Scenes from the Eastern Woodlands: A Virtual Tour, ca. 1550*. www.nativetech.org/scenes/ buildingwigwam.html.

Pryor, Mrs. Roger A. "The Mount Vernon Association." *The American Historical Register* 1 (1895): 407–20.

Ramsey, David. "Drawings on Banks, Silsbee's Artful Chaos Anchors Clinton Square." Syracuse, N.Y. *Post Standard*, Aug. 25, 2002. Final Edition H1.

Rapley, Mark A. *Quality of Life Research: A Critical Introduction*. London: Sage, 2000.

"Real Adventures," Paddle Cape Cod, East Falmouth Massachusetts Ecotour. www. realadventures.com/listing/1021727-Paddle-Cape-Cod.htm.

The Recent Past Preservation Network. "Mission 66, Modern Architecture in the National Parks." www.mission66.com/mission.html.

Reilly, Brandy. "Split Level, 1950's–1960's." Univ. of Wisconsin. http://www.uwec. edu/Geography/Ivogeler/w367/styles/S43.htm.

Reorganization Plan No. 3, 12. FR 4981, 61 Stat. 954 (1947).

Reorganization Plan No. 3 of 1970, 35. FR 15623, 84 Stat. 2086. www.access.gpo. gov/uscode/title5a/5a_4_93_html

Revenue Reconciliation Act of 1993. Public Law 66. 103rd Cong., 1st sess., Aug. 10, 1993.

"Richard Norman Shaw." Great Building Collections, Great Architects, 2006. www. greatbuildings.com/architects/Richard-Norman-Shaw.html.

Richmond Libraries. "Horace Walpole 1717–1797 and Strawberry Hill." *Local Studies Collection, Local History Notes* (2005): 1–8. www.richmond.gov.uk/local_history_h_ walpole.pdf.

Riley, Mayor Joseph P. "State of the City Address, Charleston, South Carolina" (Jan. 2006). www.charlestoncity.info/dept/content.aspx?nid=4468cid=4620.

Robinson, Janet. "Art Deco 1920s-1940s." www.uwec.edu/Geography/Ivogeler/w367/ styles/s4.htm.

Rossi, Peter H. *Why Families Move*. Glencoe: Free Press, 1955.

Roth, Leland M. *A Concise History of American Architecture*. New York: Harper and Row, 1980.

Roth, Ronica. "Built in a Day: Capturing the Era of Catalog Architecture." *The Magazine of the National Endowment for the Humanities* 19, no. 5 (Sept.–Oct. 1998). www.neh.gov/news/humanities/1998–09/aladdin.html.

Rusk, David. *Inside Game, Outside Game: Winning Strategies for Saving Urban America.*
Washington, D.C.: Brookings Insitution Press, 1999.

Ruskin, John. *The Seven Lamps of Architecture.* New York: Dover, 1989.

Rypkema, Donavan. *Preservation and Property Values in Indiana, Historic Landmarks Foundation of Indiana.* Indianapolis: Indiana Landmarks Foundation, 1997. www.nps.gov/phso/sources/readhp/htm.

———. *The Economics of Historic Preservation.* Washington, D.C.: National Trust for Historic Preservation, 1994.

Sandvick, Jonathan. "Important Tools in Building Community Through Preservation," presented at Cleveland Restoration Society Preservation Conference, Oberlin, Ohio, 2003.

Sax, Joseph L. "Heritage of Preservation as a Public Duty: The Abbe Gregoire and the Origins of an Idea." *Michigan Law Review* 88 (1990): 1142–43.

Scott, Mel. *American City Planning since 1890: A History Commemorating the 50th Anniversary of the American Institute of Planners.* Berkeley: Univ. of California Press, 1969.

Scully, Vincent J., Jr. *The Shingle Style and the Stick Style Architectural Theory and Design from Richardson to the Origins of Wright.* New Haven: Yale Univ. Press, 1971.

Sears, Roebuck, and Company. *Small Houses of the Twenties: The Sears, Roebuck 1926 House Catalog.* New York: Dover, 1991.

Seeman, Mark, ed. "Cultural Variability in Context: Woodland Settlement of the Mid-Ohio Valley." *Mid-Continental Journal of Archaeology Special Papers* 7 (1992). http://upress.kent.edu/books/Seeman.htm.

Sen, Ashish K., and Tony E. Smith. *Gravity Models of Spatial Interaction Behavior: Advances in Spatial and Network Economics.* New York: Springer, 1995.

Servicemen's Readjustment Act of 1944. Pub. Law 346. 78th Cong., 2nd sess., June 22, 1944.

Silveira, Stacy J. "The American Environmental Movement: Surviving Through Diversity." *Boston College Environmental Affairs Law Review* 28, nos. 2–3 (2001): 503–4.

Simons, Robert A. *Turning Brownfields into Greenbacks.* Washington, D.C.: Urban Land Institute, 1998.

Society for the Preservation of New England Antiquities (1910–1960). *Old-Time New England, The Bulletin of the Society for the Preservation of New England Antiquities,* 1–50.

Steinberg, Stephen, ed. *Race and Ethnicity in the United States, Issue and Debates.* Malden, Mass.: Blackwell Publishers, 2000.

Stern, Robert A. M. *The Architecture of St. Paul's School and the Design of the Ohrstrom Library, Henry Vaughn Legacy.* http://library.sps.edu/exhibits/stern/vaughn.shtml.

"St. Paul's: Lowertown New Urban Village: Layers of History." http://www.lowertown.org/LRC/heritage1.html.

Stipe, Robert E. *Legal Techniques in Historic Preservation.* Washington, D.C.: National Trust for Historic Preservation, 1972.

———. "Why Preserve Historic Resources?" In *Readings in Historic Preservation: Why? What? How?* Edited by Norman Williams Jr., Edmund H. Kellogg, and Frank Gilbert. New Brunswick, N.J.: Rutgers Univ. Press, 1983.

Stipe, Robert E., and Antoinette J. Lee, eds. *The American Mosaic: Preserving a Nation's Heritage.* Washington, D.C.: U.S. Committee/International Council on Monuments and Sites, 1987.

Stoney, Samuel G. *This is Charleston: A Survey of the Architectural Heritage of a Unique American City.* Charleston, S.C.: Carolina Art Association, 1960.

Strawbery Banke Museum. Portsmouth, N.H. www.strawberybanke.org/museum/history/history.html.

Suberman, Stella. "Addison Mizner and the Boca Eaton House," *Spanish River Papers* 7, no. 1 (Oct. 1, 1978): 5–11. www.boca.history./br_history_spanish_river.asp.

Taylor, Holly. "April 2004: The Preservation of Grandmother's Hill." *Preservation Seattle: Historic Seattle's Online Monthly Preservation Magazine* (Apr. 2004): 1–5.

The Thomas Jefferson Foundation. "The Levys at Monticello." Levy Family History. www.monticello.org/about/levy.html.

The Thomas Jefferson Foundation. "Mission." www.monticello.org/about/index1.html.

Torre, L. Azeo. *Waterfront Development.* New York: Van Nostrand Reinhold, 1989.

"True Splits: A Primer on Three-Level and Four-Level Homes also Raised Splits and Split Entry Homes." 2004. www.splitlevel.net/split-level.htm.

Turner, Scott. "New Market Tax Credits Hit the Community." Federal Reserve Bank of San Francisco. www.frbsf.org/publications/community/investments/0308/article1. html.

Tyler, Norman. *Historic Preservation: An Introduction to Its History, Principles and Practice.* New York: Norton, 2000.

UNESCO, *World Heritage Centre.* http://whc.unesco.org/heritage.htm.

United States Advisory Council on Historic Preservation. *Contributions of Historic Preservation to Urban Revitalization. Section 106 Regulations Summary.* www.achp. gov/106summary.html.

University of Wisconsin. "Styles." http://uwee.edu/geography/Ivogeler/w367/styles.htm.

"USA 2000: More People, More Diversity." *State Legislatures* 27, no. 5 (2001).

U.S. Census, 2000. www.access.gpo.gov/su_docs/fedreg/a020823c.html.

U.S. Congress. House. *Monticello.* Debate on HR 740, 62nd Cong., 2nd sess. *Congressional Record* 49, no. 1 (Dec. 9, 1912): 345–49.

U.S. Department of Transportation. Federal Highway Administration. "Environmental Transportation Enhancements." www.fhwa.dot.gov/environment/te.

U.S. Department of Transportation. Federal Highway Administration. "U.S. Transportation Secretary Mineta Names Thirty-Six New National Scenic Byways All-American Roads." June 13, 2002: 1. www.dot-gov/affairs/fhwa2702.htm.

U.S. Department of Transportation. "TEA-21-Transportation Equity Act for the 21st Century, Moving Americans in the 21st Century-Fact Sheet: National Scenic Byways Program." www.fhwc.dot/gov/TEA21/factsheets/scenic.htm.

U.S. Department of the Treasury. *Fact Sheet on the History of the U.S. Tax System.* www. treas.gov/education/fact-sheets/taxes/ustax.shtml.

U.S. Department of the Treasury. Internal Revenue Service. Keynote Speaker, Accelerated Depreciation. www.irs.ustreas.gov/business/page/0/id=134133.00.htm.

U.S. Department of the Treasury. "What We Do, New Market Tax Credit, NMTC." *Community Development Financial Institutions Fund.* www.cdfifund.gov/what_we_ do/programs_id.asp?programID=5.

U.S. Environmental Protection Agency. "What is Sustainability?" www.epa.gov/ sustainability/basicinfo.htm.

U.S. Internal Revenue Code, sec. 501 (c)(3). http://www.irs.gov/charities/charitable/ article/0.id-96099.00.html.

Valle, Erick. "Florida Vernacular Architecture." *Traditional Neighborhood Design: Building a Better Place to Live.* www.tndhouses.com/phd05.htm.

Washington, D.C. National Mall. www.nps.gov/nr/travel/washdc70.htm.

Waterman, Thomas T., and John A. Barrows. *Domestic Colonial Architecture of Tidewater Virginia.* New York: Scribner's, 1932.

Whiffen, Marcus. *American Architecture since 1780: A Guide to the Styles.* Cambridge: MIT Press, 1992.

White, Sammis, Richard Bingham, and Edward Hill, eds. *Financing Economic Development in the Twenty-first Century*. London: M.E. Sharpe, 2003.

"William Sumner Appleton, 1874–1947." *Old-Time New England, The Bulletin of the Society for the Preservation of New England Antiquities* 37 (1948): 71–72.

Williams, Norman, Jr., Edmund H. Kellogg, and Frank B. Gilbert, eds. *Readings in Historic Preservation: Why? What? How?* New Brunswick, N.J.: Rutgers Univ. Press, 1983.

Wills, Royal Barry. *Houses for Good Living*. New York: Architectural Book Publishing Company, Inc., 1940.

Wilson, James Q., and George L. Kelling. "Broken Windows, the Police and Neighborhood Safety." *Atlantic Monthly Magazine Online* 249, no. 3 (Mar. 1982): 29–38. www.codinghorror.com/blog/files/AtlanticMonthly.BrokenWindows.

Wilson, William H. "Moles and Skylarks." In *Introduction to Planning History in the United States*. Edited by Donald A. Kruckenberg. New Brunswick, N.J.: Rutgers Center for Urban Policy Research, 1987.

Winter, Robert, ed. *Toward a Simpler Way of Life: The Arts and Crafts Architects of California*. Berkeley: Univ. of California Press, 1979.

Ziegler, Arthur P., Leopold Adler II, and Walter Kidney. *Revolving Funds for Historic Preservation*. Pittsburgh: Ober Park Association, 1975.

Index